Tyranny in Shakespeare

APPLICATIONS OF POLITICAL THEORY

Series Editors: Harvey Mansfield, Harvard University, and Daniel J. Mahoney, Assumption College

This series encourages analysis of the applications of political theory to various domains of thought and action. Such analysis will include works on political thought and literature, statesmanship, American political thought, and contemporary political theory. The editors also anticipate and welcome examinations of the place of religion in public life and commentary on classic works of political philosophy.

Lincoln's Sacred Effort: Defining Religion's Role in American Self Government, by Lucas E. Morel

Tyranny in Shakespeare, by Mary Ann McGrail

The Moral of the Story: Literature and Public Ethics, edited by Henry T. Edmondson III

Faith, Reason, and Political Life Today, edited by Peter Augustine Lawler and Dale McConkey

Faith, Morality, and Civil Society, edited by Dale McConkey and Peter Augustine Lawler

Pluralism without Relativism: Remembering Isaiah Berlin, edited by João Carlos Espada, Mark F. Plattner, and Adam Wolfson

The Difficult Apprenticeship of Liberty: Reflections on the Political Thought of the French Doctrinaires, by Aurelian Craiutu

The Seven Wonders of Shakespeare, by Michael Platt

The Dialogue in Hell between Machiavelli and Montesquieu, by Maurice Joly, translation and commentary by John S. Waggoner

Deadly Thought: "Hamlet" and the Human Soul, by Jan H. Blits

Reason, Revelation, and Human Affairs: Selected Writings of James V. Schall, edited and with an introduction by Marc D. Guerra

Sensual Philosophy: Toleration, Skepticism, and Montaigne's Politics of the Self, by Alan Levine

Tyranny in Shakespeare

Mary Ann McGrail

LEXINGTON BOOKS
Lanham • Boulder • New York • Oxford

LEXINGTON BOOKS

Published in the United States of America
by Lexington Books
4720 Boston Way, Lanham, Maryland 20706

P.O. Box 317
Oxford OX2 9RU, UK

British Library Cataloguing in Publication Information Available

The hardcover edition of this book was previously catalogued by the Library of Congress
as follows:
McGrail, Mary Ann, 1958–
    Tyranny in Shakespeare / Mary Ann McGrail.
      p.   cm. — (Applications of political theory)
    Includes bibliographical references and index.
      1. Shakespeare, William, 1564-1616—Political and social views. 2. Politics and
literature—Great Britain—History—16th century. 3. Politics and literature—Great
Britain—History—17th century 4. Political plays, English—History and criticism.
5. Master and servant in literature. 6. Kings and rulers in literature. 7 Despotism
in literature. I. Title. II. Series.

PR3017.M37   2001
822.3'3—dc21   99-045933

ISBN 0-7391-0082-3 (cloth alk. paper)
ISBN 0-7391-0478-0 (pbk. alk. paper)

Printed in the United States of America

For my mother, Ruth Ann McGrail

and

For my sisters, Katherine, Margaretha, and Elizabeth

Contents

Acknowledgments

I am indebted to my teachers, beginning with Herschel C. Baker and Harvey C. Mansfield, Jr. I wish to thank three of my advisors in particular, William Alfred, Marjorie Garber, and Barbara K. Lewalski. I never failed to learn, even from our disagreements. This book would not have made it to print without the encouragement and support of my colleagues, especially Saul Bellow, Geoffrey Hill, Roger Shattuck, and Rosanna Warren. Saul and Janis Bellow and Harvey and Delba Mansfield were, and remain, dear friends and gentle critics.

Chapter 1

Introduction: Here May You See the Tyrant

Tyrant Show Thy Face

Even the most explicitly political contemporary approaches to Shakespeare have been uninterested in his tyrants as such. But for Shakespeare tyranny was a perpetual political and human problem rather than a historical curiosity, or a psychological aberration. A recovery of the playwright's perspective challenges the grounds of this modern critical silence. Shakespeare's expansive definition of tyranny may be located between those given by classical and modern political philosophy. Is tyranny always the worst of all possible political regimes, as Aristotle argues in Book III of *The Politics*? Or is disguised tyranny, as Machiavelli proposed, potentially the best possible regime? These competing conceptions were available and alive in Renaissance thought, given contemporary expression by such political actors and thinkers as Elizabeth I, James I, Henrie Bullinger, Jean Bodin, Étienne de La Boétie, Baldesar Castiglione, Guillaume de la Perrière, John Ponet, Lydgate, and the author of *The Mirror for Magistrates*. Shakespeare's dramas of tyranny are poised between Aristotle's reticence and Machiavelli's forwardness.

This book is organized around a question: What is Shakespeare's understanding of tyranny? Shakespeare addressed the problem from many different angles: political, psychological, historical, aesthetic. Tyranny is in part, for him, an expression of underdeveloped excessive desires for love or honor. The tyrant's unrestrained, elemental desires are linked in the four plays to inner and outer distortions of language. My concern remains primarily Shakespeare's exploration of these conflicting and contradictory passions that make up the tyrant.

He shows us in *Macbeth* and *Richard III* tyrants coming to power, and in *The Winter's Tale* and *The Tempest*, the actions of legitimate rulers turned tyrants who later relinquish their tyrannies. As indicated by the order of the chapters, I am not concerned to find a justification for Shakespeare's varying interest in the tyrant within the chronology of his life or work. I begin with *Macbeth* because it sets the terms of the argument about the relation between legitimacy and tyranny. This play disposes of the most conventional objection that tyranny in the Renaissance meant usurpation and that it was tied into contemporary questions of Elizabeth I's and James I's respective claims to the British throne. Macbeth represents the unreflective, powerful attraction to tyranny of an outstanding man seduced by honor. The play complements the dramatic treatment of early historical attempts to establish an arbitrary but stable standard of legitimacy for a Christian monarchy. Divine right is explored as a solution to this problem, and the question of the relation between tyranny and founding is raised. In *Richard III*, Richard the soliloquizer is more self-aware and better able to give an account of the ends of his flawed ambitions. Using the religious mask, he is more successful than Macbeth in establishing a legitimate claim to the throne. Such a man can boast he will "set the murderous Machiavel to school." In his failure to reconcile self with soul, Richard poses a challenge to Machiavelli's thought. Leontes in *The Winter's Tale* is a study of the tyrant corrected, reeducated by art and faith. He desires to be loved by Hermione absolutely and provably. In Leontes Shakespeare offers an intensely drawn instance of the tyrannic ambition to be loved by all, for all time: ambition engendered by a desire that may be joined with or set against the desire for contemporary or future honors. In *The Tempest*, Caliban accuses Prospero of being a usurper and a tyrant on the island. Of necessity Prospero pursues a political "project", yet he reveals his understanding of the self-contradictory character of political ambition. An exploration of the relation between Prospero's Art and tyranny provides a standard by which to judge the tyrannies of Macbeth, Richard, and Leontes. It returns us to the question between Malcolm and Macduff—what does legitimacy have to do with good rule?

The questions that all four of these plays address differently are: What is tyranny? What are the aims of the tyrant, declared or undeclared? Is tyranny a necessary political evil? Is all tyranny evil? Is it possible to retrieve a tyrant from the throes of tyrannic impulses? How does one strive against tyranny?

To examine these questions about Shakespeare's view of tyranny requires a certain scale. For this reason, I omit from consideration the petty tyrants of the comedies. By petty tyranny I mean the momentary taking advantage of another's character defect or weakness, or the temporary abuse of power: Malvolio is the quintessential petty tyrant in Shakespeare. There is a difference between a tyrant and a character susceptible of tyrannic passions that he or she sustains momentarily. Tyranny is the preserve of the few though, as with the souls in Plato's Myth of Er, we may all desire or be tempted to it from time to time. To achieve a great tyranny is a feat requiring either tremendous passion (Macbeth, Leontes) or tremendous intellect (Richard, Prospero), or a powerful combination of both. In a more extensive study, a comic character such as Malvolio could be read as a parodic commentary on the tyrants of the tragedies, histories, and romances, whose sphere of ambition has been ridiculously shrunken. Such reflections offer a corrective to the dangers of heavy-handed moralizing implicit in making this question the focus for a study of Shakespeare. The opposite danger, of relativizing, withdrawing from the suggestion that Shakespeare concludes anything on such an important political topic, is more evidently unsettling as a response.

The terms of the contemporary debate about Shakespeare and politics are well expressed in the titles of two books on the subject published over twenty years apart: *Political Shakespeare* and *Shakespeare's Politics*. The first is a collection of "New essays in cultural materialism" edited by Jonathan Dollimore and Alan Sinfield, and the second is a set of essays the project of which is to make "Shakespeare again the theme of philosophic reflection and a recognized source for the serious study of moral and political problems."[1] As the title of the first collection implies, for its contributors, Shakespeare and his plays are to be found within a political context, which must be examined in order to better understand the ways in which his plays either subvert or contain the representations of power in his society. As the title of the second collection implies, for Bloom and Jaffa, Shakespeare occupied a reflective position somewhere beyond the realm of politics that enabled him to represent politics as he understood them in his plays.

These two opposed approaches are in agreement explicitly and implicitly, however, in a rejection of that traditional criticism which has come to be known as essentialist humanism.[2] This criticism located political thought in Shakespeare in the history plays or Roman plays almost exclusively. H. M. Richmond's *Shakespeare's Political Plays* included the two tetralogies, *King John, Julius Caesar*, and *Coriolanus*. His reading is straightforwardly historicist, reflecting Shakespeare's contemporary historical circumstances; the plays were "under the impetus of Tudor policies, calculatedly political," but according to him, Shakespeare, after *Coriolanus*, retreated from politics to examine the individual.[3] Of course the most widely criticized exponent of this approach, E. M. W. Tillyard, argues in his *Shakespeare's History Plays* that the Histories were a celebration of an attractive and carefully ordered Elizabethan world picture, and that there is always "a larger principle of order in the background."[4]

Even among those falling under the rubric of "essentialist" criticism, there is a range of theoretical approaches. Tillyard views Shakespeare as the standing reflection of the politics of his time, which he interprets as static. There is a second approach, which is even more "essentialist," deriving universal truths about the human condition, hence politics, from the plays. L. C. Knights states this broadly when he argues for Shakespeare's interest in politics, which "included questions of power and subordination, of mutual relations within a constituted society, of the ends and methods of public action, so that we may properly speak of Shakespeare's political philosophy—so long, that is, as we remember that this philosophy is not something ready formed once for all, and applied or exhibited in varying circumstances, but a part of that constant search for meanings that informs his work as a whole."[5] Critics such as George Wilson Knight and A. C. Bradley advocate what William Empson defended in his *Essays on Shakespeare*: "The history of the drive against character-mongering in Shakespearean criticism, personality in actors and actresses, and eventually against any indulgence in human interest while art-work is in progress, is complex but is evidently intertwined with the anti-humanist movement of Pound, Wyndham Lewis, Eliot, etc. . . . the inhumanity and wrongheadedness of the principle was bound to shine through in the end."[6] Still these critics imply an ease of access to the political questions in Shakespeare that can be misleading.

Terry Eagleton in *Criticism and Ideology* argues against these views of Shakespeare's politics as either a mirror of his time, or a philosophic statement for all time: "It is true that Shakespearean drama does not merely 'reproduce' a conflict of historical ideologies; but neither does it merely press a particular ideology to the point where it betrays its significant silences. Rather it produces, from a specific standpoint within it, the severe contradictions of an ideological formation characterised by a peculiarly high degree of 'dissolution': dissolution produced by a conflict of antagonistic ideologies appropriate to a particular stage of class-struggle."[7]

This poses the problem of how you get to this "specific standpoint" within the plays—where or in which character the standpoint is placed. In *Macbeth*, for example, Eagleton argues that that standpoint is to be found in the Witches.[8] But the moment of ideological breakdown is less easy to identify. As I will argue throughout this book, such a static moment, conscious or unconscious on Shakespeare's part, is not to be found. Rather, all varieties of ideologies (if by that term is meant a systematically applied set of beliefs or ideas) break apart and are broken apart by characters in the plays. Kevin Sharpe and Steven N. Zwicker in *Politics of Discourse: The Literature and History of Seventeenth Century England* also attempt to repatriate Shakespeare, with others, back to his age, "not to confine them to the past" but "to release them into the rich complexities of their historical moment."[9] The text is made richer when seen in its connection and response to contemporary history. Leonard Tennenhouse, praising such a contextual analysis, detects the cultural bias of previous essentialist critics: "This ahistorical Shakespeare is, in other words, quite clearly a construct who speaks the politics of culture in the tradition of Arnold and Eliot."[10] The Marxist and new historicist critics with whom Tennenhouse allies himself are correspondingly frank about their underlying political projects.

My project, like those of Tennenhouse and Eagleton, examines a political question while overlooking generic boundaries. But, unlike them, I do not conclude that Shakespearean drama was as passive to the political exigencies of the volatile, contemporary historical moment. I try to indicate that there is more extreme subversion occurring in the plays than is recognized, even by those who are looking for it, though I would agree with Stephen Greenblatt in his conclusion to *Renaissance Self-Fashioning* that Shakespeare's relation to his culture was not "defined by hidden malice."[11] Greenblatt, however, stops short of eliciting political judgments from Shakespeare, because "that more than exploration [of power relations in Shakespeare] is involved is much harder to demonstrate convincingly."[12] Shakespeare did not apologize for the undemocratic politics of his day, nor did he disguise a vituperative critique—he thought about politics (not just Elizabethan or Jacobean politics) deeply, with alternative political systems available for his consideration through Plutarch, Montaigne, Plato, Aristotle, Machiavelli, and the Bible.

Along these lines, in his introduction to *Literary Theory/Renaissance Texts*, David Quint speaks of the theoretical underpinning of the essays in his book which "remotivates the idea of a humanist canon: one whose function would be to distinguish literature, as a discourse that foregrounds problems of writing and reading and suspends questions of ultimate meaning and truth, from other discourses that are more mechanical, more dogmatic, more ideologically manipulative."[13] This approach to the pedagogic problem seems to me, in an important way, to hedge. Quint wishes to say that there is a basis, even if only a pragmatic, pedagogic one, for canon formation, but he cannot say that this basis is the idea that literature might actually offer instruction or guidance about questions of "ultimate meaning and truth." But how does one arrive at the point where one may recognize such a suspension within literature? At least, it seems, the question of "ultimate meaning and truth" must be held open a little longer, which this argument about Shakespeare's dramas of tyranny tries to do.

In contrast to criticism, such as Quint's, which poises on a question, there was a certain refreshing boldness in the approach of Marxist and materialist critics such as Eagleton, Dollimore, and Sinfield, who announced their ideological cast presented what they believed to be evidence of Shakespeare's ideology. They turned critical attention back to the political questions in the plays and kept such an interest from being confined to the Histories or Roman plays. Their attention to *The Tempest*, for example, introduced a whole new level of debate about Shakespeare's white magician.

Their criticism has also been helpful in bringing out from under the cloak of historicist criticism the radical political ideas expressed in Shakespeare's plays, as Dollimore states in the opening chapter of *Radical Tragedy*: "a significant sequence of Jacobean tragedies, including the majority of Shakespeare's were more radical than has hitherto been allowed. Subsequent chapters will show how the radicalism of these plays needs to be seen in the wider context of that diverse body of writing which has been called 'the greatest intellectual revolution the Western world has ever seen' and also identified as 'the intellectual origins' of that actual revolution in the English state in 1642."[14] In his introduction to *Political Shakespeare* he writes that "All the contributors to this book would endorse Frank Lentricchia's contention that 'Ruling culture does not define the whole of culture though it tries to, and it is the task of the oppositional critic to re-read culture so as to amplify and strategically position the marginalised voices of the ruled, exploited, oppressed, and excluded.'"[15] The forceful political project behind such oppositional rereadings is stated differently in Catherine Belsey's introduction to *The Subject of Tragedy*: "The object of beginning with tragedy is not to privilege these plays but to put them to work for substantial political purposes which replace the mysterious aesthetic and moral pleasures of the nineteenth-century criticism."[16]

This frank statement of a critical political project presented two difficulties in practice. There was a preference among the critics, most notably Eagleton, to identify Shakespeare with the ruling culture of his time, for which he became an occasional unwitting apologist. The second difficulty was the distortion implied in the effort to bring forth the "marginalized voices" Dollimore refers to, a distortion which, as we will see in *The Tempest* tends to mislead. One need not make the Witches the heroines of *Macbeth* or Caliban the hero of *The Tempest* in order to explore the misunderstandings and injustices they endure. The question remains as to why Macbeth and Prospero occupy more of Shakespeare's dramatic time in these two plays. Again Dollimore argued that the critics in his anthology were motivated by "the need to disclose the effectiveness and complexity of the ideological process of containment," which does not mean political passivity.[17]

This was, at core, a very optimistic and commendable statement about the power inherent in "disclosing" processes of containment. But it overlooked the question of why that containment existed. Why is Caliban forgotten at the end of *The Tempest*? Is it because Shakespeare forgot him? Is it because Shakespeare's character, Prospero, forgot him? Is it because the audience is being tempted to forget him? The answer assumed by the above-mentioned critics is that Shakespeare was either unaware of his own elaborate artistic strategies for apparent submission to political authority, or was simply writing in a time in which particular arguments could not be made on stage.

There is another alternative. Shakespeare may have been keenly aware of the political (not just historical) imprudence of casting too much light on political injustice. It would be imprudent, at least, not to ask why Shakespeare discloses, and even points to certain political injustices, and makes others harder to see. The delight in demystification, in taking apart ideologies, may obstruct our view of the deliberateness of Shakespeare's dramatic construction—the plainness with which he shows some things and the discretion with which he obscures others. In this discussion of four of Shakespeare's dramas of tyranny, I attempt to suggest reasons for the playwright's "mystification" of certain political problems, or, as I prefer to call it, his reticence.

I'll Not Call You Tyrant

It is helpful to begin with the variety of definitions of tyranny in relation to which Shakespeare's may be located. The sheer volume of material addressing the problem of tyranny and the justification of tyrannicide in the Renaissance alone, would, from the historian's perspective, encourage us to look at what Shakespeare had to say about it. An exhaustive catalogue of these definitions is not necessary, but I offer a few of them to set the range of opinions in the background.

These definitions are organized, not chronologically, but theoretically, to stress the complexity of the political problem Shakespeare chose to treat from different angles. There is the tyrant as illegitimate ruler, as scourge (a test from god, which could be meant to ascertain either the spiritedness or the submissiveness of his people), as a being opposed to divine will (simply evil), and as self-serving ruler who ruled without popular consent. These definitions all derive from a classical, Aristotelian view of the tyrant as one who ruled without complete regard for the common good. They are opposed by the modern, Machiavellian attempt to eradicate the idea of tyrannical rule as distinct from monarchial rule. As I will argue, Shakespeare's dramas of tyranny display familiarity with all these points of view and offer critiques of them.

There is, of course, the simple definition that Macduff advocates, that the tyrant is a usurper, an illegitimate ruler. The sixteenth-century republican, George Buchanan, uses this in his *The Powers of the Crown in Scotland [De Jure Regni Apud Scotos]*: "It is of the Nature of Tyrants that they Seize Office without Being Legally chosen, and Rule autocratically. Such Rulers are to be Counted as Tyrants, Even though they do Many Things which Benefit Their Subjects."[18] Buchanan goes on to cite the Greek and Latin uses of the word tyrant: "Consequently in both languages, as you know, not only heroes and most eminent men, but also the greatest of the Gods, even Zeus himself, are called tyrants; and this was done by persons who both think and speak of the Gods with reverence."[19] As he points out, a classical tyrant was not necessarily an evil ruler—though the word came to be strongly associated with evil (not just absolute, or illegitimate ruler) in the Renaissance.[20] This is a narrowing of the original definition of the Greek *tupannos*: "a lord and master; hence an absolute sovereign, unlimited by law or constitution; it was applied to *anyone who had made himself king by force*; not to hereditary monarchs, as (for instance) not to the kings of Sparta, nor to the King of Persia; and it did not necessarily imply cruel or overbearing conduct: later however the term was used as our *tyrant* or *despot*; and in poets it was taken loosely for a *king*."[21] A tyrant could also mean a lawless or unconstitutional ruler.[22]

The tyrant also came to be interpreted as a scourge or test from God. This understanding of the tyrant frequently relied on an interpretation of Proverbs 8:15-16: "By me kings reign, and princes decree justice. / By me princes rule, and nobles, *even* all the judges of the earth." The fifth-century theologian, St. Augustine, writes, "We must ascribe to the true God alone the power to grant kingdoms and empires. He it is who gives happiness in the kingdom of heaven only to the good, but grants earthly kingdoms both to the good and to the evil in accordance with his pleasure, which can never be unjust."[23] Henrie Bullinger repeats this in *The Tragedies of Tyrantes Exercised upon the Church of God, from the birth of Christ unto this present yeere, 1572.* As he argues, tyrants are for the express purpose of persecuting the Church to better glorify God: "For in persecutions, the power of God is declared whereby hee preserveth his in the midst of afflictions, and when hee seeth time, delivereth them with great glory, as it is evidently expressed in the stories of Daniell, Hester and Efdras . . . There is also another cause of persecutions for that it pleaseth God through them to reveale the trueth unto men: namely, when the faithfull being apprehended in persecutions, and brought into judgement: do plainly and openly profess the Gospell."[24]

The idea of the tyrant as scourge, as we will see, seems to be the definition most distant from Shakespeare's own. Elizabeth I and James I echo this doctrine, derived from Augustine, though Elizabeth's defense of absolute kingship is more unqualified, or less clearly articulated than James's. In the *Homily Against Disobedience and Wilful Rebellion* (1571), the Tudor theory is set forth: "As in reading of the holy Scriptures we shall find, in very many and almost infinite places as well of the Old Testament as of the New, that kings and princes, as well the evil as the good, do reign by God's ordinance, and that subjects are bounden to obey them . . . that God defendeth them against their enemies, and destroyeth their enemies horribly."[25] This piece also refers to the king as scourge. James I recalls this doctrine in his *Trew Law of Free Monarchies*: "Not that by all this former discourse of mine, and Apologie for Kings, I meane that whatsoever errors and intollerable abominations a sovereigne prince commit, hee ought to escape all punishment, as if thereby the world were only ordained for kings, and they without controlment to turne it vpside down at their pleasure: but by the contrary, by remitting them to God (who is their onely ordinary Iudge) I remit them to the sorest and sharpest schoolemaster that can be deuised for them."[26]

A variation on such an understanding of tyranny as punishment from God was the idea that the scourge of the tyrant could be eliminated by tyrannicide. John of Salisbury's *Policratus: The Statesmans Book* (1159) was the first English work to center on theoretical justification of tyrannicide:

> [E]ven in secular literature, the caution is given that one must live one way with a friend and another with a tyrant. For it is lawful to flatter him whom it is lawful to slay. Further it is not merely lawful to slay a tyrant, but even right and just.[27]

John Ponet, in *A Short Treatise of Politic Power* (1556) writes "And wher the people have not utterly forsaken God and his worde, but have begonne to be weary of it: there hath not God suffred Tyrannies by and by to rush in, and to occupie the hole, and to suppresse the good ordres of the common wealthe, but by litel and litel hathe suffred them to crepe in, first with the head, than with an arme, and so after with a lege, and at leynight, (were not the people penitent, and tyme converted to God) to bring in the hole body, and to worke the feates of tirannes, as hereafter it shalbe declared."[28]

Perhaps the most moving (and most radical) work against tyrants in the Renaissance was Étienne de la Boétie's *Discours sur la servitude volontaire*. For la Boétie, legitimacy had nothing to do with tyranny, and he sees clearly the dangers of a religious and deterministic interpretation of the tyrant's rule. He offers a psychological portrait of the tyrant:

> C'est celà, que certainement le tyran n'est jamais aimé, ni n'aime. L'amitié c'est un nom sacré, c'est une chose sainte, elle ne se met jamais qu'entre gens de bien . . . De ma part, je pense bien et ne suis pas trompé, puisqu'il n'est rien si contraire à Dieu tout libéral et débonnaire, que la tyrannie, qu'il réserve bien là-bas à part pour les tyrans et leurs complice, quelque peine particulière.[29]

The tyrant might also be simply an evil ruler. Lydgate has a wonderful caricature of the tyrant in his *Fall of Princes* (composed ca. 1439):

> Who can or may tirauntes wil descryve,
> Whos marcial suerdis be whet ay for vengaunce?
> Ther bloode thrustes doth thoruh ther hertes ryve,
> Ther eris ay open to heere of sum myschaunce,
> Ther furious merthe, ther mortal wood plesaunce,
> Ther pale smylyng, ther laughtre of fals hatrede,
> Concludeth evere upon sum cruel deede.

And he offers a warning to prospective tyrants,

> For tirannye and fals oppressioun
> Causeth princis to stande in gret hatreede.
> And what is worth ther domynacioun
> Without love lat preve it at a neede?
> Men for a tyme may suffre hem weel and dreede:
> But whan that dreed constrayned is and goone,
> Than is a prince but a man allone.[30]

The Mirror for Magistrates (first circulated ca. 1559) continues this tradition of the tragedies of ambitious men, writing to discourage the ambitious from seeking office, quoting, as he says, Plato" "Wel is that realme governed, in which the ambicious desyer not to beare office."[31] Lydgate's *Fall of Princes* and *The*

Mirror for Magistrates after it, both emphasize the ultimate humiliation of tyrants and evil rulers to discourage the ambitious from attempting to oppress others, as Baldwin says in his dedication to the *Mirror*, this is the "chiefest ende" of the book: "Howe he [God] hath plaged euill rulers from time to time, in other nacions, you may see gathered in Bochas booke intituled the fall of Princes, translated into Englishe by Lydgate: . . . For here as in a loking glas, you shall see (if any vice be in you) howe the like hath bene punished in other heretofore, whereby admonished, I trust it will be a good occasion to move you to the soner amendment. This is the chiefest ende, whye it is set furth, which God graunt it may atteyne."[32]

This evil rule, examined more closely, may be the result of overriding self-interest. This is argued in the *Secreta Secretorum*, a collection of letters supposedly sent from Aristotle to Alexander the Great, compiled from an eighth-century Syriac source and translated into Arabic then turned into Latin by Philip of Paris in the thirteenth century:

> In fowre manners kynges ham demenyth. Some byth fre to hamselfe and to har subiectis, otheris byth scars to ham-selfe *and* to har sugettes. Of this two the ytaliance sayth, that in a kynge hit is noght worthe by yf he be large to hym-Selfe and to his sugettes. But amonge al othyrs, he is worste and most reprovabill, that is large and fre to hym-Selfe, and scars *and* hard to his sugettes. For his roilalme may not endure.[33]

The author also argues that the tyrant is a scourge of God.[34] What is most interesting is that these claims are made in Aristotle's name. There is foundation in the *Politics* for regarding the tyrant as one who rules against the common interest, just after his description of the six kinds of political regimes (kingship, aristocracy, polity, tyranny, oligarchy, democracy): "Tyranny is monarchy with a view to the advantage of the monarch."[35] This is an even stricter view than it first appears to be since a monarch whose interest coincides with the common interest would also be a tyrant according to this definition. Or perhaps Aristotle means to say that the interest of the monarch will never coincide with the common interest.

An Aristotelian, Marsilius of Padua, in his *Defensor Pacis* (composed 1324), added rule over willing subjects to Aristotle's rule for the common good: "A *kingly monarchy*, then, is a temperate government wherein the ruler is a single man who rules for the common benefit, and in accordance with the will or consent of the subjects. *Tyranny*, its opposite, is a diseased government wherein the ruler is a single man who rules for his own private benefit apart from the will of his subjects."[36] John of Paris in the thirteenth century emphasized the argument that the tyrant ruled in his own self-interest: "Hence the philosopher [Aristotle *Ethics* 8.12] says that, among the rulers seeking their own interest, that of the tyrant is the worst, because what he seeks is more proper and what he scorns is more common."[37] By "proper" is meant here proper to himself.

Aristotle's cycle of regimes was much referred to in Renaissance treatises on politics. One in which it was extensively used was Guillaume de la Perrière's "Le Miroire Politique," equipped with careful tables of Aristotle's cycle of regimes. A translation, *The Mirrour of Policie* was published in 1598:

> Aristotle in the eleventh chapter of his third booke of Politickes, disputing of this matter, maketh a comparison of the government of a particular house, unto a kingdome or cittie: For like as in the house of a good husband, set in good order, there is but one head and maister, whom we call the father of the household, so in this kind of commonweale, the king is as a father of a familie in his kingdome or cittie, and ought to rule over his subjects and Cittizens with such love and care, as a father over his children, otherwise hee loseth the precious and royall name of king, and instead thereof purchaseth to himselfe the title of a Tyrant, which is odious both to God and man. Of this word Tyrant, tyrannie is derived, which is the first kind of a depraved Commonweale.[38]

Castiglione also repeats Aristotle's cycle of regimes in Book IV of *The Book of the Courtier* (1528):

> And the degenerate and lawless forms taken by these systems when they are ruined and corrupted are, in place of monarchy, tyranny, in place of the best, a government by a few powerful men, and in place of the citizens, government by the common people, which wrecks the constitution and surrenders complete power to the control of the multitude. Of these three bad forms of government, there is not doubt that tyranny is the worst.[39]

Bodin, too, defines the tyrant as one who "treading under foot the laws of God and nature, abuses his free-born subjects as his slaves: and other men's goods as his own."[40] This suggestion that tyranny necessarily enslaves those tyrannized over is also found in Dante's *De Monarchia* (composed 1312): "perverted forms of government—namely, democracies, oligarchies, and tyrannies—which force the human race into slavery, as is obvious to anyone who runs through all of them."[41] Aquinas, too, relied on Aristotle. But he goes further to distinguish types of tyrants, according to the passions that motivate them. His description of tyranny pushes Aristotle's deceptively simple one towards Lydgate's caricature of the menacing, insanely jealous man:

> Since a tyrant, despising the common good, seeks his private interest, it follows that he will oppress his subjects in different ways according as he is dominated by different passions to acquire certain goods. The one who is enthralled by the passion of cupidity seizes the goods of his subjects; whence Solomon says: "A just king setteth up the land; a covetous man shall destroy it." If he is dominated by the passion of anger, he sheds blood for nothing; whence it is said by Ezechiel" "Her princes in the midst of her are like wolves

ravening the prey to shed blood." Therefore this kind of government is to be avoided as the Wise man admonishes: 'Keep thee far from the man who has the power to kill,' because, forsooth, he kills not for justice sake but by his power, for the lust of his will . . . Nor does the tyrant merely oppress his subjects in corporal things but he also hinders their spiritual good. Those who seek more to use than to be of use to their subjects prevent all progress, suspecting all excellence in their subjects to be prejudicial to their own evil domination. For tyrants hold the good in greater suspicion than the wicked, and to them the valor of others is always fraught with danger.[42]

Xenophon has several definitions of tyranny, his most famous contained in the *Hiero*, a dialogue between the poet, Simonides, and the tyrant, Hiero. In it, Simonides suggests to Hiero how he might improve the lot of those he rules without diminishing his rule. Hiero laments the lot of the tyrant, diminishing the attractions of tyranny to a wise man (Simonides) who, he suspects, might be tempted by the pleasures of tyranny.[43] In his *Memorabilia*, Xenophon quotes Socrates's definition of tyranny:

Kingship and despotism, in his judgment, were both forms of government, but he held that they differed. For government of men with their consent and in accordance with the laws of the state was kingship; while government of unwilling subjects and not controlled by laws, but imposed by the will of the ruler, was despotism.[44]

Xenophon includes the willingness and unwillingness of subjects in his definition of monarchy and tyranny.

These all represent variations on the classical view of tyranny as a bad regime both for the ruled and the ruler, but Machiavelli's political realism introduced the idea that tyranny was not only nor uncommon, but was not to be condemned. Tyranny is never mentioned in *The Prince*, and in the *Discourses on Livy* he discusses it in light of the new modes and orders a modern prince should adopt.[45] He concludes a chapter on how the reformer of an old government should retain old customs with the ominous remark that there is another way of reforming practiced by the tyrant:

But he who proposes to set up a despotism [una potesta assoluta], or what writers call a "tyranny", must renovate everything, as will be said in the next chapter.

He goes on to describe this practice, dropping his reference to the tyrant, who is now a "new prince":

Such methods are exceedingly cruel, and are repugnant to any community, not only to a Christian one, but to any composed of men. It behooves, therefore, every man to shun them, and to prefer rather to live as a private citizen than as a king with such ruination of men to his score. None the less, for the sort of man who is unwilling to take up this first course of well doing, it is expedient, should he wish to hold what he has, to enter on the path of wrong doing. Actually, however, most men prefer to steer a middle course, which is very harmful; for they know not how to be wholly good nor yet wholly bad.[46]

Elsewhere, of course, Machiavelli says that a good man will come to ruin among many who are evil (*Discourses* I.27). It is a measure of the success of Machiavelli's ideas that the English philosopher, Hobbes, could later ridicule Aristotle's cycle of regimes, eliminating the distinction between just and unjust regimes along the lines of the Florentine:

There be other names of Government, in the Histories, and books of Policy; as *Tyranny*, and *Oligarchy*: But they are not the names of other Formes of Government, but of the Same Formes misliked. For they that are discontented under *Monarchy*, call it *Tyranny*.[47]

Twentieth-century literary and political writers have an interesting reluctance to use the word tyranny. The word has been replaced by authoritarian, totalitarian, despot, and most strongly dictator. Shakespeare, however, used the term with great frequency, and, as I will argue, both with great variety and with great precision. His plays dramatize tyranny as a political entity, encountered more frequently than most others in world history, as well as a state of being. Unlike modern writers such as Orwell or Solzhenitsyn, who are very concerned to detail the oppressiveness of particular systems, Shakespeare is most interested by what happens to and within the tyrant. In these four dramas of tyranny he is most concerned with portraying the soul or soulessness of the tyrant. What tyranny does to the state qua state and to its individual subjects is not important, but is best understood by looking within the disordered mind and passions of the tyrant himself.

Orwell, for instance, explores modern totalitarianism from the perspective of a citizen of Oceania. The tragedy of *1984* is the final, complete destruction of Winston's will: "Obedience is not enough. Unless he is suffering, how can you be sure that he is obeying your will and not his own? Power is in inflicting pain and humiliation. Power is in tearing human minds to pieces and putting them together again in new shapes of your own choosing."[48] Is this kind of reinvention of the human being a new phenomenon of a technological and democratic age? Hannah Arendt described the new power as

the means of total domination are not only more drastic but . . . totalitarianism differs essentially from other forms of political oppression known to us such as despotism, tyranny and dictatorship. Wherever it rose to power, it developed entirely new political institutions and destroyed all social, legal and political traditions of the country.[49]

But isn't this definition of the new totalitarianism—what replaces tyranny for Arendt—reminiscent of what Machiavelli neglects to call tyranny in his *Discourses*?

Such a political topic as Shakespeare's dramas of tyranny invites the question of whether a Renaissance playwright has anything to teach about contemporary politics. If, as Arendt argues, the oppressions we experience and have experienced in the twentieth century are wholly new phenomena, enabled by modern technology, we might be discouraged from looking to Shakespeare for any sort of understanding of current politics. But if, as I argue, Shakespeare had available to him, thought about, and criticized a comprehensive variety of tyrannies in his plays, his dramatic explorations might have more than aesthetic value to us. They also respond to definitions ranging from Aristotle's sober and strict categorization of tyranny, through Machiavelli's calculated forgetfulness, to Lydgate's startling caricature. Is there such a thing as tyranny? Or is it name-calling that can be made to disappear from our vocabulary and our understanding as Machiavelli and Hobbes imply? These four dramas of tyranny insist that such a forgetfulness seriously diminishes our understanding of the political world and of ourselves.

Notes

1. Alan Bloom with Harry Jaffa, *Shakespeare's Politics* (Chicago: The University of Chicago Press, 1981), 3. Bloom's approach, in its treatment of philosophic problems in Shakespeare, interprets the dramatist as a profound thinker, whose thought was not ultimately subject to the prejudices of his historical time period. A clear statement of the grounds for this theoretical approach is given by Leo Strauss in *Natural Right and History* (Chicago: The University of Chicago Press, 1971). He opens the question of the validity of the historicist approach, which confines a thinker to the general "thought" of his historical circumstance, suggesting that "we need . . . an understanding of the genesis of historicism that does not take for granted the soundness of historicism" (33).

2. For an unsympathetic but careful examination of the problem of essentialist criticism see Victoria Kahn's essay, "Humanism and the Resistance to Theory," which concludes the collection *Literary Theory/Renaissance Texts*, eds. Patricia Parker and David Quint (Baltimore: The Johns Hopkins University Press, 1986), 373-396. Hereafter referred to as Parker/Quint.

3. H. M. Richmond, *Shakespeare's Political Plays*, Studies in Language and Literature (New York: Random House, 1967), 13, 235.

4. E. M. W. Tillyard, *Shakespeare's History Plays* (New York: Collier Books, 1944), 363.

5. L. C. Knights, *Further Explorations* (Stanford: Stanford University Press, 1965), 13.

6. William Empson, *Essays on Shakespeare* (Cambridge: Cambridge University Press, 1986), 243. For examples of this see A. C. Bradley's *Shakespearean Tragedy*

(London: Macmillan, 1957) and George Wilson Knight, *The Crown of Life* (London: Methuen, 1952) and *The Imperial Theme* (London: Methuen, 1951). Though his symbolic approach aims at finding an "essential" meaning in the plays, Knight, of course, recommends specifically against Bradley's approach: "we give attention always to poetic colour and suggestion first, thinking primarily in terms of symbolism, not 'characters,'" *The Shakespearean Tempest* (London: Methuen, 1953), 4.

7. Terry Eagleton, *Criticism and Ideology* (London: NLB, 1975), 96.

8. Terry Eagleton, *William Shakespeare* (New York: Basil Blackwell, 1986), 3.

9. Kevin Sharpe and Steven N. Zwicker, eds., *Politics of Discourse: The Literature and History of Seventeenth-Century England* (Berkeley: University of California Press, 1987), 20.

10. Leonard Tennenhouse, *Power on Display: The Politics of Shakespeare's Genres* (New York: Methuen, 1986), 1.

11. Stephen Greenblatt, *Renaissance Self-Fashioning* (Chicago: The University of Chicago Press, 1980), 253.

12. Greenblatt, *Renaissance Self-Fashioning*, 254.

13. Parker/Quint, 16.

14. Jonathan Dollimore, *Radical Tragedy* (Chicago: The university of Chicago Press, 1984), 3.

15. Jonathan Dollimore, *Political Shakespeare: New Essays in Cultural Materialism* (Ithaca, NY: Cornell University Press, 1985), 14.

16. Catherine Belsey, *The Subject of Tragedy: Identity and Difference in Renaissance Drama* (New York, Methuen, 1985), 10.

17. Dollimore, *Political Shakespeare*, 15.

18. George Buchanan, *The Powers of the Crown in Scotland [De Jure Regni Apud Scotos]*, trans. Charles Flinn Arrowood (Austin: University of Texas Press, 1949), 89. He wrote another historical/political account entitled *The Tyrannous Reign of Mary Stuart*.

19. Buchanan, 89.

20. See William A. Armstrong, "The Elizabethan Conception of the Tyrant," *Review of English Studies*, 22.87 (July 1946), 161-181.

21. *A Lexicon Abridged from Liddell and Scott's Greek-English Lexicon* (Oxford: Clarendon Press, 1974).

22. James I also held this view; see chapter 2, footnote 19.

23. St. Augustine of Hippo, *City of God* V.21.15. That Shakespeare was acquainted with this idea of the tyrant is evident from the reference to Talbot in 1HVI: "Thou ominous and fearful owl of death,/Our nation's terror and their bloody scourge!/The period of thy tyranny approacheth" (IV.ii.15-17).

24. Henrie Bullinger, *The Tragedies of Tyrantes Exercised upon the Church of God, from the birth of Christ unto this present yeere, 1572*. Containing the causes of them, and the just vengeance of God upon the authours. Also some notable convertes and exhortations to pacience. Written by Henrie Bullinger and now Englished. Inprinted at London by William How, for Abraham Welae, dwelling in Paules Churchyard at the sign of the Lamb, 1575, 115b, 116a.

25. As quoted in William Armstrong, "The Elizabethan Conception of the Tyrant," 164.

26. Charles Howard McIlwain, ed., *The Political Works of James I* (New York: Russell & Russell, 1965), 69.

27. John of Salisbury, *Policratus: The Statesmans Book*, ed. Murray F. Markland (New York: Frederick Ungar Publishing Co., 1979), 40.

28. John Ponet, *A Short Treatise of Politic Power* (Yorkshire, England: The Scholar Press, Ltd., 1970), Avi verso. He argues for tyrannicide by natural law, "The lawe testifieth to every mannes conscience, that it is naturall to cutte awaie an incurable membre, which (being suffred) wolde destroie the hole body," Gvi recto.

29. Étienne de la Boétie, *Oeuvres Politiques*, les Classiques du Peuple, ed. Francois Hincker (Paris: Editions Sociales, 1963), 76. This circulated widely in the original French, between 1574-78, and Montaigne refers to it at the end of his essay "Of Friendship." For a discussion of the interesting history of the manuscript see Harry Kurz's introduction to his 1942 translation, entitled *Anti-Dictator* (New York: Columbia University Press, 1942), xiv-xix. He uses la Boétie's work as a call for people to rise up against Hitler.

30. Lydgate, *Fall of Princes*, ed. Henry Bergen (Washington, D.C.: The Carnegie Institution of Washington, 1923), 3.3949-62: 439.

31. *The Mirror for Magistrates*, ed. Lily B. Campbell (New York: Barnes and Noble, Inc., 1938), 63.

32. *Mirror*, 65-66.

33. Robert Steele, ed., *Three Prose Versions of the Secreta Secretorum*, Early English Text Society Extra Series LXXIV (London: Kegan Paul, 1898), 130.

34. Steele, 199.

35. Aristotle, *Politics*, trans. Carnes Lord (Chicago: The University of Chicago Press, 1984), 1279b5-6. Earlier, Aristotle says, "It is evident, then, that those regimes which look to the common advantage are correct regimes according to what is unqualifiedly just, while those which look only to the advantage of the rulers are errant, and are all deviations from the correct regimes; for they involve mastery, but the city is a partnership of free persons," 1279a17-21.

36. Marsilius of Padua, *Defensor Pacis*, Mediaeval Academy Reprints for Teaching, trans. Alan Gewirth (Toronto: University of Toronto Press, 1980), 27-28.

37. John of Paris, "On Kingly and Papal Power," (composed 1302) trans. Ernest L. Fortin, in *Medieval Political Philosophy*, eds. Ralph Lerner and Muhsin Mahdi (Ithaca, NY: Cornell University Press, 1972), 407. Hereafter referred to as Lerner.

38. G. de la Perrière, *The Mirrour of Policie: A Worke nolesse profitable than necessarie, for all Magistrates, and Governours of Estates and Commonweales* (London: Printed by Adam Islip, 1598), ai recto. He later gives one cause of tyranny as follows: "This coveting of Honour was the cause of great trouble and alteration in the common-weale of Rome, chaunging it from Aristocratie into tyrannie, and the government of one alone: which happened when as Iulius Caesar scorning a Superior and Pompey stomacking to have any equall to himselfe, did both strive for the principallity." This is useful in thinking about *Macbeth*.

39. Baldesar Castiglione, *The Book of the Courtier*, trans. George Bull (Middlesex, England: Penguin Books, 1967), 298.

40. Jean Bodin's *Six Livres de la République* (1576) as quoted in Oscar Jaczi and John D. Lewis, *Against the Tyrant: The Tradition and Theory of Tyrannicide* (Glencoe, IL: The Free Press, 1957), 72.

41. Dante, *On Monarchy* (trans. Philip H. Wicksteed), in Lerner, 430.

42. St. Thomas Aquinas, *The Political Ideas of St. Thomas Aquinas: Representative Selections*, ed. Dino Bigongiari (New York: Hafner Publishing Co., 1953), 183.

43. All citations from the *Hiero* will be taken from *Xenophon*, Loeb Classical Library, 7 vols., Vol. 7 (Cambridge: Harvard University Press, 1979).

44. *Xenophon*, Loeb Classical Library, 7 vols., Vol. 4, *Memorabilia, Oeconomicus. Apology, Symposium*, trans. E. C. Marchant (Cambridge: Harvard University Press, 1979), 4.6.12-113: 343-345.

45. There have been many views taken on Elizabethan knowledge of Machiavelli. Among them are Felix Raab's *The English Face of Machiavelli*, which rejects the notion that Machiavelli was known only indirectly through Gentillet's attacks on him in *Discours sur les Moyens de Bien Gouverner*. For an exhaustive enumeration of references to Machiavelli in the Renaissance see Edward Meyer's *Machiavelli and the Elizabethan Drama* (New York: Burt Franklin, 1897) and Federico Chabod, *Machiavelli and the Renaissance*, trans. David Moore (New York: Harper and Row, 1958). See also Mario Praz's "Machiavelli and the Elizabethans," Proceedings of the British Academy, Vol. 13 (London: Humphrey Milford Amen House, 1928). Praz refers to the sixteenth-century Italian dramatist Geraldi Cinthio who developed the "Senecan tyrant brought up to date on the lines supplied by *The Prince*" (23), a villain later used by Elizabethan dramatists. This argument is also made by William A. Armstrong in his article on "The Influence of Seneca and Machiavelli on the Elizabethan Tyrant" (*Review of English Studies*, 24.93 [January 1948]) where he includes *Richard III* and *Macbeth* among what he calls "tyrant-tragedies": the Senecan villain given a basis in Machiavellian political theory (32). Finally, he detects a "Renascence synthesis of Roman, Christian, and Machiavellian ideas," which I believe overlooks Shakespeare's profound comprehension of the incompatibility of those three ways of life (35). He gives a general treatment in "The Elizabethan Conception of the Tyrant" (*Review of English Studies*) Vol. 22 [July 1946] no. 87). Tracy B. Strong suggests that Shakespeare knew enough of Machiavelli to offer a criticism of his political ideas ["Shakespeare: Elizabethan Statecraft and Machiavellianism" from *The Artist and Political Vision*, eds. Benjamin R. Barber and Michael J. Gragas McGrath (New Brunswick: Transaction Books, 1982)]. My understanding of Shakespeare's critique of Machiavelli differs significantly from Strong's. He concludes: "only when we have settled with those around us do power, authority and kingship become possible, and not, as the Machiavellians would have it, the other way around"" (218). See chapter 3 for a discussion of Shakespeare's response to Machiavelli.

46. Niccolo Machiavelli, *The Discourses*, ed. Bernard Crick, trans. Leslie J. Walker (Baltimore, MD: Penguin Books, 1974), 176, 177.

47. Thomas Hobbes, *Leviathan*, ed. C. B. Macpherson (New York: Penguin Books, 1968), II.19: 240-241.

48. George Orwell, *1984* (New York: Signet Classics, 1983), 220.

49. Hannah Arendt, *Totalitarianism*, pt. 3 of *The Origins of Totalitarianism* (New York: Harcourt Brace Jovanovich, 1968), 158.

Chapter 2

Macbeth: What Does the Tyrant?

The Title Is Affeer'd

Contemporary approaches to *Macbeth* treat the central problem of tyranny as an historical aberration or, in one notable instance, as an apparently archaic term, antecedent of the modern bourgeois individualist.[1] *Macbeth* provides an excellent starting point for recovery of Shakespeare's teaching about tyranny, and what it has to do with an attempt to find natural limitations to human desire. In particular, Macbeth's fate describes a very direct but unexpected path to tyranny, that of the patriot, or lover of honor. The authoritative man, authoritative because unbeatable on the field of battle and so the necessary prop of any regime, must often be subordinate to men whom he considers his inferiors. They are inferior to him primarily in courage.[2]

There is lengthy dialogic exploration of tyranny in act 4, scene 3, a scene that has been largely ignored or dismissed by critics. Of all the scenes in *Macbeth*, this scene is most difficult to place within the thematic framework of the play. Malcolm attempts to persuade Macduff that he is tyrannical by nature. Dramatically, it seems a peculiar place to situate the longest expository scene in the play, a lengthy deception that does not immediately further the action. But this conversational interlude occurs just before the denouement, the accelerated movement of act 5, and invites reflection on the issue of good and bad kingship. No one has yet satisfactorily explained the presence of this, the longest scene in the shortest tragedy. The absence of any prolonged analysis of this undramatic scene in a tightly constructed, highly dramatic play, can perhaps be explained by a reluctance to regard the play as an exploration of the evolution of a tyrant. The scene takes on importance and makes most sense as drawing the audience's attention to the question, What is a tyrant? Or, what does a tyrant do that sets him apart from others of great political ambition, Malcolm or

Banquo, for instance? Menteth's question about military strategy in act 5, scene 2 might be extended—What does the tyrant want?

One may either interpret Malcolm's self-libel to Macduff as his insecurity in a moment of crisis (he is, after all, first seen as ineffectual or at least immature in acts 1 and 2), or it may be seen as a sign of his necessary subtlety in Macbeth's world of spies. E. K. Chambers attributes it to a loss of nerve:

> I think there is a touch of deeper psychological insight in this [than a trial of Macduff's patriotism]. Is it not true that in the critical moments of life one is often suddenly oppressed with a sense of one's own weaknesses, and dormant, if not actual, tendencies to evil, which seem to cry aloud for expression, confession?[3]

The editors of the Clarendon edition dismiss this encounter with a comment on dramaturgy: "The poet no doubt felt that this scene was needed to supplement the meager parts assigned to Malcolm and Macduff."[4] A. W. Verity, in his notes to *The Pitt Press Shakespeare* (1901) says,

> Dramatically this scene seems, at first sight, more open to criticism than any other in the play. . . . The real design is, I think, to mark the pause before the storm. . . . The denouement must be led up to gradually; there must be an antecedent period in which the storm clouds gather: and this long scene as it were, fills the period.[5]

No doubt, but this comment, too, avoids the significance of the discussion of tyranny. Most recent critics make no mention of the scene at all. E. A. J. Honigmann, a rare exception, argues that the scene is designed to moderate the audience's condemnation of Macbeth (excited by the murder of Lady Macduff and her children in the scene just before), "blunting its edge by first directing it upon a false target."[6] But this complex and indirect psychological account does not help account for the brief concluding description of the "King's Evil." It would be more powerful if the discussion between Malcolm and Macduff were not immediately succeeded by Rosse's reminder of the slaughter.

None of the above explanations is implausible, but none is complete, because all overlook the critical element of the scene. It presents a definition of what the tyrant is—one who rules oppressively, solely in his own self-interest, and for the satisfaction and excitement of his own desires. And along with this definition it offers a glimpse of a standard of good rule.[7]

Not only does Malcolm force a discussion of what constitutes a tyranny, but, within the scene, he holds conference with a doctor and gives a detailed account of a remarkable, presumably divine aspect of the king of England: he can cure the "king's evil." This scene is recollected three scenes later in Macbeth's conversation with his wife's doctor. In the first reference to medicine's powers, the king cures the people, in the second, Macbeth, king of Scotland, turns to a doctor for a "purgative drug" (V.iii.55)[8] for his country. He, too, sees the realm as diseased, but not in the same way that Malcolm and Macduff do. The disease of Scotland, "my land" (51), is the English force which, in support of Malcolm, has invaded Scotland. Macbeth does not mention Malcolm; it is the English who infect Scotland. He understands the final conflict not as a civil war, but, from a nationalist perspective, as a foreign invasion. Malcolm spends some time in England and he has learned about monarchial politics there, as we might gather from the fact that he renames his Thanes Earls at the end of the play ("the first that ever Scotland/In such an honour nam'd," V.ix.29-30.)[9] The scenic paradox of Malcolm's deception and the Doctor's description of the King's Evil affords an anecdotal account of the differences between good and bad kingship. Why call our attention to the question of good rule here? Or why call our attention to the problem so fully this late in the play?

The scene takes place between the execution of Lady Macduff and her children—the most pathetic instance of Macbeth's increasing inhumanity in the play—and Lady Macbeth's sleepwalking scene, with commentary by another doctor. The execution scene is such a startling excess that Coleridge felt compelled to defend it as dramatically necessary from the accusation that Shakespeare "wounds the moral sense by the unsubdued, undisguised description of the most hateful atrocity—that he tears the feelings without mercy, and even outrages the eye itself with scenes of insupportable horror."[10] The bloodiness of the play as a whole is striking; we witness at least two murders and overhear another being committed. (By contrast in *Richard III*, with the exception of the murder of the guilty Clarence, Richard's atrocities are talked of rather than shown.) This discussion, then, is preceded by a scene of utmost physical brutality and followed by a scene of mental anguish (Lady Macbeth overheard by her Doctor and Gentlewoman). The first scene exemplifies the consequences of tyrannical action for society as a whole (the cold-blooded murder of innocents and the destruction of the family), and the second scene examines the consequences of tyrannical rule for those who exercise it. The point of connection between the destructive act and the ensuing guilt comes in the midst of Lady Macbeth's disjointed utterances, "The Thane of Fife had a wife, where is she now?" (38) She calls Macbeth by his original, unsullied title. Underlying this question is Lady Macbeth's implied loss of self, her guilty fears, and her collapse back into the role of vulnerable wife.

In the play we are shown two unsuccessful versions of rule, Duncan's and Macbeth's. Duncan is credulous, kindhearted, generous, and apparently ineffectual militarily. Macbeth is victorious in the short term, but bloody. In this scene we have brief reference to a third standard, Edward's kingship—one which seems to work well. He is a strong king, honored and given a semi-divine status by the people—some sort of elevated mean between the two kinds of kingship we observe more carefully in Scotland.

Perhaps the most interesting passage in the portion of Holinshed's *Chronicles* pertaining to *Macbeth* is the passage in which Duncan and Macbeth are compared. Macbeth is described as

> One that if he had not beene somewhat cruele of nature, might have beene thought most woorthie the government of a realme. On the other part, Duncane was so softe and gentle of nature, that the people wished the inclinations and maners of these two cousins to have beene so tempered and enterchangeablie bestowed betwixt them, that where the one had too much clemencie, and the other of cruelte, the meane vertue betwixt these two extremities might have reigned by indifferent partitions in them both, so should Duncane have proved a woorthie king, and Makbeth a excellent capteine.[11]

Shakespeare interprets this difference in character at several points in the play and act 4, scene 3 presents us with an alternative to the overly ambitious captain, Macbeth, and the unsuspecting, pious Duncan in the persons of Malcolm and Macduff. This curiously placed, nondramatic scene instructs us in how the tragedy might have been averted, and in so doing offers an analysis of the component vices of tyranny and its effects.

Malcolm's Correction of Macduff

Malcolm, unlike his father, who finally concludes that there is no art "To find the mind's construction in the face" (I.iv.12), straight off acknowledges "that which you are, my thoughts cannot transpose: /Angels are bright still, though the brightest fell: /Though all things foul would wear the brows of grace, /Yet grace must still look so" (21-24). This emphasizes how highly thought of Macbeth originally was, a fact often overlooked. Malcolm echoes not only his father, but also Macbeth: "False face must hide what false heart doth know." He conflates these two teachings. He serves as a correction to Duncan—there is an art to finding the mind's construction, though not through simple appearances. One must search out intentions by indirect means, such as the test of loyalty and intellect he administers to Macduff.

In offering his services, Macduff twice refers to Macbeth as a tyrant:

> Bleed, bleed, poor country!
> Great tyranny, lay thou thy basis sure,
> For goodness dare not check thee! wear thou thy wrongs;
> The title is affeer'd! —Fare thee well, Lord:
> I would not be the villain that thou think'st
> For the whole space that's in the tyrant's grasp,
> And the rich East to boot.
> (IV.iii.32-37)[12]

But what does Macduff mean by "tyrant"? The central lament of this sincerely self-righteous outburst is that "the title is affeer'd," which means the title is confirmed, Macbeth has won the title "king" by default, he has succeeded in usurping the legitimate heir.[13] Macduff assumes the simplest definition of tyranny, that it is illegitimate rule. Macbeth is a tyrant because he has usurped the throne from Malcolm, the rightfully appointed heir.[14] But Malcolm's understanding of tyranny is significantly more complicated. He begins with a list of seven of Macbeth's supposed vices, recalling the cardinal sins, with the notable omission of pride (II.57-66).[15] Yet Macbeth seems, if anything, somewhat plain, even Spartan, except in his desire to gain and secure the crown.[16] When Malcolm speaks of Macbeth as "luxurious," does this refer to his excessive desire for power? He certainly does not seem to mean it in the narrow sense in which he applies it to himself (physical lust). Macbeth, after all, speaks contemptuously of the "English epicures" before the decisive battle (V.iii.8). "Luxurious" is a curious term to apply in the midst of all the other epithets he uses, most having immediately to do with the crimes Macbeth has committed—regicide, infanticide, treason.[17]

Malcolm dwells as well on Macbeth's being "false, deceitful," and "sudden," those characteristics most absent from his father and most responsible for Macbeth's success as usurper. To speak of someone, or of an action, as "sudden" may be a commendation (see *King John* V.vi.26, *Richard III* I.iii.345, *Julius Caesar* III.i.19, *Hamlet* V.ii.46). If Duncan is to be found lacking in any royal qualities it is these—he is too trusting and he is slow to act. We first see Duncan in act 1, scene 2 completely ignorant of the battle events, depending on a wounded soldier for information on whether the rebellion has succeeded. He is well behind battle lines, and his son, Malcolm, has just been rescued from enemy soldiers by a sergeant. He has apparently had no presentiment of the revolt of Cawdor, which allowed or furthered the invasion of King Sweno of Norway. Duncan presents himself as wholly dependent on his soldiers for success, without any sense that a strong subordinate military leader is as much a danger as a necessity to the throne. Malcolm emphasizes about Macbeth, then, several of the traits he himself must acquire in order to regain the throne and to secure it as his father could not. Malcolm's first deceitful act is one of self-preservation when he urges his brother to fly and says that he, too, will secretly escape Scotland to avoid being killed. His second, more elaborate deceit is the one he practices on Macduff in this scene.

Malcolm accuses himself of sins in the same order in which he applies them to Macbeth, excluding the first epithet "bloody" since the prince has yet to show himself as murderous. First he describes the extent of his voluptuousness (recalling his description of Macbeth as "luxurious" just before). He describes all his vices in terms of immoderate sexual desire, or limitlessness: "confineless harms" (55), "there's no bottom" (60), "could not fill up" (62), "my desire . . . would o'erbear" (63-64). Macduff's response to this circumvents the point at issue: "boundless intemperance in nature is a tyranny" (66-67). This line is usefully glossed by Delius, a nineteenth-century German commentator, as follows: "This belongs to 'tyranny;' such organic intemperance is compared with the political tyranny of Macbeth."[18] But this is a theoretical argument; Macduff does not relate it to fitness for political rule. Malcolm is trying to bring him to make this connection, as Shakespeare is trying to bring his audience to this connection. Tyranny is not simply a political or historical aberration but a particular human condition. Macduff understands these as private vices unrelated to the political evils of tyranny. Malcolm is forcing Macduff to acknowledge the connection between private and public vice, showing that legitimacy does not mitigate vicious character.

What would it prove to Malcolm that Macduff concede this point? Macduff's first response to Malcolm's self-accusation (that he is too lustful for Scotland to sustain his desires), is to say that this vice will cost Malcolm his life, possibly his throne. The implication that he will die an early death from his excesses is stronger than that he will be overthrown for it. Still it will not cause fatal or even critical harm to Scotland, only to the occupant of the throne. He insists "fear not yet/To take upon you what is yours: you may/Convey your pleasures in a spacious plenty" (69-71). Again Macduff sees no connection between the world of private vice and public rule; legitimacy is everything. He goes on to suggest that Malcolm might "hoodwink" the time, drawing our attention back to Macbeth's decision to "mock the time" (I.vii.82, see also I.v.61). He still has a right to the throne, as legally appointed heir to it, even though his vices rival Macbeth's. The usurpation of reason by boundless intemperance is equated, implicitly, with Malcolm's usurpation by Macbeth (see note 14). The word tyranny here has the same connotation of illegitimacy as in Macduff's earlier speech, but it has become associated with unnatural rule (rule that is not according to nature, or rule by a disordered soul—where reason, in the Platonic tripartite division of the soul, has been overthrown) as well as rule that goes against conventions of legitimacy. Macduff's position has implicitly altered. But Malcolm is still the ruler of choice, argues Macduff, because he is legally heir to the throne, and Macbeth, whatever his tyrannical qualities, is responsible for "our down-fall birthdom" (14). Clearly such an argument is not sufficient to convince Malcolm; and it is in order to gain near certain conviction that he has presented himself as weak (weeping) and vicious in this critical moment before a battle for which he is eminently well-prepared, as we are immediately to learn.

Macduff's adherence to a legal formality that overlooks a potential for greater evil could be construed in many ways. Macduff might simply be a traitor, or he might support Malcolm for the wrong reasons, as Macbeth supported Duncan against the traitorous Thane of Cawdor and Norway—with less thought for the right of Scotland and Duncan's merits than for military honor. (This scene is preceded, of course, by the discussion between Lady Macduff

and her son as to what a traitor is, with Macduff's son arguing for realpoli
Macduff concludes that kingly vice can play on ordinary human vice, wom
willing to sell themselves to powerful men, and can satisfy itself more easily by
virtue of its station. In other words, there is no difference in character between
the vices of a king and those of a commoner, only a difference of degree and
ability to indulge. This conclusion could not explain the existence of tyranny. If
every self-indulgence were taken as tyranny, we would all be named tyrants.
Why is Malcolm forcing Macduff into the position of choosing between two
evils? This dialogue points up the paradoxical notion of all-important legitimacy. Is it enough that a legitimate ruler be considered a monarch and a usurper
be termed a tyrant, that arguments of merit be ignored for the sake of formality
and custom? On a historical note, the issue of the status of legitimacy can more
easily be raised in a play about the Scottish line at a time before it became one
with the English line (at a time when royal primogeniture was not firmly established) without immediate political risk to the playwright.

James I, of course, spoke and wrote extensively on the question of proper
rule. He gave a speech before Parliament on his "Opinion of a king, of a
Tyrant," which makes Malcolm's point:

> I do acknowledge that the special and greatest point of difference that is be-
> twixt a rightful King and a usurping tyrant, is in this: That whereas the proud
> and ambitious Tyrant doth think his Kingdom and People, are only ordained
> for satisfaction of his Desires, and unreasonable appetites; The righteous and
> just King doth by the contrary acknowledge himself to be ordained for the
> procuring of the Wealth and Prosperity of his People; and that his great and
> principal worldly Felicity, must consist in their Prosperity.[19]

What is interesting about this excerpt from James's speech is that he begins by
denoting the tyrant a "usurping tyrant" thereby further distancing the tyrant
from the king, just as Macduff does. James begins with the implicit assumption
that a tyrant is primarily a tyrant by virtue of his illegitimacy. The dangers of
expanding the definition of tyrant to include legitimate rulers who rule solely in
their own interest must have been obvious to him.[20]

Malcolm explains next that he is avaricious as well, the second vice he
attributes to Macbeth. He vows he will "cut off the nobles" for their lands (79),
something Macbeth has not yet done (though he has apparently killed those he
considered a danger to his power). Macduff responds that former Scottish kings
have used their "sword" to fill their coffers: imperialism prevents abuse of
one's subjects (consider Shakespeare's account of Henry V's decision to invade
France). Both these vices are excusable, so long as a legitimate king possesses
"other graces."

Malcolm denies he possesses any of the king-becoming graces and names
them.[21] All are public, political virtues appropriate to a Christian king as well
as private moral virtues. At this, Macduff succumbs, and, for the first time,

"an untitled tyrant," rather than speak, as before, of
yrant" because he is a usurper. The addition of "un-
is a distinction to be made between titled and untitled
ـgitimacy is not the only grounds for, or definition of,
ـan be a tyrant irrespective of one's title.

ــــauff then lapses into pious exclamations, nearly canonizing Duncan, pronouncing himself "banish'd" from Scotland. This convinces Malcolm of two things. First, that he is not Macbeth's spy, and second that his allegiance is to a proper occupant of the throne, not just to anyone with a legitimate claim. Macduff's quarrel with Macbeth is not an individual one, but one based on principle, a principle that Malcolm brings out through his deception. This principle is also important to our view of the play. Macduff's speech shows that he can, and does, without realizing it, make the distinction between legitimacy as an unqualified claim to the throne, and capacity for good rule. Macduff's abhorrence of Malcolm's description of himself also convinces him that Macduff's is not a personal quarrel with Macbeth. Had it been so, Macduff would be a far more dangerous man, likely to use Malcolm's rightful claims to the throne to promote his own interest, another Macbeth perhaps. In his final speech of the play, Macduff refers no longer to the tyrant, but to "Th'usurper's cursed head" (V.ix.21), a technically correct understatement demonstrating what he has learned from Malcolm, which the newly restored king immediately corrects.

Malcolm brings to light the distinction between tyranny as the exercise of rule by an illegitimate king and tyranny as bad rule by a king whether legitimate or illegitimate. This is fitting since he defines Macbeth's reign in the final speech of the play as "watchful tyranny" (V.ix.33). Malcolm's deception exhibits the superiority of his political understanding to that of his father. As Pierre Sahel points out in "Machiavélisme Vulgaire et Machiavélisme Authentique dans *Macbeth*," "Malcolm a remplacé pour un temps ses vertus personnelles par la *virtu* indispensable à la réussite de son entreprise imminente."[22] Sahel argues that in this scene Malcolm practices an authentic Machiavellianism, whereas Macbeth's Machiavellianism is crude and so fails.[23] The superficially tedious dialogue of act 4, scene 3 forcefully introduces a moment of reflection on the question of what tyranny means and so is an appropriate starting point for a discussion of Shakespeare's understanding of tyranny. The tyrant, for Shakespeare, is no mere usurper.[24]

The King's Evil

Malcolm calls upon "God above" to deal between himself and Macduff. He puts himself in Macduff's hands—proclaiming his honesty, not asserting his kingly virtues, but denying all the tyrannical vices. The confrontation between Malcolm and Macduff under these circumstances provides us with alternative courses of action to those taken by Duncan, Banquo, and Macbeth earlier in the play. Malcolm is more cautious than Duncan, and Macduff is more cautious than Banquo, less ambitious than Macbeth. Malcolm is a more prudent statesman than his father and Macduff is a soldier whose ambitions are circumscribed by his patriotism. There is a pause and a Doctor enters to tell them of the imminent arrival of the English king (in a show of support for Malcolm and Siward). While a brief announcement would have been adequate to establish dramatically the forceful presence of England, Malcolm instead offers commentary on the manner of the king. J. P. Collier, in agreement with other early editors, notes that this entire intrusion was "struck out by the MS corrector" and suggests it was included only as a compliment to King James, during his lifetime, since he had revived the practice.[25] Arden editor Kenneth Muir suggests, rightly I think, that it is integral and provides a contrast of good supernatural force with evil supernatural force—a counter-poise to the witches.[26] The dramatic importance of Malcolm's account of this supernatural healing process is not simply the scientific miracle or the potentially valuable flattery of King James, however, but the illustration of an aspect of kingship wholly lacking in Macbeth's reign, and just barely attempted by Duncan during his rule (see I.ii.48, I.vi.10-14).

The mythology of the king's semi-divine powers has been extended to his heirs as well, suggesting his concern with founding a stable monarchial line. As Malcolm notes prudently, "How he solicits Heaven/Himself best knows" (149-150). Already word has spread that Edward's heirs will possess the same virtue, as Malcolm reports: "'tis spoken/To the succeeding royalty he leaves/The healing benediction" (154-156). He takes this from Holinshed's account: "He used to help those that were vexed with the disease, commonlie called the kings euill, and left that vertue as it were a portion of inheritance into his successions the kings of this realme."[27] Malcolm has apparently come to learn the importance of the continuity of such a myth. Shakespeare emphasizes this with the change of one detail; in Malcolm's account the king also hangs a golden stamp around those he has cured—he does not simply depend on word of mouth to enhance his reputation as healer. Malcolm also mentions Edward as having a "gift of prophecy" (157), merely a rumor in Holinshed.

This is yet another indication that Malcolm has learned something during his enforced sojourn in England; he is well-acquainted with helps such as these (popular superstition) to royal authority. If we are to take his renaming of the thanes at the end of the play as a serious sign of the British influence on him, we could expect a greater attention to the semi-divine trappings of kingship during Malcolm's reign as well.[28]

Malcolm's bitter experience might lead him to look to Edward's more successful reign for a solution to the problem of succession (next to founding, the greatest problem of kingship).[29] This account of Edward's convenient godly gift is in stark contrast to the open criminality of Macbeth's reign. This is one of the rare instances in the play where the commons are mentioned; Shakespeare's Macbeth (unlike Holinshed's) seems wholly unpersuaded of the importance of the high regard of his subjects, making oblique reference to them only once when he speaks, with some contempt, of having "bought/Golden opinions from all sorts of people" (I.vii.32-33). The honors Duncan has accorded him have purchased rather than earned him the good opinion of others.

According to Holinshed, Duncan seems to have been a weak king, overly pious, too scrupulous and lenient with offenders.[30] There is immediate evidence of this in his handling of the revolt of Cawdor as the play begins. Shakespeare emphasizes Duncan's saintly nature (I.iv.15, I.vi.12-14, I.vii.16-25, IV.iii.108-111). Malcolm's exposure to Edward contrasts with his knowledge of the private character of Duncan's piety.

Macbeth, on the other hand, is heedless of reputation for sanctity altogether, openly acknowledging his consultation of the witches (IV.i.136-139, V.iii.5). In doing so he violates one of the most infamous and important of all Machiavelli's teachings, that, since it is the case that princes cannot truly possess all moral virtues, (including piety), "it behooves a prince to use that discretion whereby he maye avoyde the infamie especiallie of such vices as maye weken his power, or hazarde the losse of his principalitie."[31] Malcolm's exposition of this curious detail about the English king draws attention to the problem Macbeth ignores, that of making the kingship appear to the people to have some foundation aside from that of superior strength. From this perspective Macbeth is not only a tyrant, but also his unselfconscious superstition causes him to be an incompetent one. The complete self-confidence inspired in him by the witches causes him to act in contempt of popular opinion. There are kings of private piety and kings who take pains to publicize their piety. Drawing on the problems with Duncan's and Macbeth's experiences respectively, we are shown the advantages of the latter in Edward's gold stamps.

The Succession Crisis

This suggestive rumor about the divinely sanctioned powers of the English line is in marked contrast to the justification Duncan gives for appointing Malcolm his heir. In the past, the Scots throne had been transferred from generation to generation by appointment or election, nominally on the basis of merit. (The English throne historically was passed on by the same means, election by the Witan, a council of leaders.) The one strong indication Shakespeare gives us in the play that primogeniture was not solidly established is Duncan's appointment of Malcolm as heir in act 1, scene 4. There is no comparable instance in the rest of Shakespeare. If a ruler has a legitimate son, the line of succession is clear.

Here Duncan provides no other justification (to quiet resentment or envy) for his choice of Malcolm than that he is "our eldest." To forestall the most superficial objections, he promises that others, too, will be invested with "signs of nobleness," though we never learn what these are (I.iv.38). Certainly Duncan cannot justify his choice of Malcolm on the basis of military valor or proven merit. We know from the first that, while Macbeth and Banquo are fighting against all odds, Malcolm has been captured by the enemy and has barely been saved.

In act 1, scene 2 we get a very indistinct first impression of Duncan—his first line is a question: "What bloody man is that?" In contrast to his apparent confusion, we first learn of Macbeth by hearing of his bloody deeds, his having "unseam'd" a traitor and beheaded him (I.ii.22-23). Duncan terms this blood-thirsty warrior a "valiant Cousin, worthy Gentleman": these are euphemistic, courtly terms for our first heroic introduction to Macbeth. This description may derive in part from Holinshed's reference to Macbeth's cruelty.[32] Our first impression of Malcolm is that he shares his father's unmilitary manner. The early depiction of this great disparity in temperament between Duncan and his son on the one hand, and Macbeth on the other, prepares us to view more sympathetically the latter's strong reaction to Duncan's announcement.

Duncan is apparently in the process of founding his hereditary line in a country where hereditary succession is not yet established. Primogeniture has not yet entirely replaced the former procedure of appointment or election by merit. Shakespeare draws our attention to this necessary and troublesome aspect of founding a dynasty in this scene when Duncan announces to whom he will give his crown (33-34).

The fact that public appointment of an heir is necessary should also moderate our response to Macbeth's outburst. He would be less justified in his apparent resentment of Malcolm if royal primogeniture were an established custom. The inclusion of this scene suggests that Shakespeare wished us to consider that Malcolm's succession was not a given. Though it might be expected, it had to be formally and publicly announced.[33] Holinshed emphasizes Macbeth's rival claim to the throne by his mother rather than his reasonable or unreasonable expectations of reward for service in battle. While Shakespeare alludes to this (Duncan calls Macbeth "cousin" at I.iv.14), Macbeth never asserts he has a right to the throne by blood lines. The reasons for Macbeth's accession to the throne in the absence of Malcolm and Donalbain are left obscure. We could assume he succeeds in part because of general consensus about his superior power and reputation (after his recent victory against Norway) rather than because he is a blood relation. But that he will succeed on Duncan's death and Malcolm's flight, is a foregone conclusion (II.iv.30). (Characteristically, Macbeth has not thought ahead to the possibility that Malcolm might have stayed and claimed the throne.)

The hopes Macbeth reveals when he reacts to this announcement are not then, from this perspective, so entirely unreasonable. By merit he might con-

sider—his ambition having been piqued by the witches—that he ought to be
made Prince of Cumberland since he has saved Scotland from conquest by
Norway. This is not to say that Duncan's appointment of Malcolm is surprising
or unexpected, only that Macbeth's experience with the Witches seems to have
expanded a slender, unarticulated hope into a strong desire. They provide
Macbeth with a twisted reasoning for imposing or re-introducing a standard of
selection by merit that existed in Scotland within recent memory. By such a
standard he would be heir apparent.

Historically, no Scottish monarch was succeeded by his own son or grand-
son until the accession of Duncan after Malcolm II in 1034.[34] According to
Holinshed, royal primogeniture had been introduced in Scotland by Kenneth I,
Duncan's great-great-grandfather by this account, who murdered the rightful
heir, Malcolm Prince of Cumberland, and "got the nobles to agree that succes-
sion should henceforth be by primogeniture."[35] George Buchanan in *Rerum
Scoticarum Historia* gives an account closer to historical fact, noting that Kenneth III slew the rightful heir to the throne (again Malcolm) and persuaded the
nobles to pass a new law, "That as the Kings Eldest Son should succeed his
Father; so, if the son died before the Father, the Nephew should succeed the
Grandfather."[36] At best it would have been an imperfect system at the time
Duncan became king and Shakespeare could reasonably have chosen this point
in Scottish history to pose dramatically the problem of the institution of royal
primogeniture rather than succession by appointment. In any event the succession of Duncan before Macbeth posed a problem historically as both were the
sons of princesses. But Shakespeare does not draw our attention to Duncan's
questionable succession (as he does to that of King Edward IV in *Richard III* or
to Prince Hal's in the Henriad), but to the necessity of his appointing an heir,
and to his appointment of his eldest son.

Shakespeare's refashioning of his historical sources only supplements the
evidence within the play that he is interested in this aspect of the founding, the
problem of succession and how the transition from succession by appointment
or election to succession by inheritance occurred in Scotland.[37] This is one way
of presenting the problem of the creation of kingship by divine right out of the
superstition of the many and the founding ambition of an individual. This helps
explain the pointed reference to Edward's divine healing powers.

Of all Shakespeare's kings, Macbeth seems the least concerned, in a positive sense, with succession. He is at pains to eliminate rivals to the throne, he
goes to great lengths to exterminate Macduff's line lest it prevent his act of
founding, and he attempts to kill Fleance (Banquo's son). He does not, however, mention his own childlessness (except indirectly when he mentions that
he has "fil'd his mind" for "Banquo's issue"). Only once in the play is Macbeth's
lack of an heir mentioned: by Macduff in the scene following his interview with
Malcolm. Macbeth appears wholly unconscious of what or who will succeed

him, except in the abstract. His reign, as we see it, is spent, because of its origins, in securing his throne and not in preparing for more than the immediate future. This focus on the immediacy of power is part of his implicit assumption that the moment of his supreme power as tyrant may be frozen in time, and in this sense he may overcome his own mortality.

The problem of the founding or refounding (with which Malcolm is faced) is rivalled by this problem of succession, which Macbeth addresses only in the negative. The absence of explicit attention to his childlessness is a striking example of the supreme confidence Macbeth derives from the witches. Much like Coriolanus, who aspires to godhead, he comes to believe himself wholly self-sufficient; after all, he cannot be killed by man "of woman born." Just as he does not doubt he will win the battle, he does not entertain the idea that he will remain childless, until his wife dies. He understands his task to be eliminating obstacles (such as Fleance, Macduff's household, and the English), not as taking positive steps to insure his rule.

If it is unclear that he makes a serious attempt to found a line of kings, are Macbeth's aims, then, merely instantaneous gratification? If so, he fails utterly and we are left with Shakespeare's unattractive portrait of an honor-seeking tyrant and the conclusion Macbeth draws from this way of life that life "is a tale/Told by an idiot, full of sound and fury, /Signifying nothing" (V.v.26-28). But he is not the egotistic individualist that Richard III is; the tone of his other speeches and the nihilism of this one indicate he had hopes for greater satisfactions—satisfactions derived from a community, "As honour, love, obedience, troops of friends" (V.iii.25). The play invites us to examine how reasonable these hopes are. To do this we must account for their genesis.

It is important to see that Macbeth has a claim to rule on the basis of merit—a claim no longer admissible in a country coming to be ruled by one dynastic line. Still, he is a far stronger ruler, potentially, than Duncan was, or than Malcolm promises to be (even in his moment of greatest perspicuity in act 4, scene 3). Consider the problematic character of Rosse, whose reluctance to commit himself to one side or the other indicates the strength of Macbeth's claim to the throne.[38] This capacity, coupled with his seduction by the witches, engenders a growing, irrational belief in his own complete self-sufficiency. He falls into evil not all at once, but more and more rapidly. The indications that Scotland is in a vulnerable state and that Macbeth is the man to lead his country increase the tension of the tragedy, but do not soften the delineation of his destruction of his own soul. But it is critical that we see at the beginning of the play that Scotland might be better off under Macbeth, because he is encouraged to view this reasonable alternative in a compellingly favorable light by the perverse and elliptical logic of the Witches' pronouncements. As Holinshed (as well as his predecessor Machiavelli) points out vividly, cruelty is often a valuable commodity in a prince. This is a quality that has no bounds for Macbeth.

Vaulting Ambition

Holinshed says of Macbeth after he has killed Duncan that he

> used great liberalitie towards the nobles of the realme, thereby to win their
> favour, and when he saw that no man went about to trouble him, he set his
> whole intention to mainteine justice, and to punish all enormities and abuses,
> which had chanced through the feeble and slouthfull administration of Duncane
> [Macbeth punished murderers sternly] in such sort, that manie yeares after all
> theft and reiffings were little heard of, the people injoieng the blissefull ben-
> efit of good peace and tranquillitie.[39]

Shakespeare follows the tempo of Macbeth's inner dynamic, not historical reality, and so he omits the first ten good years of his reign.[40] This inner dynamic
is constituted by what he describes as "vaulting ambition," which does and
must "o'erleap" (I.iv.49, I.vii.27).

Holinshed says that Macbeth reconciled the nobles and paid court to the
commons, reinstituted harsh penalties, and successfully restored order in the
kingdom for ten years before he grew into insolent tyranny. Why omit any
mention of the advantages of Macbeth's rule? Shakespeare's intent seems to be
to focus on the inner motions of Macbeth's desire for and attainment of the
throne, or on the tyrannical impulse itself. I do not claim that the tragic hero's
interior world is an isolable point of interest in the play. Such a dramatic frac-
ture has led at least one critic to dismiss the consequences of Macbeth's tyranny
altogether. With a peculiarly modern apolitical resistance to the term "tyrant,"
E. A. J. Honigmann argues that, "Hearing him [Macbeth] described as a *tyrant, usurper, butcher* and so on, an audience . . . cannot but feel that a man's
outer life is a tale told by an idiot, full of sound and fury, signifying very little,
and that the inner life is all in all."[41] But the name "tyrant" is not accidentally
applied to Macbeth more than to any other Shakespearean character. In Macbeth,
he presents us with a tyrant distilled to his essentials, and a tyrant in abeyance
for ten years is still a tyrant.

One of the more surprising aspects of Macbeth's condensed reign in the
drama is that he never seems to be greatly concerned with the effects of his
rule, of his beliefs, or of his manner on the commons or the nobles. His mar-
ginally successful cover-up of Duncan's assassination is followed dramatically
two scenes later by his bold plot to murder Banquo and his effective confession
of guilt at the banquet. He apparently stops making a pretense of honoring the
nobles and respecting their property soon after this murder (III.vi.33-37, IV.iii.4-
5), and he is increasingly and dangerously open about his reliance on the Witches.

Macbeth grows careless of appearances, overconfident of his innate powers and takes no pains to solidify positive support or to justify his claim to the
throne properly—he consistently asserts superior force. Malcolm acts in opposite fashion. A weaker ruler from the first, he has no grounds to claim that he

merits the throne of Scotland except through appointment by his murdered father.

Shakespeare implicates, in his exploration of political rule in Macbeth, as elsewhere, the question of sexual difference, a focus of much critical interest in the play. There is, however, a fundamental question underlying debate about sexual difference in *Macbeth* that has been avoided. This question is at the core of such attacks on feminist criticism as Richard Levin's "Feminist Thematics and Shakespearean Tragedy."[42] The question is, Does Shakespeare understand sexual difference as natural, and therefore determinant, or as mostly conventional and so malleable?[43]

The Witches provide an escape from or confusion of sexual identities—a standard which does not judge Lady Macbeth's unsexing of herself or Macbeth's striving to be more than a man. Yet both Lady Macbeth and Macbeth end tragically—what does this suggest is Shakespeare's view of their attempts to redraw sexual boundaries? An answer to this question would help establish whether the playwright was an adherent of a patriarchal notion of sexual difference (even sexual hierarchy) given currency in his day, or whether he attempted to subvert this. Janet Adelman asserts the former in "'Born of Woman': Fantasies of Maternal Power in *Macbeth*." She argues that the end of the play reasserts the primacy of the masculine against the frightening power of the maternal, replacing Macbeth's masculinity with the only slightly less mysogynistic masculinity of Macduff. Terry Eagleton asserts that the Witches are an example of the latter kind of subversion in *Macbeth* and that they are the play's true heroines.

We are offered three versions of sexual difference in the play, with minor variations: first, the Witches, whose sexual nature is obscure, though they incline towards the womanly; second, Lady Macbeth, who wishes to "unsex" herself in order to commit deeds to which she believes femininity is unsuited; and third, Macbeth, who is urged to be more than a man, fears losing his humanity by being so, and ends describing himself as an animal, "bear-like."

Malcolm, Duncan, and Macduff, present variations on the problem of how one may possess the "womanly" virtues of pity and charity and still be a strong king or warrior—still be manly. The final success of Malcolm, in his state of sexual innocence ("yet unknown to woman" IV.iii.125-126)[44] and unproved manhood, suggests a preference for some androgynous standard. As many critics have pointed out, Duncan's meekness allows Macbeth to view him and treat him as a woman—speaking of the murder in terms of a rape, as he approaches with "Tarquin's ravishing strides" (II.i.55). Macduff, like Macbeth, the warrior who must save Scotland, must learn to "feel it as a man" (IV.iii.221), to grieve at the slaughter of his family. Lady Macduff—a woman who has not only "given suck" but has children—offers an alternative view (to Lady Macbeth's) of femininity and its vulnerability.

If we still incline to forget that sexuality is fundamentally at issue in *Macbeth*, we are asked to "remember the Porter" and the provoking and unprovoking of sexual desire. (II.iii.21). In support of his assertion that "the murderers are taken out of the region of human things, human purposes, human desires," Thomas De Quincey in his famous essay "On the Knocking at the Gate in *Macbeth*," points to the fact that Lady Macbeth has been "unsexed" and Macbeth "has forgotten that he was born of woman"—the latter a neat interpretive inversion of the dramatic facts. He attributes their "fiendishness" in part to attempts to escape their own sexuality—Lady Macbeth wishes to be unburdened of her femininity and Macbeth to forget the connection between his masculinity and the feminine process of generation. The movement beyond "human desires" De Quincey describes is an abandonment of sexuality.

This movement beyond sexual definition results, of course, in their sterility, which is never explained and on which Macbeth is the last to comment obliquely just before he commands Banquo's murder, referring in a dual sense to his "barren sceptre" (III.i.61). This sterility is connected to both Lady Macbeth's and Macbeth's seeking empowerment by escaping sexuality. After the murder of Duncan, Macbeth loses any positive concern for establishing a line of his own. His last affirmative remark about the succession is "bring forth men-children only"—after that his purpose becomes exclusively negative. He is intent on eliminating all other possible heirs to the throne rather than producing one of his own. Other than in her famous speech on infanticide, Lady Macbeth never mentions children. One might expect that the tyrant Macbeth, so concerned to ensure the throne for his progeny by eliminating all potential threats—Banquo and his son, Macduff's wife and children—would be concerned about an heir—but he never shows such concern. Macduff offers it as an explanation for Macbeth's cold-blooded killing of Lady Macduff and her sons: "He has no children" (IV.iii.216).

The confusion of sexual roles begins just before the murder of Duncan and results in a "fruitless crown" (III.i.60). Jointly Lady Macbeth and Macbeth attempt to detach themselves from procreative cycles. Lady Macbeth, hearing that her husband has come, impels herself into the frame of mind for murder:

>   unsex me here
> And fill me, from the crown to the toe, top-full
> Of direst cruelty! make thick my blood,
> Stop up th'access and passage to remorse;
> That no compunctious visitings of Nature
> Shake my fell purpose, nor keep peace between
> Th'effect and it!
> (I.v.41-47)

Janet Adelman suggests, rightly I believe, that there are allusions to menstruation here. Lady Macbeth wishes to divest herself of all natural differences she possesses as a woman—especially her reproductive cycle, or her connection with generation. According to Lady Macbeth, her sex stands as a barrier to the commission of a crime such as regicide. She views her sexuality as the root of that "Nature" which impedes her ruthlessness. Lady Macbeth concludes with the boastful challenge

> I have given suck, and know
> How tender 'tis to love the babe that milks me:
> I would, while it was smiling in my face,
> Have pluck'd my nipple from his boneless gums,
> And dash'd the brains out, had I so sworn
> As you have done to this.
> (54-58)

I say that this challenge is boastful because Lady Macbeth is not able to sustain it—she cannot kill Duncan and she cannot support the guilt she feels at her complicity in his murder.

In her husband, Lady Macbeth sees the impediment as high-mindedness "what thou wouldst highly, /That wouldst thou holily" (I.v.20-21). After he has faltered for the first time she says, "When you durst do it, then you were a man; /And, to be more than what you were, you would/Be so much more the man" (I.vii.49-51). She argues that by intensifying his manly qualities he will be more masculine.[45] Macbeth will echo this argument later in act 3 when he challenges the murderers to prove they are not "i'th'worst rank of manhood" (i.95-97). There are different kinds of men as there are different kinds of dogs, he argues, though they are all the same species. If Macbeth falters then he must have been a "beast" when he proposed the plan to her, says Lady Macbeth—and this is precisely what he becomes by the end of the play, likening himself to a bear being baited by his enemies (V.vii.2). Like his wife, Macbeth rejects the procreative process (and his own sexuality), but on a cosmic scale. He is willing to see "the treasure/Of Nature's germen's tumble all together" (IV.i.58-59)—to have all nature's procreative potential destroyed in order to know his destiny.

Lady Macbeth's and Macbeth's attempts to exceed sexual boundedness are connected to their sterility and eventual dehumanization in the play. They become like the farmer who "hang'd himself on th'expectation of plenty" (II.iii.5)—profoundly unnatural in their rejection of natural cycles. Ambition prompts the desire to exceed natural and conventional boundaries. But what results from these excesses is sterility—domestic and public.

Though Macbeth's "bear-like" end has drawn significant critical attention, Lady Macbeth's apparent guilt-ridden suicide tends to be slighted. It is a dramatic fact that is difficult to reconcile with any reading of the play as a praise of the attempt to escape sexuality. Janet Adelman, for example, briefly mentions the suicide as indicative of loss of interest in the character, "Lady Macbeth becoming so diminished a character that we scarcely trouble to ask ourselves whether the report of her suicide is accurate or not." But there is an entire scene between Doctor and Gentlewoman devoted to describing her collapse. Though Macbeth has no time for such a "word,"[46] he is a man who no longer places any value on his own life; much less is he able to weigh the import of his wife's death, as he watches the Witches' prophecies turn against him. I think the suicide is critical to an understanding of whether the play deconstructs or reinforces sexual roles.

A way of generalizing this question is to ask whether natural differences determine other differences—the ability to divest oneself of conscience, for instance? To fully answer this question in Shakespeare one would have to look beyond the "fiend-like Queen" at least to Shakespeare's other women "fiends" (Katherina Minola, La Pucelle, Goneril, Regan and Cymbeline's Queen).[47] Goneril and Cymbeline's Queen also kill themselves and confess all in the last instant. Shakespeare conceives of no ultimate woman villain—no female Iago, who, even if caught, can maintain silence about her crimes and motivations. What does this imply about his representation of the naturalness of sexual boundaries? Of the natural limits of femininity? Obviously we have to look outside this play for a complete answer to the question. The Macbeths are particular examples of failed attempts to exceed sexual boundedness, attempts which result in sterility and self-destruction. But the question of the stability of sexual differences arises within each of Shakespeare's dramas of tyranny as intimately connected to the tyrannical problem.

Lady Macbeth dehumanizes herself by trying to escape her own sexuality—to become like a man, to lose those traits most associated with woman—pity and remorse—to lose all frailty and to dissociate herself from natural cycles. Macbeth, in trying to be more than a man, becomes a beast. With all their concern for succession and lineage in the play, the Macbeths remain childless and never speak of children after the murder scene. The judgment of the play against Macbeth and Lady Macbeth seems to be that the attempt to escape one's sexuality is foredoomed. The woman who attempts to become a man in order to commit the ultimate crime destroys herself and the man who is urged to go beyond himself, to be more than a man, becomes like an animal. What is interesting is that the play begins with such remarkable erotic tension between Lady Macbeth and her lord: she taunts him sexually to force him to the crime of regicide and he challenges her to "bring forth men-children only" in complimenting her boastful fortitude. After the first crime is committed, this erotic tension disappears, or, more accurately, dissipates; nor is there further mention of children, no further articulated concern with establishing a royal line.

One could describe the efforts of Lady Macbeth and Macbeth as attempts to step out of conventionally determined sexual roles.[48] But if these roles are merely founded on convention, if there are no natural differences, why aren't they able to succeed? Macbeth's erotic attention shifts to the Witches (who "drain him dry as hay," I.iii.18, as Dennis Biggins has pointed out), and Lady Macbeth collapses in on herself. Their failures to escape sexuality suggest that Shakespeare presents sexual difference as having its foundations in nature, and as being determinate in some fundamental way of what we are. There is a strong connection in the play between loss of sexuality and loss of humanity. The play is filled with allusions to and images of disruption of natural, procreative cycles. These disruptions are directly related to the criminality of the Macbeths, and to their sterility, which is in turn related to their mutual attempts to go beyond their sexuality. The only proffered alternatives to this sexual boundedness are the Witches. But are they attractive alternatives?

Lady Macbeth is thrown back on her conception of womanliness from the instant of Duncan's murder: "Had he not resembled/My father as he slept, I had done't.—My husband!" (II.ii.12-13). She has both a father and a husband (the only time in the play she refers to Macbeth as such). But Macbeth rejects his original understanding that one may "dare do all that may become a man; / Who dares do more, is none" (I.vii.46-47). He aspires to be, as Lady Macbeth puts it, "so much more the man" (51), and ends as less than one, "bear-like" (V.vii.2).

Just before the murder of Duncan he asks that the earth be deaf to his "steps" and earlier he has asked nature to be blind to the inner workings of his soul ("Stars hide your fires," I.iv.50). In his anxiety before Banquo's assassination, Macbeth swears, "But let the frame of things disjoint, both the worlds suffer, /Ere we will eat our meal in fear, and sleep/In the affliction of these terrible dreams, /That shake us nightly. Better be with the dead."[49] After Banquo's death his pronouncements become even more fatalistic: "For mine own good, /All causes shall give way: I am in blood/Stepp'd in so far, that should I wade no more, /Returning were as tedious as go o'er" (III.iv.134-137). The image of the river of blood betrays the fact that Macbeth is still hopeful—there is a shore to be reached; there are a finite number of murders he must yet commit to land himself safely on the other side. His belief that he can secure himself by a certain number of discreet actions implies his basic misunderstanding of the ever tenuous position of an illegitimate ruler (consider the complete distrustfulness and ultimate exhaustion of Henry IV, or the constant watchfulness of Richard III). Like the previous images, it is not clearly thought through. He knows what he wants, but he does not know how to get it; more importantly, he does not know that what he wants he cannot obtain. His desires themselves are surprisingly simple, even barren. He does not fit Malcolm's caricature of the tyrant in act 4, scene 3; he expresses no desire to indulge vices gratuitously. Instead, he wishes to rule, to be honored, to be truly loved, to be the most admired man in Scotland. How is it that his methods so directly defeat his aims? Is what he wishes for possible?

His oaths become more desperate as he aspires to know what he takes to be the truth about his future from the Witches and Hecate. To this end, he is willing that nature rebel and human science and religion be overthrown:

> Though you untie the winds, and let them fight
> Against the Churches; though the yesty waves
> Confound and swallow navigation up;
> Though bladed corn be lodg'd, and trees blown down;
> Though castles topple on their warders' heads;
> Though palaces, and pyramids, do slope
> Their heads to their foundations; though the treasure
> Of Nature's germens tumble all together,
> Even till destruction sicken, answer me
> To what I ask you.
> (IV.i.52-61)

Human monuments to political and religious power, the science of navigation, nature's procreative potential—manifestations of human reason, civilization, and the natural cycle—may all be destroyed in order for him to know. He is willing to sacrifice forever all of human achievement—all that which gives his ambitions context and meaning.

Ironically, he subverts his own elaborate oath not forty lines later. Having been told that he will not be defeated till Birnam wood come to Dunsinane, he confidently asserts, "That will never be" (94)—an assertion that relies on the predictability of natural forces. Finally, when the prophecy proves true he defies nature altogether, "I'gin to be aweary of the sun, /And wish th'estate o'th'world were now undone. —/Ring the alarum bell! —Blow wind! come, wrack!" (V.v.49-51).

The self-defeating images in Macbeth's oaths underscore the contradiction between his desires and the means he uses to satisfy them. He cannot discover how to achieve what he truly wants because he comes to regard himself as beyond humanity, as more than a man (as Lady Macbeth argues he must do in act 1, scene 7), with superhuman capacities. Above, he offers that the world be destroyed to satisfy his desire to know his fate. He appears wholly unaware of the self-contradiction such desire betrays. Macbeth seems remarkably devoid of any impulse to self-justification, even from the point of view of political expediency, once Banquo is murdered. Why does he wish to rule?

He has no far-reaching plan such as Richard's, nothing like Prospero's project, no interior yearning for a purity of soul such as Leontes. If he is not simply covetous or licentious, why isn't he content with his original position as king's favorite? He speaks remarkably little about what he hopes to gain in achieving the "golden round"; Lady Macbeth mentions only once the increased honors and power ("shall to all our days and nights to come/Give solely sovereign sway and masterdom," I.v.70), a prediction proven exactly wrong. Is his "vaulting ambition" simply unharnessed desire? What is it he hopes to gain? He does not clearly reveal his desires until they have been frustrated, in a rare reflective moment in act 5, scene 3, after he has learned of battle reverses.

Macbeth articulates what he has lost:

> —This push
> Will cheer me ever, or disseat me now.
> I have liv'd long enough: my way of life
> Is fall'n into the sere, the yellow leaf;
> And that which should accompany old age,
> As honour, love, obedience, troops of friends,
> I must not look to have; but in their stead,
> Curses, not loud, but deep, mouth-honour, breath,
> Which the poor heart would fain deny, and dare not.
> (V.iii.20-28)

The way of life he has led is the life of a man who dies young, not the way of life of someone who wishes to be loved and enjoy honors. The logic he has followed is simple. His military successes spur him on to greater glories: he is the greatest warrior in Scotland, "Valour's minion," "Bellona's bridegroom." But he perceives that the greatest honors in the kingdom are reserved for the king. He cannot be king by direct means; Malcolm bars his succession. He takes a quicker route and achieves the crown, but with it neither the honor nor the loving regard he sought—there can be no sense to life. How could he be given overpowering ambitions that he could never satisfy?

This moment of clarity is coupled with his persistent misunderstanding—he reasons, if I only manage to overcome this last obstacle it will "cheer me ever" (see also I.iii.53-56, III.ii.13-15, III.iv.28-30, III.iv.134-139). There is no last obstacle for the tyrant—this is the superiority of Richard III's understanding. He comprehends that to be tyrannical is to be supremely powerful, and as a consequence to live in fear and to be in ceaseless turmoil. Macbeth is not self-aware in this way—he is a simpler man, credulous, superstitious, of preeminent martial ability, of overreaching ambition, with only occasional moments of self-understanding (after the murder of Duncan, he wishes to shut out self-knowledge altogether, II.ii.72). But with Macbeth, who does not possess Richard's soliloquizing gloss of self-consciousness, the tyrannical impulse is more visible in its raw, primitive form—an urge to immediate domination without well-defined, far-reaching goals. By releasing his ambition, Macbeth is successful in destroying his own conscience—a feat of great difficulty—and in gaining the Scottish kingdom for a time, but to what further end? Simple dreams of power and certain knowledge of an unbroken succession, such as that promised Banquo, are shown to be finally impossible by the death of his wife. He strives to know what he can never know—that he has captured the throne of his heirs who will possess it uninterruptedly. It is as if he expects to witness this inheritance from that realm he intimates exists beyond the life to come. Learning of Lady Macbeth's suicide, he despairs of this ultimate satisfaction (the ability to view, after death, his own achievement) and so life can only be "a tale told by an idiot." His necessary rejection of any attempt at reflection or self-knowledge is done in order to commit the crimes that his ambition directs. This leaves him with only the externalities—the incoherence of possessing the crown and winning "Curses, not loud, but deep, mouth-honor, breath"—and a soul that neither horror, nor its counterpart, grace, can touch.

> I have supp'd full with horrors:
> Direness, familiar to my slaughterous thoughts,
> Cannot once start me.
> (V.v.11-13)

The compact Macbeth believes he has established with the Witches allows him to set free all his forceful, irrational desires, but it offers him no guidance as to how to satisfy them. To the extent that he believes in the superficial meaning of the prophecies, he does not see himself as susceptible to human exigencies. Without this susceptibility he has no reason to reflect on his situation, his passions, or his goals. Without such reflection he embodies the crude tyrannical impulse to power, blind to the contradictory nature of its ends, and standing in the way of any attempt at self-understanding or self-justification. The Witches provide the seductive refrain that questions the status of honor and nobility in the play: "Fair is foul, and foul is fair." Macbeth, in distinguishing "mouth-honor" from true honor, incidentally confronts the problem posed by the desire to be first in honors: natural superiority is not reflected in conventional rewards. Macbeth is superior to everybody in the play, his closest rival, Macduff is too conventional (as IV.iii points up) to have the imagination necessary for great ambition, and Malcolm's very intellectual superiority seems to deplete him of the grand and attractive passion Macbeth experiences for rule.

From the unthinking passion for tyranny we move to the more refined, sophisticated, and carefully laid plottings of Richard III. The fundamental urge to "solely sovereign sway and masterdom" remains the same, but the methods are far more immediately successful. Richard is self-aware, a tyrant looking forward to growing old in crime and glory, with little concern for his progeny, but clever enough to assure himself the throne with less difficulty and less compunction than Macbeth. Where Macbeth is passionately, misguidedly hopeful, Richard is detachedly pragmatic.

Notes

1. Terry Eagleton, *William Shakespeare* (New York: Basil Blackwell, 1986), 5. Eagleton opens his book with a discussion of *Macbeth* in the first chapter. He speaks of the Macbeths' "impulse to transgress" and refers in this context to "the different but related disruptiveness of bourgeois individualist appetite" (5). This reading implies an underestimation of both Macbeth's and Lady Macbeth's ambitions to power. I will argue that the tyrant, for Shakespeare, is far rarer than the "bourgeois individualist" and far more deadly.

2. José A. Benardete argues this: "According to Aristotle courage and justice are both moral virtues—for the simple reason that a moral virtue is taken to be any praiseworthy trait of character, and it is not to be doubted that courage as well as justice is a praiseworthy trait of character. If we accept that account of moral virtue we may venture to say (doubtless with exaggeration) that Macbeth kills Duncan for the sake of virtue, for the sake—at any rate—of one of the virtues." "Macbeth's Last Words," in *Interpretation* 1 (Summer 1970), 69.

3. Horace H. Furness, ed., *Macbeth* by William Shakespeare, Vol. 2 of *A New Variorum Edition of Shakespeare* (New York: American Scholar, 1963), 281, n. 60-65. This edition of the variorum will subsequently be referred to as Variorum 2. (cf. *Hamlet* III.i.124.)

4. Horace H. Furness, ed., *Macbeth*, Vol. 2 of *A New Variorum Edition of Shakespeare* (Philadelphia: J. B. Lippincott & Co., 1873), 226, note to scene iii. This edition of the Variorum will subsequently be referred to as Variorum.

5. Variorum 2, 276.

6. E. A. J. Honigmann, "*Macbeth*: The Murderer as Victim," *Shakespeare: The Tragedies* (Englewood Cliffs, N. J.: Prentice-Hall, 1984), 145.

7. Three other scenes contain dialogues seemingly outside the main current of events and themes in the plays: the famous Porter scene (II.iii), Rosse's conversation with the Old Man (II.iv), and the brief scene where Old Siward is told of his son's death (V.ix). Of these only the first is generally recognized as setting up a thematic resonance. I will argue later that the other two scenes serve similarly to reconnect us with another question central to the play, that of the importance of military valor.

8. Kenneth Muir, ed., *Macbeth*, the Arden Edition (New York: Methuen, 1962). All citations from this play will be taken from this edition.

9. Geoffrey Bullough, ed., *Narrative and Dramatic Sources of Shakespeare*, Vol. 7 (New York: Columbia University Press, 1973). A fact that Holinshed notes with great interest, as signifying the start of English influence over the Scots crown: "He created manie earles, lords, barons, and knights. Manie of them that before were thanes were at this time made earles, as Fife, Menteth, Atholl, Levenox, Murrey, Cathnes, Rosse, and Angus. These were the first earles that have bene heard of amongst the Scotishmen, (as their histories doo make mention.)" (506). Holinshed also translates from "Vol. II. The Description of Scotland by Hector Boece" concerning the English influence: "In processe of time . . . and cheeflie about the daies of Malcolme Canmore, our manner began greatlie to change and alter. [Through contact with the English the Scots began] through our dailie trades and conversation with them, to learne also their maners, and therewithall their language." (507). See note 23 for an interpretation of this renaming.

10. Variorum, 226, n. 84.

11. Bullough, Vol. 7, 488.

12. The word, or forms of it, is used more in this scene than in any other. It is used seventeen times in this play, substantially more than in any other play.

13. There are two competing glosses to this line offered in the Arden edition (124) and the Variorum (230-231). I take the more popular definition of "confirmed" for "affeer'd." The suggestion that there is a pun on "feared for" strengthens my argument.

14. The Clarendon editors correctly gloss "tyranny" as Macduff uses it here to mean "usurpation in consequence of which the rightful king loses his throne" (Variorum 2, 282). Shakespeare uses the term to suggest oppressive or wrongful rule elsewhere (consider *Measure for Measure* II.ii.108; *The Winter's Tale* III.ii.

15. There seems to be a suggestion of the seven deadly sins (Variorum 2, 281, n. 69-71), though pride, gluttony, and sloth are omitted. This is balanced by the later enumeration of the "King-becoming Graces" (106); see note 19.

16. George Wilson Knight notes that Malcolm deliberately emphasizes the vices of lust and avarice by the imagery he uses, in *The Imperial Theme* (London: Methuen & Co., 1951), 132. These two vices, as they refer to man's attitude towards material things, seem inappropriate to Macbeth, though Malcolm applies them to himself with this specific sense.

17. *The Rape of Lucrece* might serve as a gloss on *Macbeth* in this regard. Luxuriousness is a tyrannical passion. The connection that Malcolm draws is particularly important because Macbeth recognizes this in himself: before he is about to murder Duncan he likens himself to Tarquin (II.i.55).

18. Variorum, 233.

19. "K. James's Opinion of a King, of a Tyrant, and of The English Lawe, Rights, and Priviledges In Two Speeches The first to Parliament, 1603, the second, 1609" (London: printed for R. Baldwin near the Black Bull in the Old-Bailey, 1689), [1]. This quote is from the first speech; in the second speech he argues that a king rules according to the laws, and the tyrant does not, leaving open an appeal (by the king) to divine law, which is higher than human law. See also "The Trew Law of Free Monarchies" (1603) in *The Political Works of James I*, 53-70.

20. This scene alone compared with James's speech on the difference between kings and tyrants should be enough to suggest why the play cannot simply be regarded as a compliment to James I, Banquo's descendent. Several other critics have explored Shakespeare's revision and subversion of contemporary political views and historical accounts, for example, David Norbrook's "*Macbeth* and the Politics of Historiography" in *Politics of Discourse: The Literature and History of Seventeenth-Century England*, eds. Kevin Sharpe and Steven N. Zwicker (Berkeley: University of California Press, 1987), 78-116, and Jonathan Goldberg's *James I and the Politics of Literature* (Baltimore: The Johns Hopkins University Press, 1983). But neither Norbrook nor Goldberg notes the radical politics of the debate between Malcolm and Macduff. Arthur Melville Clark's *Murder Under Trust or The Topical Macbeth and Other Jacobean Matters* (Edinburgh: The Scottish Academic Press, 1981) catalogues detailed topical references within the play but cautiously maintains that Shakespeare's contemporary and other political insights stayed in service "to the purely dramatic requirement" (3). This begs the question of the purposefulness of political observations in Renaissance literature altogether. An earlier and even more theoretically circumscribed approach is made by Lilian Winstanley in *Macbeth, King Lear and Contemporary History* (New York: Octagon Books, 1970). She makes the essential historicist argument that, "A

dramatic poet appeals first and foremost to the mentality of his audience and it is through the mentality of his audience that his plays must consequently be interpreted" (1).

21. There may be a reference here to Spenser's twelve proposed virtues in the "Letter of the Authors" introducing *The Faerie Queene* (i.e. a Christian revision of Aristotle's ten virtues in the *Nicomachean Ethics*) [*Complete Poetical Works*, The Cambridge Edition of the Poets, ed. R. Neil Dodge (New York: Houghton Mifflin, 1908), 136-138] or, as suggested in a Variorum reading, to the twelve virtues in the Vulgate of Galatians 5:22-3; love, joy, peace, patience, gentleness, goodness, long-suffering, meekness, faith, modesty, temperance, chastity (Variorum 2, 285, nn. 106-109).

22. Pierre Sahel, "Machiavelisme Vulgaire et Machiavelisme Authentique dans *Macbeth*," *Cahiers Élisabéthains: Études sur la Pre-Renaissance et la Renaissance Anglaises*, no. 14 (October 1978), 17.

23. This interpretation depends implicitly on a view of Machiavelli, or at least Machiavellianism, as preeminently concerned with patriotism and civic republicanism. The end justified by any means is the end which secures a nation's good. The most forceful advocate of this interpretation of Machiavelli's writings is J. G. A. Pocock, in *The Machiavellian Moment: Florentine Political Thought and the Atlantic Republic Tradition* (Princeton: Princeton University Press, 1975). For Pocock, as for Sahel, the *virtú* of Machiavelli's prince is civic virtue that had to be divorced from the corrupting influence of Christian values: "The truly subversive Machiavelli was not a counsellor of tyrants, but a good citizen and patriot" (505, 218). As chapter 3 will suggest, this understanding of Machiavelli underestimates his Machiavellianism. I am indebted to Harvey C. Mansfield's argument for the "vulgar" interpretation of Machiavelli as a teacher of evil in his *Machiavelli's New Modes and Orders: A Study of the "Discourses on Livy"* (Ithaca: Cornell University Press, 1979): "The true Machiavelli is more Machiavellian, not less, than the vulgar Machiavelli" (11).

24. There is a variation on this question in *Measure for Measure*, when Claudio speaks to the imprisoned Lucio about Angelo, who stands in for the true Duke Vincentio. Claudio speculates "Whether the tyranny be in his place/Or in his eminence that fills it up" (I.ii.163-164). Is it the illegitimacy of the office or the abuse of it which makes for tyranny?

25. Variorum, 242-243 and Variorum 2, 289-90, n. 157. This surmise is supported by the fact that Macduff's speech before the entrance of the doctor makes a perfect verse with the entrance of Rosse.

26. Muir, 130-131, nn. 140-159.

27. Bullough, vol. 7, 508.

28. Malcolm might be thinking of Duncan's remark when he appoints him Prince of Cumberland, "which honour must/Not unaccompanied invest him only, /But signs of nobleness, like stars, shall shine/On all deservers" (I.iv.39-42). All honors are to derive from the king. Malcolm's renaming of the thanes emphasizes his power over the dispensation of honors and it also serves as a reminder, to other ambitious nobles, of the foreign power that helped enthrone him. The renaming of the thanes is also mentioned as symbolic of Scotland's coming under English influence. The thanes of Cawdor have so tainted the title that Malcolm may feel called on to impose an outside hierarchy to centralize monarchial power. See also page 4 above.

29. Consider the problem of succession Lear faces in act 1, scene 1 of *King Lear*, the problem of Cymbeline with his daughter Imogen, the problem Leontes has with a lost heir, the problem King Henry IV has with his apparently recalcitrant son, the

problem of the quarrel over succession in *King John*, as well as the question of who will succeed the founder of the Roman Empire in *Julius Caesar* and in *Antony and Cleopatra*.

30. See page 6.

31. Hardin Craig, ed., *Machiavelli's "The Prince": An Elizabethan Translation* (Chapel Hill: The University of North Carolina Press, 1944), 67. This manuscript translation of *The Prince* was in circulation in the late sixteenth century. The first published translation, by Henry Dacres, was not issued until 1640. It is conceivable that Shakespeare could have known the work itself, not just Gentillet's distorted version of it, which was very popular in England at the time (*Discours Sur les Moyens de Bien Gouverner*, first pub. 1576, translated: *A Discourse Upon the Meanes of Wel Governing and Maintaining in Good Peace, A Kingdome, or Other Principalitie*, first pub. 1602). For subsequent citations I use Harvey C. Mansfield's literal translation of *The Prince* (Chicago: University of Chicago Press, 1985), 62. The Elizabethan edition of *The Prince* will be referred to as Craig.

32. Both the Sergeant's and Rosse's account of Macbeth's achievements contain telling ambiguities to which Duncan is apparently oblivious. The implicit comparisons between Macdonwald and Macbeth in Rosse's speech are made in such a way that the traitor and the defender are syntactically confused (I.ii.55-59). Given Rosse's duplicity, the confusion might well be intentional.

33. I have found only one parenthetical reference to this curiously overlooked circumstance, in Graham Holderness's article "Radical Potentiality and Institutional Closure: Shakespeare in Film and Television" in *Political Shakespeare* (Ithaca: Cornell University Press, 1985), 190. I quote: "When Duncan declares Malcolm his successor (a declaration which indicates that this is not a hereditary dynasty) he is simultaneously creating a hierarchy and rendering it open to assault by suppressing the very power, vested in the thanes, which sustains his authority."

34. "Scotland," *Encyclopedia Britannica*, 1911 (eleventh edition), Vol. 24, 431.

35. Bullough, Vol. 7, 485. Editorial paraphrase.

36. Bullough, 510.

37. For a treatment of Shakespeare's use of Buchanan see Norbrook (in *Politics of Discourse*), who emphasizes the historian's republican sympathies and concludes, "As a regicide who was condemned equally by Buchanan and by conservatives, and yet had half-buried associations with constitutionalist traditions, Macbeth was a figure bound to evoke ambivalent responses from a Renaissance humanist," 116.

38. Rosse enters describing Scotland as a country "almost afraid to know itself!" (165) (an analogy is invited with Lady Macbeth's insanity and Macbeth's inner soul turmoil). Rosse is certainly the play's slipperiest character, an opportunist par excellence. Significantly, Malcolm does not recognize Rosse when he enters (IV.iii.159). Rosse repeats of Scotland his earlier words of consolation to Lady Macduff. He says Scotland is "Almost afraid to know itself." It is a grave rather than a mother, and he confirms Macduff in that Macbeth has been slaughtering his opposition and the best men no longer die natural deaths. Macduff, a man of fewer words, comments on Rosse's elaboration (174). Rosse does not at first tell Macduff of the murder of his family. It is not plausible that he hesitates for humanitarian reasons. He reveals the slaughter to Macduff only after he has learned that Malcolm has English support and so is in the stronger military position. Once he has decided to throw his lot in with Macduff and Malcolm it is safe for him to tell Macduff of Macbeth's actions. Had he told him earlier, he could not then have expected to return unhindered to Macbeth's troops. Rosse is here

still waiting to see which will be the stronger of the two. This suggests how very close to ultimate success Macbeth is—Rosse is too prudent a man to consider siding with Macbeth for reasons of loyalty or patriotism (to keep the English out). He manages to play both sides and survive. The ambivalence of the most politically astute observer in the play implies that Rosse believes Macbeth could succeed in ruling Scotland, however oppressively, and in keeping the English out. See Variorum 2, 194 for a suggestion that this interview shows Rosse's circumspection. Rosse is a survivor (see chapter 6).

39. Bullough, 497.

40. Gustav Landauer, *Shakespeare* (Hamburg: Rutter and Loenig Verlag, 1962), 238. "Shakespeare who here proceeds as always, doesn't measure the time of Macbeth's reign according to astronomical time, but according to the inner workings of his fate, the tempo of his life-force and intensity; he doesn't present the reality, the relativity and heterogeneity of political society, but rather the truth of the basic individual drives *sub specie aeternitatis*; he doesn't need the long interval between Duncan's and Banquo's murder, or the hypocrisy and normality. In Holinshed, by contrast to Shakespeare, Banquo remains peacefully in his grave." Unpublished translation by James H. Read.

41. E. A. J. Honigmann, "*Macbeth*: The Murderer as Victim," *Shakespeare: The Tragedies*, ed. Robert Heilman (Englewood Cliffs, NJ: Prentice-Hall, Inc., 1984), 148.

42. Richard Levin, "Feminist Thematics and Shakespearean Tragedy," *PMLA* 103, no. 2 (March 1988), 125-138.

43. See Dennis Biggins's "Sexuality, Witchcraft, and Violence in *Macbeth*," *Shakespeare Studies* 8 (1975) 255.0. See also Terry Eagleton's *William Shakespeare* (New York: Basil Blackwell, 1986); Janet Adelman's "Fantasies of Maternal Power in *Macbeth*," *Cannibals, Witches, and Divorce: Estranging the Renaissance*, ed. Marjorie Garber (Baltimore: The Johns Hopkins University Press, 1987), 90-121; and Marjorie Garber's *Shakespeare's Ghostwriters: Literature as Uncanny Causality* (New York: Methuen, 1987).

44. There is here perhaps some recollection of Elizabeth, the Virgin Queen. Sir Thomas Elyot in *The Book Named the Governor* (Menston, England: Scolar Press, Ltd., 1970), advises the education of a child above seven: "For though there be no perille of offence in that tender and innocent age/yet in some children nature is more open to vice than to vertue/and in the tender wittes be sparkes of voluptuositie: whiche norished by an occasion or objecte/encreace often tymes in to so terrible a fire/that ther with all vertue and reason is consumed. Wherefore to eschewe that daunger/the most sure counsaile is/to withdrawe him from all company of women," folio 21 verso.

45. The argument is reversed by Antonio in *Measure for Measure* when he says "Be that you are, /That is, a woman; if you be more, you're none" (II.iv.143-35), as Terry Eagleton points out in *William Shakespeare*, p. 4. There it is equally insidious. See also Michael Taylor's "Ideals of Manhood in *Macbeth*."

46. See Joan Larsen Klein's "Lady Macbeth: Infirm of Purpose" for a version of the feminine/masculine debate surrounding Lady Macbeth (in *The Woman's Part*, eds. Lenz, Greene, and Neely, Chicago: University of Illinois Press, 1983). This volume is after referred to as Lenz.

47. The word "fiend" is significant here since it is used of only these five female characters in Shakespeare, in every case to suggest a lack of femininity and an unnaturalness. See W. Moelwyn Merchant's "His Fiend-Like Queen" for a discussion of lady Macbeth's connection with the supernatural and for the supernatural associations of the word "fiend."

48. Marjorie Garber states what I am calling the "conventional" argument when she identifies in the play a "Medusa complex" that centers on "gender undecidability and anxiety about gender identification," 97. She argues that feminist critics and others "merely replicate the fundamental resistance we have seen in Freud, the refusal to regard the enigma as such, to gaze upon the head of the Medusa, to recognize the undecidability that may lie just beneath the surface of power—and perhaps of sexuality itself," *Shakespeare's Ghostwriters*, 119.

49. Abraham Lincoln read this speech to a party with him on the boat returning to Washington after a visit to the fallen confederate capital, Richmond, in 1865, three days before he was shot. He found *Macbeth* Shakespeare's most powerful play. As quoted from Lincoln's letters by Harry V. Jaffa in *Shakespeare As Political Thinker*, eds. John Alvis and Thomas G. West (Durham, NC: Carolina Academic Press, 1981), 283.

Chapter 3

Richard III: That Excellent Grand Tyrant of the Earth

And Set the Murderous Machiavel to School

*R*ichard III is the only play by Shakespeare that begins with the title character on stage speaking alone. Without the repeated insights into Richard's energetic malevolence, which this and his later soliloquies afford us, the play would make most sense as a straightforward dramatization of the Tudor myth.[1] Richard offers us just such an oversimplification of historical fact in the first few lines of the play: "Now is the winter of our discontent/Made glorious summer by this son of York."[2] This is the official version of how the *Henry VI* plays might conclude had there been no Richard. The Yorkists have rightly recovered the throne. But in the fourteenth line the outrageous sarcasm of this panegyric becomes apparent as Richard turns to his most interesting subject, himself: "But I, that am not shaped for sportive tricks." He speaks of the action of the play being motivated and controlled from within him:

> And therefore, since I cannot prove a lover
> To entertain these fair well-spoken days,
> I am determined to prove a villain,
> And hate the idle pleasure of these days.
> (28-31)[3]

As critics of all persuasions have continually noted, the interest of this play lies mostly in the character of Richard. This interest depends on the contradiction of self with soul in Richard that surfaces, devastatingly, in his final soliloquy on the night before the battle of Bosworth Field. Richard reveals that he does not know whether to regard himself as having a soul (and therefore a conscience), which connects him with the cosmos, or as being a self—a material being without any responsibility to man, nature, or a divinity.

Richard's "schoolmarmish" soliloquizing (as Laurence Olivier termed it)[3] suggests how much more self-aware he is than Macbeth. Macbeth depends on his relations to the supernatural (the witches) and to Lady Macbeth to reveal his quality and his destiny to him. Richard, by contrast, appears to understand himself fully and appreciate his deformities and limitations from the beginning. He even appears to accept being "Cheated of feature by dissembling Nature" (19). This acceptance, however, would seem to arise from the opinion out of Machiavelli which Shakespeare embodies in his character's every action: that it is possible to circumvent or conquer nature and achieve one's ends by bringing to perfection imperturbably a private villain and a public tyrant. This requires that he regard himself as a man without hidden or uncontrollable longings, without a soul. He must see clearly that the opinions (about conscience, guilt, and the watchfulness of some divinity) that restrain most men from complete criminality are false. He must possess a clinical understanding of how to get what he wants. This is what makes the courtship scene between Richard and Anne so chilling. It is not only that he woos her over the corpse of her father-in-law, but that he shows us afterwards that his success is all due to technique.

As a consequence of this realism, Richard has none of the sense of guilt or loss of Macbeth when he speaks of "mine eternal jewel/Given to the common Enemy of man" (III.i.67-68). Instead, in his final moment of supreme crisis Richard does not confess or express regret: he debates himself. He does not discover himself in a quagmire of guilt, but in what Machiavelli calls a "confusion of the brain."[4] After his murders of Duncan and Banquo, Macbeth finds himself "in blood/Stepp'd in so far, that, should I wade no more, /Returning were as tedious as go o'er" (III.iv.135-137). He resigns himself stoically to stand firm through what may be eternal torment (like a chained bear, V.vii.1-2). Richard, on the other hand, speaks knowingly of the unending cycle of crime that usurpation entails, just before he orders the murder of the young princes "But I am in/So far in blood that sin will pluck on sin; /Tear-falling pity dwells not in this eye" (IV.ii.63-65). Unlike Macbeth who has little foresight, less prudence, and only a few late glimpses of self-understanding, Richard, self-aware, always has a plan. We know already in *Henry VI, Part 3* that he plots to ascend the throne.

Is Coleridge correct in classing Richard with Iago and Falstaff, as a consummate and perfectly unrepentant villain?[5] Is he a poor draft of the later "mature" tragic heroes and so not psychologically real?[6] Freud, by contrast, finds him convincing. His interpretation points up the internal conflict Richard faces. On the one hand, it is Richard's intellectual understanding that the world is there to be manipulated, that it regards human beings indifferently, that there is no such thing as either divine or natural right, and so there is no possibility that conscience is anything more than a "convenient scarecrow."[7] On the other hand, he finds in nature a deliberate malevolence towards himself that suggests that nature or divinity takes an interest in human affairs.[8] In his last soliloquy, Richard understands that he may have made a mistake about his own nature and falls into confusion: Why do I feel in danger? Am I in danger from myself? Who loves me? Do I love myself? This soliloquy has been overlooked or ignored by critics fascinated with Richard's psyche, including the first to offer a psychological interpretation of him, Sigmund Freud. Freud rests his argument (about Richard's sexual perversion and power complex) on the opening soliloquy, concluding that he is "a figure in whose character the claim to be an exception is closely bound up with and is motivated by the circumstances of congenital disadvantage."[9] Freud rephrases this soliloquy as follows:

> Nature has done me a grievous wrong in denying me the beauty of form which wins human love. Life owes me reparation for this and I will see that I get it. I have a right to be an exception, to disregard the scruples by which others let themselves be held back. I may do wrong myself, since wrong has been done to me.[10]

Freud's summary, with its reference to "right," injects into Richard's speech a moralism, which it is not clear that he possesses. I will argue that what Freud overlooks in his insightful analysis is that Richard is actually struggling with the notions of "soul" and "right." Richard's definitions are uncertain rather than static. Richard's determination to be a villain is not the same as a conviction of the "right to be an exception." Instead, Richard attempts to move, as he believes Machiavelli teaches, beyond notions of moral right and wrong.

The psychoanalytical approach of Freud (and those who borrow from and interpret him[11]) is particularly useful in pointing to a greater complexity in the protagonist than was earlier appreciated.[12] But because it does not consider that Richard calls into question the nature and existence of his psyche, it is incomplete. Freud does not discuss Richard's character in the light of his final tortured soliloquy on conscience, because the speech is a speech about the existence of soul. The question that should precede the psychoanalysis of Richard is: Does Richard have a conscience or even a soul? One indication that this is a concern of the play is that "soul" is spoken of more in *Richard III* than in any other Shakespearean play.

A version of Richard's project is to "set the murderous Machiavel to school" (*Henry VI, Part 3*, III.ii.193). Richard seems, for much of the play, to be a perfect machiavel. Machiavelli is referred to twice in the first tetralogy (*Henry VI, Part 1*, V.iv.74 in reference to the Duke of Alençon, and Richard's boast that he will "set the murderous Machiavel to school," *Henry VI, Part 3*, III.ii.193).[13] It is reasonable to suspect that *Richard III* represents a Shakespearean comment on whether it is possible for a man to be completely evil to further his own ends—for a man to be a true "machiavel."[14]

In addition to the difference in characterization, *Macbeth* and *Richard III*
contrast politically. *Macbeth* shows usurpation at an historically early point in
the establishment of divine right, and *Richard III* shows usurpation at a time
when the much abused myth of divine right begins to require radical revision or
reinforcement. This accounts, in part, for the discrepancy between the carefully crafted arguments for legitimacy in *Richard III* and the simple assertion of
a right to rule in *Macbeth*.

Richard is not, then, simply a "scourge,"[15] nor is he dismissable as an
example of an immature Shakespearean tragic hero. Does Richard have a conscience or even a soul? This overlooked question seems to be behind all critical
debate about the play.

Thy Self is Self Misus'd

Dive, thoughts, down to my soul.

Richard admonishes himself at the end of the opening soliloquy. He con-
signs "thoughts" of his fraternal treachery to the repository of his "soul" just
before he is to encounter and sympathize with his doomed brother, Clarence.
The "soul" that his thoughts inhabit is an unusual one. He speaks as though his
soul were a place in which to hide what he does not wish known. This conception is the antithesis of the Christian conception of soul, which may always and
everywhere be examined by God.[16] This is not a theological error on Richard's
part because, of course, he knows well how to profess belief and "clothe" his
"naked villainy" with scripture (I.iii.336-7). Far from fearing divine scrutiny,
Richard appears to regard his soul as like the body in that it gives him individuality and separates him from all other souls.[17] Richard's final non-rhetorical
reference to "soul" suggests, too, that the soul is like the body (V.iii.217), a
separate entity, with no connection to anything outside itself. As he goes through
his Protean changes, what he terms his "soul" (I.i.41) is where he keeps his
self-consciousness and his own counsel. He notes that his "counsel" is his "shield"
(IV.iii.56)—his intellect (rather than any divinity) protects him.

The word "soul" is used more often in this play than in any other, a third
again as many times as in *Hamlet* or *Othello*. And Richard speaks of it more
often than any other character in the play.[18] It is spoken of so much, I contend,
because its existence is in constant doubt. Richard speaks of his own soul eight
times, altogether. With two exceptions (the first and last usages, I.i.41 and
V.iii.217), he makes reference to his soul only in the context of deceiving
others, as to the court: "I do not know that Englishman alive/With whom my
soul is any jot at odds," II.i.71, also I.ii.180, III.v.27, III.vii.225, IV.iv.256,
IV.iv.263. Elizabeth later catches him up on this rhetorical usage as he tries for
the hand of her daughter in order to consolidate his power and unite the kingdom:

K. Rich. Then know that from my soul I love thy daughter.
Eliz. My daughter's mother thinks it with her soul.
K. Rich. What do you think?
Eliz. That thou dost love my daughter from thy soul;
So from thy soul's love didst thou love her brothers, [*the slain Princes*]
And from my heart's love I do thank thee for it.
K. Rich. Be not so hasty to confound my meaning:
I mean that with my soul I love thy daughter,
And do intend to make her Queen of England.
                                        (IV.ib.256-263)

Richard is forced to rephrase his profession: he does not love "from" his soul (in the sense of "apart from" or "at variance with"),[19] but "with" his soul. His deceitful, pietistic language of love no longer works with the woman whose sons he has killed. He is reduced to speaking not of his "soul" but of his "self." This scene is an inversion of the earlier wooing scene between Richard and Anne, where he draws her into his syntactic constructions and so gains her consent.[20] But here, Elizabeth reverses the linguistic game and forces Richard to use her formulations, challenging his every oath and finally asserting "Thy self is self-misus'd" (376). Richard realizes it would be too ambiguous for him to swear by his "soul" at this point, and so he begins to speak openly of his "self" and the "selves" he will produce with Elizabeth's daughter (425). He is willing to say anything to convince her, and he offers his most extreme pledge yet, if he does not fulfill his promises, "Myself myself confound" (399). Words are only words, but Richard's have turned on him.

Richard, in his manipulations of women, appears inhumanly frigid. He laments his incapacity to fully delight in romantic or sexual play (*Henry VI, Part 3*, III.ii.146-164 and *Richard III*, I.ii.16-31). As he sees it there are two alternative lives open to a noble: the life of the lover and the life of the politician. Given his enforced choice of a political life, it is particularly interesting that he is shown wooing two women in the play, Anne and Elizabeth. The women in the play, the Duchess of York, Queen Margaret, Queen Elizabeth, and Queen Anne, are all without political power, but Richard's three longest dialogues in the play are with Margaret, Elizabeth, and Anne. They alone confront him with his villainy (I.ii.70; I.iii.221, 330; IV.iv.144, 195-6). Unlike his male victims, they are permitted to survive and reflect on Richard because they pose no threat to him politically or militarily. His attitude towards the curses of women is simply reflected in his response to his mother's disowning him:

A flourish, trumpets! Strike alarum, drums!
Let not the heavens hear these tell-tale women
Rail on the Lord's anointed. Strike, I say!
Either be patient and entreat me fair,

Or with clamorous report of war
Thus will I drown your exclamations.
(IV.iv.149-154)

For Richard the ultimate arbiter is war, which can silence all speech. Why then do the speeches of "tell-tale women" have such importance in this play? They are temporarily protected by their powerlessness and so able to observe Richard's machinations, learn from them, and comprehend them. It is through the women in the play, especially Elizabeth, that we can understand Richard's struggle to achieve selfhood and to void himself of soul. Coppelia Kahn argues in *Man's Estate: Masculine Identity in Shakespeare* that "the patriarchal world of Shakespeare's history plays is emphatically masculine. Its few women are relatively insignificant, and a man's identity is determined by his relationship to his father, son, or brother." She argues that the play emphasizes, negatively, the importance of the mother in the "formation of masculine identity" and that the entire tetralogy traces "the decline of the father-son bond."[21] This approach slights the importance of the women in the play, not as participants in the action of the plot, but as knowers of its significance.

The women in *Richard III* know Richard through their relations with him as mother, wife, mother-in-law, and tormentor more completely than any of his male allies or challengers. As Madonne M. Miner puts it, they represent a "humanity apparent nowhere else in the play."[22] Miner understands the increasing camaraderie of the women in the play as a "counterprocess, one that insists on the inherently positive value of women," against Richard's destructive momentum.[23]

Elizabeth is the only one of these women who, having understood Richard's ambitions and intentions, is able to act on this understanding. The second wooing scene of the play in act 4, scene 4 is a dramatic revision of the earlier courtship of Anne. Richard begins by attempting the same tricks with Elizabeth in seeking the hand of her daughter. But rather than slip into Richard's rhetoric she forces him into one of his most self-damning lines: "Myself myself confound." How is she able to entangle him in his own rhetoric?

Elizabeth's conversation with Richard in act 4, scene 4 shows her drawn quickly into his rhetorical power, as Anne was:

K. Rich. Wrong not her birth; she is a royal princess.
Eliz. To save her life I'll say she is not so.
K. Rich. Her life is safest only in her birth.
Eliz. And only in that safety died her brothers.
K. Rich. Lo, at their birth good stars were opposite.
Eliz. And only in that safety died her brothers.
K. Rich. All unavoided is the doom of destiny.
Eliz. True, when avoided grace makes destiny.
(212-219)

She is soon trapped within Richard's language and syntax, just as Anne was (343-353). But she manages to escape his rhetorical stratagems. By speaking in Richard-like riddles of his professions of "soul's love," she compels him to untangle his own verbal tropes.

The flow of Richard's repartee is interrupted, and he, having failed at the game of courtship in which he seduced Anne, speaks to Elizabeth more plainly than he does to anyone else in the play. If she has lost sons, she should welcome their replacement with grandchildren, and grandchildren are better since she will be spared the physical labor of children. Richard relies on his standard repertoire of oaths, which Elizabeth challenges one by one until he attempts to swear by his "self" and Elizabeth points out, "Thy self is self-misus'd." She assumes mastery of the exchange by line 418.

It is indicative both of Richard's underestimation of women and his final hopefulness that he is confident at the end of Elizabeth's submission ("Relenting fool, and shallow, changing woman!"). But as is apparent in Richmond's speech after his victory at Bosworth, she has made other arrangements for her daughter as well (V.v.29-31). Elizabeth understands her weak position, unlike Anne, but does not rail against it, as Margaret does. She exposes Richard's appeals to her desire for security and political power and reduces him to the argument that his political survival coincides with hers. This is the only point in the play where a character understands the action better than Richard himself.

In the first courtship, Richard offers himself as a replacement for her father and her husband and she accepts. In the second courtship scene, Richard offers to replace Elizabeth's children with the promise of grandchildren who are, from the political perspective of lineage, just the same, he argues. His argument makes sense on the level of rational self-interest, but it makes no sense on the level of the heart (Elizabeth's "heart-love," 261). Richard's soulless soul, the repository of his thoughts, is capable only of rational affiliation. He allies with Elizabeth and her daughter out of political necessity. Elizabeth, however, possesses not just "soul" in Richard's unchristian sense of the word, but also "heart." She remains unpersuaded by the cold logic that substitutes grandchildren for children.

From the first we see of him, Richard is interested to separate himself from natural and conventional ties, which, for him, are most strongly represented by women. In *Henry VI, Part 3*, act 5, scene 6, after killing King Henry VI in cold blood (having become impatient with Edward's inconvenient and impolitic compunctions, V.v.49) Richard says that he has "neither pity, love, nor fear"—that he has "no brother", and is "like no brother."[24]

He concludes the self-reflective part of the soliloquy "I am myself alone," affirming his selfhood. He says he wins Anne with "dissembling looks" (*Richard III*, I.ii.241). The description is ironic, since his looks—how he appears physically—cannot be dissembled and exclude him from ladies' chambers. He has managed, through his art of speech, to disguise his true nature (both physi-

cal and mental), defeating "dissembling Nature" (I.i.19) itself. He describes
how he foments civil strife: "And thus I clothe my naked villainy/With odd old
ends stol'n forth of Holy Writ, /And seem a saint, when most I play the devil"
(I.iv.336-8). And, finally, after the dialogue confusion of the nightmare in act
5, scene 3, he echoes his first self-revelatory speech in *Henry VI, Part 3*: "I
myself/Find in myself no pity to myself" (203-204). What his remarks about
himself all have in common is that they all state what Richard is not. He is most
obviously not a saint, but neither is he a devil—he merely plays one. He is
incapable of pity, love, or fear—rejecting love as beyond his natural capacities.
He can also play comedian, tragedian, Mermaid, basilisk, Nestor, Ulysses,
Sinon, chameleon, Proteus, and Machiavelli's master. Given that we know all
he is capable of playing, all he is capable of metamorphosing into—son, brother,
friend, lover, husband, father, king—we are led to ask who or what he is.

For a character who so frequently explains himself in soliloquy and asides,
there is remarkable critical disagreement about just who he is. The problem
behind this critical uncertainty is the questionable status of "soul" for Richard.
Commentators such as Sir Thomas Whately and John Philip Kemble refer to his
"character";[25] E. M. W. Tillyard and Lily B. Campbell speak of symbolic
accoutrements; Freud understands him as possessing a psychology;[26] David L.
Frey refers to the "internal process"; and Robert N. Watson discusses the "internal logic" of Richard as a symbol.[27] But the difficulty is that they do not
fully explore why Richard is at odds with himself—what the contradictions
between his first and last soliloquies mean. Richard attempts to understand
himself outside the Judeo-Christian framework, and outside the Aristotelian/
Platonic framework, as a being who consists in self rather than soul. Unlike
Marlowe's Faustus, he does not wait until his last desperate moments to ask,
"Why wert thou not a creature wanting soul?" (V.ii.182).[28] Richard tries, at
least from the beginning of his ascent to the crown, to see himself as without
soul in the classical or theological sense.

Richard, instead of understanding himself as possessing a soul, which can
be watched over by an omnipotent, all-seeing dispenser of divine justice, views
himself as in possession of a "self."[29] He is a selfhood rather than a body and
soul in tension with one another. The very existence of a soul implies a disjunc-
tion between material and spiritual being. Richard wishes to escape this notion,
which brings along with it notions of love, pity, guilt, and conscience. To
escape "soul" means that he must understand it as an externally imposed religious, or philosophical, construct and liberate himself from the notion. This
means that there will be no constraints on his actions imposed from without.

A notable instance of this new, Machiavellian way[30] of looking at the
world is his public denunciation of conscience just before the final battle in act
5, scene 3: "Conscience is but a word that cowards use/Devis'd at first to keep
the strong in awe" (310-311). This is quite a different notion from Hamlet's
regretful, "Thus conscience does make cowards of us all" (III.i.83).[31] For

Hamlet conscience is an innate impediment to forceful action. Richard argues to his captains that it is an external construct imposed by the weak on the strong.[32] If conscience exists, then to escape detection for a crime is not to escape punishment for it—this is what Richard, along with Machiavelli's prince, wishes to go beyond.[33]

Given Richard's level of metaphysical competence, it is surprising to learn that he is subject to nightmares. Anne refers to his "timorous dreams," which keep her awake (IV.i.82-84). And it is even more puzzling when Richard, on the eve of the decisive battle of his reign, is woken into his final soliloquy on conscience. His troops outnumber Richmond's three to one (V.iii.11). He is nearly certain of military triumph. Yet he finds himself in the throes of what is generally taken to be an attack of conscience, but what is actually confrontation with deep uncertainty.

Richard has a consistently clear view of himself, which is shattered only on his awakening from a nightmare of ghosts charging his "soul" to despair and die. The difficulty is that this clear view of himself includes a deep contradiction that Richard does not recognize until too late; it is one that he never resolves. We are not presented, as in *Macbeth*, with the destruction and loss of a soul, but with the rupture of a man's belief about who he is. Richard discovers a contradiction in his understanding of human nature and its relation to external nature.

Richard is even utterly indifferent to guilt, referred to more in this play than in any other. Whether or not guilt exists is a question central to the play. Guilt, Richard argues, need not necessarily exist. It is not necessary to feel guilty for assassinating a brother, a wife, a cousin, kings, small children, friends. In fact, the truly strong and successful man must dispense with such feelings, understanding them to be conventions built into men by rulers and priests and given support by religion or superstition. Richard is so good at adopting the appearance of piety to persuade others because he himself is not at all pious.

One instance in which our attention is drawn to this dramatically is in the quiet entry of Prince Edward and Richard into London. Richard, with typical convoluted but perfectly accurate logic, warns the Prince "Nor more can you distinguish of a man/Than of his outward show, which—God knows—/Seldom or never jumpeth with the heart" (III.i.9-11). Hastings enters immediately after with the news that the Queen and the young Duke of York have taken sanctuary and Richard uses the same oath, "On what occasion God he knows, not I" (26). Richard explains himself—only God knows that a man's professions and his actual intentions are never the same. But, of course, Richard believes that he, rather than God, knows this of himself. The doomed Hastings repeats the oath sincerely and unthinkingly.

If Richard has succeeded in ridding himself of guilt, though, how does he understand himself? Only a soul (fearing some justice) is subject to guilt or attacks of conscience; a self is free of them. A self, unlike a soul, has no links with others—it can be hidden behind different masks (religious, romantic, loyal, patriotic).

My interpretation starts from the premise Richard gives us in the opening soliloquy: that guilt is unnecessary and that the soul, otherwise empty, is simply the private repository of thought or consciousness.[34] From this perspective the price for the success of Richard's project of usurpation is nothing; he has no "jewel" to lose like Macbeth.

Just before the summary execution of Hastings, Buckingham—the last to be betrayed—describes what is most dangerous about Richard:

> We know each other's faces; for our hearts
> He knows no more of mine than I of yours,
> Or I of his, my lord, than you of mine.
> (III.iv.10-12)

He means to cast aspersions on Hastings's loyalty, to make his execution seem less precipitous to the Bishop of Ely; but, like so many deliberately prophetic moral pronouncements in the play (Queen Margaret's curses), it falls back on the speaker. He can no more read Richard than Hastings can. His allusion to the masks of conspiracy comes very close to Machiavelli's advice in *The Prince*, chapter 18, "In What Mode Faith Should Be Kept by Princes":

> Men in general judge more by their eyes than by their hands, because seeing is given to everyone, touching to few. Everyone sees how you appear, few touch what you are; and these few dare not oppose the opinions of many, who have the majesty of the state to defend them; and in the actions of all men, and especially of princes, where there is no court to appeal to, one looks to the end.[35]

Most men never penetrate beyond appearances to the truth about another, or their motivations. Most men cannot "touch" Richard's essence, or see him for what he really is behind his various masks. Machiavelli concludes that because you cannot know the essential truth about motive you can only adequately judge the ends or results. Richard notes of Buckingham, after he has sounded him on the murder of the Princes, "none are for me/That look into me with considerate eyes" (IV.ii.29-30). He understands how rare and dangerous those who can "touch" are and accordingly dooms Buckingham. Richard is a master of appearances—of being seen rather than touched—as we learn when he first reveals his ambition in his first significant soliloquy in the tetralogy:[36]

> Why I can smile and murder while I smile,
> And cry 'Content!' to that that grieves my heart,
> And wet my cheeks with artificial tears,
> And frame my face to all occasions.

I'll drown more gazers than the basilisk;
I'll play the orator as well as Nestor,
Deceive more slily than Ulysses could,
And, like a Sinon, take another Troy.
I can add colours to the chameleon,
Change shapes with Proteus for advantages,
And set the murderous Machiavel to school.
Can I do this, and cannot get a crown?
Tut! Were it further off, I'll pluck it down
                    Henry VI, Part 3 (III.iii.182-195).

Richard claims he is capable of being anything, and makes here the one direct reference to the author of *The Prince* in all of Shakespeare. It is significant that he refers to the Florentine himself, rather than to the bastard creations that took his name on the Renaissance stage. Richard will not simply rival the followers of Machiavelli, but will strive to outdo Machiavelli himself. He is Shakespeare's version of a true student of Machiavelli, rather than the static stage machiavel of the period. He is a brilliant political and military strategist who understands Machiavellian policy and holds with Marlowe's Machevill "there is no sin but ignorance" (*The Jew of Malta* prologue, 15).[37]

At one point, Richard is described by Buckingham as a "Christian Prince" (III.vii.95), one of three figures in Shakespeare's dramas to receive that honor (the other two are Henry V at I.ii.24.pr.6; and Henry VI pt. 1 at V.iii.172). The epithet might be chosen with the teachings of Machiavelli's *Prince* in mind since Richard uses the appearance of humility and charity to achieve power. Though this mask wears thin, it enables him to become Protector under his simplistically pious brother, King Edward IV. It is Machiavelli's understanding that the pretense of complete humility and virtue may be the most effective way to power—that Christianity has much to teach the modern prince. The tragedy is, on this level, a philosophical response to the implicit Machiavellian contention that such rare and wholly evil men must be politically successful.[38]

John F. Danby speaks of the "prime significance of Machiavellianism" for the Elizabethans: "there is a new sense of the fissuring of man, of a gap between the external and the internal, a possible dichotomy between the social and the spiritual." The man who is conscious of the mask of society "will be the hypocrite—a man superior in degree of consciousness to his fellows." Danby sees Richard's final fit of guilt as a criticism of this type of new man.[39] In part, this is true, but the criticism is not that bad men will always have their comeuppance, despite Machiavelli's teaching. Instead, the criticism is directed at the forwardness of Machiavelli and the openness with which he teaches political realism. This openness invites imitation by those not suited to, or capable of, being fit princes. Machiavelli addresses his *Prince* to those who are princes and his *Discourses* to those who ought to be. This does not mean that he could not be understood and used by those who neither were nor ought to be princes.

Harry V. Jaffa calls Richard "a nearly perfect symbol of Machiavellian modernity."[40] He falls short of perfection because he is not a perfect student of Machiavelli.

He does, however, seem to have studied "policy." He reminds himself to attend to the reality of the moment—not to count on tactical success until he is certain of it (I.i.120, "but yet I run before my horse to market," I.i.160). He knows how to get the crown, how to foment civil strife, who to befriend, who to test, who to execute, who to marry, who to ally with and when to drop the alliance—all from the very beginning of the play, even before Edward is assured of the crown (*Henry VI, Part 3*, V.vi.61-93). It is as though he has heeded Machiavelli's admonition in his chapter "On Conspiracies" in *Discourses on Livy*:

> But that lust for domination, which blinds men, blinds them yet again in the way they set about the business: for, if they knew but how to do their evil deeds with prudence, it would be impossible for them not to succeed. (*Discourses*, 404)

Richard seems to possess this complete prudence.

For Richard, there is a question as to the efficacy of the means, never the desirability of the end. Macbeth, by contrast, likens the murders that he must commit to secure his throne to the crossing of a river—a finite act (III.iv.135-7). Richard speaks more matter-of-factly. The chain of crimes to usurpation, once begun, continues on indefinitely—that is political realism. "Sin will pluck on sin" (IV.ii.63-65). He accepts assassination, execution, and private murder as a way of life. *Macbeth* is first concerned with the corruption/temptation of Macbeth to the crime of usurpation.[41] *Richard III* takes this for granted in the opening soliloquy.

Richard is always conscious of how he presents himself; he speaks in theatrical terms, and directs scenes with Buckingham. But this self-consciousness makes him self-aware rather than self-knowing. Richard's numerous revealing asides have the effect of making the audience co-conspirators in his project. Since he can confide his true plans to no other character, the silent audience, like the Scrivener, knows but says nothing. Despite all Richard's revelations, Macbeth is still more accessible to us as a moral being. Richard remains multiplicitous and ambiguous, yet nonetheless representative of the ambitions of modern political man (according to Machiavelli's account).

There is a dimension of self-consciousness that Richard does not have, and that is regard for his "fame"—a concept introduced by the young Prince Edward before he is imprisoned and killed in the Tower. He describes his royal aspirations to the Protector and questions him closely about the Tower and how it came to be believed that Julius Caesar built it:

Prince: Is it upon record, or else reported
Successively from age to age, he built it?
Buck. Upon record, my gracious lord.
Prince: But say, my lord, it were not register'd
Methinks the truth should live from age to age,
As 'twere retail'd to all posterity,
Even to the general all-ending day.
Rich. [Aside] So wise so young, they say, do never live long.
Prince: What say you, uncle?
Rich. I say, without characters fame lives long
[Aside] Thus, like the formal Vice, Iniquity,
I moralize two meanings in one word.
Prince: That Julius Caesar was a famous man:
With what his valour did enrich his wit,
His wit set down to make his valour live;
Death makes no conquest of this conqueror,
For now he lives in fame, though not in life.
(III.i.69-88)

How is the fame of a great conqueror sustained? Does it depend on "character"? That is, does it depend on writing or, as Richard puns, on character—the moral substance of a leader? The Prince argues innocently that the truth lives on without writing—a political actor is rewarded with fame or infamy. History brings about justice.

Again, Machiavelli's *Prince* is helpful on this point. In chapter 8 "Of Those Who Have Attained a Principality through Crimes," he tells the story of Agathocles, tyrant of Syracuse. Unfortunately, despite Agathocles' "virtu"— his military prowess and leadership—"his savage cruelty and inhumanity, together with his infinite crimes, do not allow him to be celebrated among the most excellent men."[42] It is not enough to gain fame: one must avoid infamy as well. This is the risk that a tyrant always runs, and is the point of the Prince's questioning concerning Julius Caesar.[43]

This is the problem facing Richard as well. If he is concerned with glory (the highest goal for man in Machiavelli), he must be concerned with his reputation. The irony is that Shakespeare's presentation of this conversation keeps alive Richard's reputation as cruel murderer of the Princes. There has been much scholarship on whether Richard himself was actually responsible for having the princes killed, an event shrouded in mystery. Shakespeare seems unconcerned with keeping open the possibility of Richard's innocence or even obscuring his complicity—the point being that, whether or not Richard actually had the princes killed, he was widely believed to have killed them. In matters of historical record, written or oral, it is one's reputation rather than the unrecoverable or little known facts of accurate biography that should concern a man who aspires to greatness and glory, according to Machiavelli. The conversation between Richard and Prince Edward emphasizes this point nicely. It may not be the truth that lives from age to age (as the Prince somewhat naively asserts), but the report of what was believed or wished true that persists. The perfect criminal/prince commits a crime that is wholeheartedly believed to be someone else's doing. Richard obviously is not able to relieve himself of the burden of blame for what may have been (from the coldly political point of view of securing the crown for the House of York) entirely necessary murders. Richard, most pleased with his own cleverness, ignores the importance of the question of how fame is created, and fails historically. The full irony is, of course, that Shakespeare's record of Richard keeps alive his reputation as a tyrant and killer of innocents. Our attention is called to another aspect of Richard's imperfect machiavellianism.

Richard's debate with himself in act 5, scene 3 is closer to disputation than to moral dilemma. It raises again the implied question of the first soliloquy: Is nature indifferent to man? If nature is indifferent to man, then it provides no guidance for human beings, no natural foundation for constraints on man's treatment of man, no necessity that all men have consciences. If nature, however, can be shown to provide guidance in human affairs, then there is a possibility of a moral standard available to all. Every man might then possess a conscience and Richard might merely have suppressed his. Given Richard's bravado after his nightmares ("Conscience is but a word that cowards use, / Devis'd at first to keep the strong in awe," 310-311), he seems to have concluded on the side of nature's indifference.

But Richard answers the question differently in his first soliloquy. There is a rationale behind nature—it may be malevolent (as in his case), but nature knows what she is doing and why. If nature is "dissembling," she possesses a deliberate intention to mislead. This unresolved contradiction between the first and last soliloquies explains why Richard finally fails, and why he is a less than perfect student of Machiavelli.

The Dregs of Conscience

Richard boasts at the end of act 5, scene 6 in *King Henry VI, Part 3* that he has "neither pity, love, nor fear" (68). In his final soliloquy, he comes to experience all three when he is afflicted by "coward conscience" (V.iii.178-207).[44] By placing this scene at the end of the play, Shakespeare has tempted us to consider that Richard's first accounts of himself are complete and true. The soliloquy is his attempt, intellectually, to convince himself that he has no conscience. If we have allowed ourselves to believe that Shakespeare's most villainous protagonist is a man without guilt or fear of retribution (discounting Anne's' reference to Richard's "timorous dreams" [IV.i.84]), we must now rethink his character.

At first, Richard tries to explain away his fear and dismiss it as groundless. The only justifiable reason for fear is imminent physical danger. From whom is he in danger? Himself? He is after all a murderer. That cannot be, unless he seeks revenge against himself. But, though he is moved to revenge himself for wrongs done him by nature (I.i.30), his desire for revenge is limited by self-love. "Richard loves Richard." He is no suicide. In another sense, he is in danger of himself; his fears may cause him to betray himself, lose heart. "Alack, I love myself" (188). But this directly contradicts the claim on which he has built his usurping and tyrannical career—that he does not possess the capacity to love.

Richard has believed himself totally devoid of love or any human attachments, but in the dream sequence he is brought to face his experience of the emotions that attach men to other human beings (love, pity, and fear) as they all surface. His unconcern with the consequences of his crimes has been based on his conviction that he is altogether indifferent to others. But, if he is self-loving and therefore sensitive to injustices don to himself (the wrongs done him by nature), he cannot be entirely indifferent to injustices done to others. Can one feel these emotions about oneself and be completely unmoved by what happens to others? To feel the injustice of the world strongly is to expect justice from it. If nature owes something to him, then nature must owe something to others. His ability to harm others and his cruelty (an example of which is his request that Tyrrel give him details of the princes' deaths, IV.iii.31-32) suggest that he is emotionally attached to other men in an important way. To be concerned with harming others is to be concerned with them, however perversely. In a sense, Richard must go out of his way to emphasize the injustice done him by nature in order to motivate and justify cruel actions.

Richard, unlike Clarence, is not consumed with guilt, but with the debate about guilt and conscience.[45] He acts on the erroneous belief that he is a creature solely of intellect,[46] capable of making himself entirely into a selfhood with no human attachments. He tries to debate his way out of a self-contradiction—to dismiss his very real nightmares, tangible evidence of his guilt. Shakespeare stages Richard's dreams, not Clarence's, to emphasize that the emotional experience (of someone who claims to have no such emotions) has substance, and that, for a human being who does not acknowledge inner struggle, the dilemma must be displaced to the outside. For Richard to be able to dismiss this experience he must believe that there is no natural reason that a human being may not, as Proteus, recreate himself into anything he pleases. Men need not necessarily feel love, pity, or fear—men may be creatures solely of intellect. In fact, Richard believes such men are by far superior, as is suggested by his contempt for all those (particularly women), who do not operate exclusively on this level. He, unlike the rest of mankind, claims to have seen through the superstitions governing men, and freed himself from the fear of divine justice, and so from conscience. Why then is he troubled with these dreams? Afterwards he says that these shadows have struck terror to his "soul." Has Richard discovered that he has a soul?

The Murderers of Clarence (I.iv) provide the best anticipatory commentary on Richard's final soliloquy (V.iii.178-207). They puzzle over whether there exists such a thing as conscience, what its origins are, and whether it can be escaped, avoided, or circumvented. Each takes a side of the debate Richard has with himself later on.[47]

The Second Murderer feels some pangs of conscience—he is worried by the "urging of that word, 'Judgment'" (104), but at the mention of a reward he theorizes:

> I'll not meddle with it; it makes a man a coward. A man cannot steal but it accuseth him; a man cannot swear but it checks him; a man cannot lie with his neighbour's wife but it detects him. 'Tis a blushing, shamefaced spirit, that mutinies in a man's bosom. It fills a man full of obstacles; it made me once restore a purse of gold that by chance I found. It beggars any man that keeps it; it is turned out of towns and cities for a dangerous thing; and every man that means to live well endeavors to trust to himself, and live without it. (I.iv.128-138)

Conscience is an unnecessary impediment to self-interest. He concludes by advising that man should "trust to himself"—serve his own ends, rather than heed conscience. Conscience is, then, another voice, one not governed by self-interest. The Second Murderer describes it as a separate individual. This is true of the experience of conscience. It is external to the individual in some way. It links man to standards beyond himself. Conscience relates man to given political or natural or theological standards.

The murderers continue accusing conscience; the Second Murderer perverts proverbial wisdom, likening conscience to the devil: "he would insinuate with thee but to make thee sigh" (I.iv.142)—it deceives men against their own best interest. Caught in this exchange of witticisms when Clarence wakes, they "reason" with him, in order to justify to themselves his execution.

Clarence, in response, appeals to divine law over human law: "The great King of kings/Hath in the table of His law commanded/That thou shalt do no murder" (184-186). This sentiment is echoed, to as little effect, in the next scene as King Edward IV attempts to reconcile his Court: "Lest He that is the supreme King of kings/Confound your hidden falsehood, and award/Either of you to be the other's end" (II.i.13-15). The idea is repeated again in the next scene (just after Clarence's murder), by Clarence's son: "God will revenge it, whom I will importune/With earnest prayers, all to that effect" (II.ii.14-15). The argument for divine vengeance is put in the mouths of the weak who seek protection, ineffectually, from the strong.

The Second Murderer has second thoughts, having failed to rid himself of conscience.[48] He does little to prevent the assassination, though, and afterwards compares himself to Pilate—another guilty bystander. He is termed a "coward" by his companion (269), echoed later by Richard's denouncement of coward conscience at Bosworth. How can cowardice be distinguished from conscience by an onlooker?

Can one completely rid oneself of conscience? The argument between the murderers represents two opposing ideas about conscience and divine justice presented in the play. Either conscience is the reasonable fear of punishment from a just God (or gods), or it is merely timidity in the face of convention, based on the incorrect opinion that justice is at work in this world or another. These are the positions of Clarence and Edward on the one hand, and Richard on the other.

Queen Margaret's cursing refrains remind us, if we had forgotten, of the murders committed by all three in order to establish the House of York on the throne. From the moral perspective, they deserve the torments of conscience. Clarence and Edward do experience these as they near death, but Richard strives, with near success, to escape them up until his nightmares in act 5, scene 3.

Clarence, sensible of the dangers of his imprisonment, ultimately comes to the belief that God does punish villains, however successful. He describes to the Keeper a complex dream in which he envisions being called to account by his victims and punished by Furies (pagan exacters of vengeance). The experience of conscience has, for him, a psychological complexity. In Edward, by contrast, conscience shows itself as simple fear of divine retribution. Worried by the thought of imminent death and judgment, Edward spends his last days arranging artificial reconciliations between nobles, for the more certain salvation of his soul. Later, he fears God's wrath for his part in Clarence's death (II.i.132-3).[49]

Richard, however, does not evince belief in a deity who concerns himself with punishing human evil. Guilt and conscience have their roots in groundless superstitions. The only punishment he understands is failure, and failure is the avoidable consequence of imprudence. What, then, are the roots of his apparent attack of conscience in act 5, scene 3? Why is he able to ignore the concerns that afflict his brothers about the usurpation of Henry VI? Either conscience is innate, an immutable part of us that connects us with the world (human and divine) beyond ourselves, or it is a convention (like divine right), carefully contrived by men to discourage questioning of political or religious authority.

Unlike Clarence's "unfelt imaginations" (I.iv.80), Richard's torments are externalized and staged. Despite these tangible manifestations (the ghosts that burden his "soul" and charge him to "despair and die"), Richard publicly denies the power of conscience (V.iii.310). But his debate with himself remains precariously unresolved. This lack of resolution is due to his conflicting views of nature, which cause him confusion about whether there is some natural standard for human behavior.

Dissembling Nature

The murderers show the terms of the debate, but this does not explain why Richard, so apparently unconcerned with moral right and wrong, is divided before the decisive battle of his reign. This division is rooted in his conflicting views about nature. Richard believes he has been "cheated of feature by dissembling Nature" (I.i.19):[50]

> Why, Love forswore me in my mother's womb:
> And, for I should not deal in her soft laws,
> She did corrupt frail Nature with some bribe,
> To shrink mine arm up like a wither'd shrub;
> To make an envious mountain on my back,
> Where sit Deformity to mock my body.
> (III.ii.153-163)

To explain his misshapenness, Richard says that nature has been corrupted by love. Consequently, he believes that nature has done him an injustice. To believe in the injustice of nature implies the attribution of intention to nature. How can a nature indifferent to man be spiteful, envious, dishonest, and dissembling? How can it intend anything towards an individual man?

Richard's egocentric view of nature requires that there be some rationale behind nature that gives men different physical natures for different ends. There must be some motivating intelligence behind it all, however malicious, or incomprehensible to human reason. According to Richard, nature gives lovers beautiful shapes. Since it has deprived him of beauty, he cannot be a lover and must pursue villainy—nature has indirectly determined his course of action. There are three choices, as he sees it in this soliloquy. He might have been a lover, but nature has precluded that (I.i.14-24). He might become philosophic or poetic, gazing at his "shadow" or attempting to describe his "deformity" (I.i.26-27), but there is no satisfaction in this. Finally, he might become what society would call a "villain" (I.i.30-31). Richard, then, is not entirely a creature of his own creation. He cannot simply make what he wants out of himself: nature has imposed certain limitations on him—limitations that he understands as guiding him, negatively, to villainy. There is some kind of natural standard, then, even if it is only as crude as beauty of form.

The other outstanding Shakespearean villain who contemplates nature as a supreme power is Edmund in *King Lear*:

> Thou, Nature, art my goddess; to thy law
> My services are bound. Wherefore should I
> Stand in the plague of custom, and permit
> The curiosity of nations to deprive me,
> For that I am some twelve or fourteen moonshines

Lag of a brother? Why bastard? Wherefore base?
When my dimensions are as well compact,
My mind as generous, and my shape as true,
As honest madam's issue? (I.ii.1-9)[51]

Edmund stands in the "plague of custom," and so vows to serve nature in-stead,[52] which has given him all her gifts: dimension, mind, and shape. He will worship her as a goddess, because he recognizes in nature rational standards by which to judge men: quality of form and mind.

Edmund is society's bastard while Richard is the bastard of nature. Edmund is deprived only by custom of the status that he might naturally claim. He intends to circumvent with his "invention" (20). He is the thrall of "custom," Richard is "the slave of nature" (I.iii.230). He notes the superiority of others in this respect: Edward, Prince of Wales is "Fram'd in the prodigality of Nature" (I.ii.248). In Richard's case nature does not reveal his true qualities in his outward form. The truth about him and his capacities is hidden. In Edmund's case custom obscures his excellent nature, his form and mind. Both attribute their misfortunes to forces external to themselves, forces they believe may be overcome by "invention" or "villainy."

Edmund decides to take nature alone as his standard for action—he is supe-rior, therefore he deserves all the honors and opportunities appropriate to that superiority. We might suspect that, like Richard, he seeks a kind of revenge—but against custom, rather than nature—for instance, by engaging himself to both Goneril and Regan. Richard's alternatives are, first, to create a "self" in opposition to, or apart from, nature, which will enable him to achieve happi-ness through conquering nature. Second, to fulfill the purpose nature has given him: he is ugly, therefore he must be villainous. He vacillates between these two opinions. Richard desires to revenge himself for what nature has done to him and finds that nature has given him a form that instructs him in this desire for vengeance. He reflects on accounts of his birth:

And so I was, which plainly signified
That I should snarl, and bite, and play the dog.
Then since the heavens have shap'd my body so,
Let hell make crook'd my mind to answer it.
I have no brother, I am like no brother.
(V.vi.71-80)

But can one be revenged on nature from within nature? Richard wants both to discover that nature determines that he will seek vengeance and to believe that he is capable of triumphing over nature by revenging himself in some way. His quest for such revenge raises the question: How should one regard one's own natural deficiencies?

Richard finds biblical guidance on this subject from St. Paul. He is the only character in all of Shakespeare to swear by this saint (six times: I.i.138, I.ii.36, I.ii.41, I.iii.45, III.iv.76, V.iii.277).[53] It is a highly unusual oath. Paul, too, suffered from imperfection of physical form and was an outsider (a Pharisee and Roman citizen converted to Christianity). Paul writes in his letters of having an invisible ailment ("a thorn in the flesh," 2 Cor. 12:7), which afflicts him terribly. In the Second Epistle to the Corinthians, Paul speaks to Richard's problem:

> Do ye look on things after the outward appearance? If any man trust to himself that he is Christ's, let him of himself think this again, that, as he is Christ's, even so are we Christ's. For though I should boast somewhat more of our authority, which the Lord hath given us for edification, and not for your destruction, I should not be ashamed: That I may not seem as if I would terrify you by letters. For his letters, say they, are weighty and powerful; but his bodily presence is weak, and his speech contemptible. Let such an one think this, that, such as we are in word by letters when we are absent, such will we be also in deed when we are present.   (2 Corinthians 10:7-11)[54]

Outward appearances are deceptive, so we should not look to outward form as an indicator of inner power. Nature dissembles the truth. Richard's motto might be Paul's defiance about his infirmity in 2 Corinthians 12:10: "Therefore I take pleasure in infirmities, in reproaches, in necessities, in persecutions, in distresses for Christ's sake: for when I am weak, then am I most strong."

This is true, in caricature, for Richard; his pretense of humility carries him far with Edward IV who makes him Lord Protector; with Clarence, who trusts him to gain his freedom; with Anne, who refuses to kill him when he is most vulnerable; and with the people of London who quietly watch him refuse and then accept the crown (echoes of *Julius Caesar*). It is the case with Richard that, when he appears most weak, he is most strong and most dangerous. Like Machiavelli he understands the power of seeming weakness in the political arena.

Richard twice refers to himself as "ordain'd" for his political role. Both times in *King Henry VI, Part 3*, V.vi.58—as he kills Henry—and V.vii.23; "This shoulder was ordain'd". Richard uses the word in the sense of being chosen by the superior power that has deformed his shoulder, so Paul is chosen by a higher power, Acts 26.

Nature, by deforming Richard, has suited him for the role of "That excellent grand tyrant of the earth/That reigns in galled eyes of weeping souls" (Margaret's epithet, IV.iv.51). According to the Queen, Richard has achieved his revenge. He tyrannizes or "reigns" in the tears of those he has injured; his victory is in their pain. More simply, he is in the "eyes of weeping souls" because he is reflected in their eyes as they look at him, fixing on the source of all their unhappiness.

Nature has taken away from Richard the possibility of private pleasures, and so he retreats into public life. Richard's political and public stance is that Nature does not determine political success or failure. One's nature (physical form, mental endowments) may always be used to advantage—as Edmund perceives.

Anne's submission to Richard (I.ii) gives him the thought that he may recast (clothe) his natural deformity with convention (tailoring) in such a way that others do not notice it. He will "entertain a score or two of tailors/To study fashions to adorn my body" (I.ii.261-2). This suggests how hopeful Richard is that man may conquer or circumvent nature. Just as deformity may be disguised by clever tailors, so the highest political ambitions may be hidden underneath the appearance of piety or weakness: "And thus I clothe my naked villainy/With odd old ends stol'n forth of Holy Writ," I.iii.336-7.

Self against Soul

Why is Richard interested in creating a "self"? He is trying to find a point outside of nature from which to revenge himself on it. On the one hand, he cannot escape his natural deformity, and so takes it as indicative of his purpose in life—to be as hideous in thought and action ("let hell make crook'd my mind to answer it," *King Henry VI, Part 3*, V.vi.79) as in form. On the other, nature has cheated him and so he must get beyond nature ("clothe" his natural deformity), in order to gain happiness. But to go beyond nature requires that he not look to nature for an end or purpose in life.

Macbeth resolves to "jump the life to come" (I.vii.7). Richard is beyond or, alternatively, below, such a concern with divine retribution. His concern in act 5, scene 3 is with whether conscience, a thing intangible, and existing only in the soul or mind (Macbeth's "dagger of the mind"), does or ought to have any effect on his actions. His debate is interrupted by preparations for battle and we never learn that he resolves it satisfactorily. One form of this debate over conscience asks whether it is possible to be entirely evil.[55] Richard's first understanding is that, if there is no natural standard for right or justice, conscience or guilt is merely conventional. Even an individual brought up in a religious society might be able to liberate himself from such conventions, by seeing them as merely imposed by a particular society in a particular historical period. If, however, there is reason to suspect that nature is not simply indifferent to man, (either that there is some divine plan, though we may not comprehend it, or that there is a natural order), then there may be more solid grounds for believing in the existence of conscience or the experience of guilt. Richard fails, in part, at what he tries to become (a self rather than a soul), because he cannot resolve himself as to whether his final pangs of conscience over those he has slain are merely the shadows of an externally imposed social morality, or whether they are rooted in some kind of natural law. Is there natural right or no?

A simple moral reading of the play would interpret it as Shakespeare's assertion that everyone has a conscience, no matter how villainous he may appear. But, as Richard's imperfect self-understanding shows, he is not the perfect villain. His flaw points to a possibility beyond himself—a tyrant who is not simply excellent, but perfect. Such a tyrant would have no nightmares.

Richard's motivation, to revenge himself for wrongs done him by nature, is based on a sense of injustice—nature has cheated him. Desire for such vengeance presupposes that the affliction is deliberate. Richard's anger against nature is rooted in an unarticulated belief that nature is not indifferent to man. Consequently, he cannot avoid entertaining the suspicion that there is a standard for human behavior. Richard, after all, acknowledges the natural standard by which he is considered deformed, by which his end (villainy rather than love) is determined.

Richard is the prototypical modern man in this sense: he believes he can conquer nature entirely by means of his intellect, forcing everyone to acknowledge him as most powerful (even imperial), despite his natural disadvantage. But by the end of the play, Richard actually believes that he "may despair" (V.iii.201). To despair in the religious sense is utterly to doubt God. For Richard, despair is the discovery that his hopes for the crown, for the House of York, and above all for revenge are utterly unrealizable. This hope ignores the fact that he believes intermittently that nature has determined his end to be that of villain rather than lover.

On a political level, an answer to the general question of whether nature provides standards for human action would influence an answer to the question posed in act 4, scene 3 of *Macbeth*: Is formal legitimacy the most important aspect of political rule, or is justice necessary as well? Malcolm argues that the tyrant is tyrannical because of his injustice rather than because of his illegitimacy. Richard, like Macduff in that scene, limits the question of rule to the question of legitimacy. By slandering his parents and removing everyone between him and the throne, he can provide himself with formal legitimacy. In this sense he is the prototypical modern tyrant and a good student of Machiavelli. He is that political gambler, offering a kingdom for a horse: "I have set my life upon a cast/And I will stand the hazard of the die" (V.iv.9-10).[56]

Xenophon, in his *Hiero* and *Education of Cyrus*, sets forth two classical models of tyranny. Respectively, they are the tyrant who pursues unlimited private pleasure and the tyrant who pursues unlimited honor and glory. In Macbeth, we have a usurper motivated by the desire for the highest honor (the Scottish throne), and he, like Cyrus, knows that he deserves it. In *The Winter's Tale*, Leontes, like Hiero, is tyrannical in the realm of private desires—especially love. He desires to be loved absolutely and provably by Hermione. Richard III follows neither classical model of tyranny: he does not seek honor or love, but revenge.

This play is the core of Shakespeare's criticism of Machiavelli, or Machiavellianism. The deformed Richard parodies Machiavelli's favorite examples of potential and actual princes—those who are not favored by nature or society (bastards, for example, Cesare Borgia). Shakespeare sees the possibility of a new species of tyrant arising from the teachings of the *Prince* and *Discourses*. Machiavelli's openness invites imitation by all sorts of brilliant but perverted minds. He may even have particular appeal to a man, like Richard, who desires to revenge himself on the world. Shakespeare's character demonstrates how an aspiring tyrant of this sort, using Machiavelli's "new modes and orders," goes very far towards achieving his ends, without understanding them.

But what does Richard want? Is it that his nature impels him towards villainy? Unlike Macbeth, Richard does not regard himself as deserving of the high honors of kingship, but only as clever enough to get them, and he has contempt for those who will not try. He desires revenge against nature because of his deformity. Yet he believes he has freed himself from the notion that there is a natural standard (natural law, natural right)—freed himself from the ferocity of conscience—which distinguishes good and evil. It emerges that Richard is driven by an unacknowledged sense of injustice: nature has injured him. As it turns out, Richard's new way of looking at the world ruptures when he cannot decide whether he is within nature or able to be outside it. This rupture occurs as he faces death.

If Richard's actions are not inspired by some belief in his natural right as a superior intellect, what moves him? It could be said that he simply wants mastery over others and over nature. It appears that he desires power for its own sake. But how is this desire for power to be distinguished from a desire for revenge, a hatred of the world? That distinction cannot be made from outside a person: no one can "touch" what another is.

If Richard does not acknowledge a standard in nature which, well understood, may offer guidance on human action, is there some other guide? Another such standard might be history. Does Richard wish to be judged by history as the unifier of England, the originator of empire, like the builder of the Tower, Julius Caesar? If so, and there is some reason to credit him on these grounds, he fails utterly, attracting instead the reputation of cruel tyrant (ironically reinforced by the surface presentation of Richard in this play).

Richard and Macbeth are not so far apart finally. There is a connection between the desire for vengeance and a love of honor (most fully explored in *Coriolanus*). Richard's desire to be revenged on nature comes out of his sense that nature owed him something in particular that he has been forced to obtain in another way: by perfect manipulation of his world, by science. But already, in his drive for mastery, Richard concedes that his invented "self" is incomplete: he needs something from the rest of the world, even if that something is infamy. For Machiavelli the desire for power is coeval or identical with the desire to conquer fortune. But Shakespeare probes this desire in order to expose the human anger at natural deficiencies—a power-seeking anger which, because he underestimates it, Machiavelli guides recklessly.

Notes

1. Both Samuel Taylor Coleridge and Henry James registered dissatisfaction with the play on this account. H. C. Robinson's *Diary* records that Coleridge believed Shakespeare "wrote hardly anything of this play except the character of Richard: he found the piece a stock play and re-wrote the parts which developed the hero's character," from *Lectures on Shakespeare*, ed. T. Ashe (London: George Bell & Sons, 1900), 27. The play was for James "a loose, violent, straddling romance . . . —a chronicle for the market-place, a portrait for the house wall." From a review in *Harper's Weekly* quoted in *Eyewitnesses of Shakespeare*, ed. Gamini Salgado (Sussex: Sussex University Press, 1975), 104.

2. All citations from *Richard III* will be taken from the Arden Shakespeare, ed. Antony Hammond (New York: Methuen, 1981) and noted in the text. This edition will be cited in notes as Hammond.

3. "Ronald Berman remarked after a screening of *Richard III* on Public Television that Richard is the only character in the play who *thinks* very much. At times he seems to be thinking about his own double performance (one for characters, one for us)," Jack J. Jorgens, *Shakespeare on Film* (Bloomington: Indiana University Press, 1977), 143. This running self-conscious commentary accounts, in part I believe, for the attraction/obsession of this part for contemporary actors. Antony Sher records this in *Year of the King* (London: Chatto & Windus, 1985).

4. In *Discourses* III.6. Translated by Bernard Crick (New York: Penguin Books, 1985), 414.

5. Coleridge, 487.

6. Michael Neill cites E. A. J. Honigmann in "Shakespeare's Halle of Mirrors: Play, Politics, and Psychology in *Richard III*," in *Shakespeare Studies* 8 (1975): 99. This is also argued by L. C. Knights in *Shakespeare, The Histories* (Essex, Longman Group Ltd., 1965); and Norman Rabkin in *Shakespeare and the Common Understanding* (Chicago: The University of Chicago Press, 1967); and Bridget Gellert Lyons, "'King's Games': Stage Imagery and Political Symbolism in *Richard III*" in *Criticism* 20.1 (Winter 1978): 17-30.

7. Colley Cibber, "Richard III. a Tragedy" in *The Dramatic Works of Colley Cibber*, Vol. 2 (New York: AMC Press, Inc., 1966), 322. Cibber introduces the association of conscience and cowardice early on in his revision of *Richard III* and abbreviates the speech on remorse from act 5, scene 3. In his version, interestingly, Gloucester complains of "tyrant Conscience" but believes himself too evil to be capable of repentance (much like Marlowe's Faustus). Cibber creates a safer Richard, more cowardly and less ruthlessly competent.

8. Francis Bacon's Essay XLIIII "Of Deformity" states this view of nature as follows: "*Deformed Persons* are commonly euen with Nature: For as Nature hath done ill by them; So doe they by Nature: Being for the most part, (as Scripture saith) *void of Naturall Affection*; And so they have their Reuenge of Nature." *Essays*, (London: Oxford University Press, 1975).

9. "Richard III" in *The Design Within*, ed. M. D. Faber (New York: Science House, 1970). Afterwards cited as Faber.

10. Faber, 345.

11. Examples of such criticisms are: James T Henke's *The Ego-King: An Archetype Approach to Elizabethan Political Thought and Shakespeare's Henry VI Plays*; Marjorie Garber's *Dreams in Shakespeare: From Metaphor to Metamorphosis*, pp. 15-25; Murray Krieger's "The Dark Generations of *Richard III*" in Faber; and Michael Neill's "Shakespeare's Halle of Mirrors: Play, Politics, and Psychology in *Richard III*,", in *Shakespeare's Studies* 8 (1975): 99-129.

12. For example, Sir Thomas Whately, in his excellent essay, "Remarks on Some of the Characters of Shakespeare" overlooks entirely the effect of Richard's deformity on him. In *Shakespeare Criticism: 1623-1840*, ed. D. Nichol Smith (London: Oxford University Press, 1961), 125-126. Freud recognizes the force of Richard's resentment and its connection with his misshapenness.

13. The first reference is particularly interesting since it suggests one source of Shakespeare's knowledge of Machiavelli, as Edward Meyer points out in *Machiavelli and the Elizabethan Drama* (1897; reprint, New York: Burt Franklin, 1969), 58. The Duke of Alençon was the noble to whom Gentillet dedicated his famous commentary on Machiavellian thought in *Discours Contre Machiavelli* [eds. A. D'Andrea and P. D. Stewart (Firenze: Casalini Libri, 1974)]. Meyer notes no less than 395 references to Machiavelli in all of Elizabethan literature. There are three in Shakespeare. The third instance is in *The Merry Wives of Windsor*, where the Host of the Garter asks "Am I too politic? Am I subtle? Am I a Machiavel?" III.i.92-93, just before undeceiving two potential combatants. Gentillet's diatribe against Machiavelli ironically did much to popularize his thought in England before the first published English translation of *The Prince* in 1666. But Felix Raab completely dispels the myth of Gentillet's version of Machiavelli as the definitive English Machiavelli in *The English Face of Machiavelli* (London: Routledge and Kegan Paul, 1964): "The common form of this myth is that those who manufactured these masters [stage machiavels] had not read Machiavelli at all and had created their villains on the basis of Gentillet's hostile distortion of his writings. . . . In the first place, although Simon Patericke translated the *Contre-Machiavel* in 1577, only a year after it was written, the translation was not printed until 1602, by which time the Machiavellian villain had been a stock figure for some time. To argue that Patericke's translation exerted this tremendous influence in manuscript is clearly ridiculous in view of the proliferation of Machiavelli's work in England, nor is there any evidence that the French edition of Gentillet was being more widely read than Machiavelli in Italian, Latin, and English before 1602 or, for that matter, afterwards" (56). For another discussion of how Shakespeare might have known Machiavelli, see Hardin Craig's introduction to *Machiavelli's The Prince: An Elizabethan Translation* (Chapel Hill: The University of North Carolina Press, 1944). There were manuscript translations of *The Prince* available before 1666 (the date of the first published English translation). Wyndham Lewis bases his otherwise interesting discussion in *The Lion*

and the Fox: The Role of the Hero in the Plays of Shakespeare on the assumption that Shakespeare knew Machiavelli exclusively through Gentillet (New York: Harper & Brothers Publishers, n.d.). See also chapter 1, note 46. The comprehension of Machiavelli's new political science in *Richard III* suggests that, one way or another, Shakespeare knew more than a caricatured version of Machiavelli.

14.   David L. Frey argues similarly in *The First Tetralogy: Shakespeare's Scrutiny of the Tudor Myth* (Paris: Mouton, 1976), 139-154. Citing Coleridge, he concludes that Shakespeare "has carefully built up the successful Machiavellian, and removed all the external causes of his defeat, in order to show us the internal process that points to the real flaw in the writings of the crafty Italian" (174). But Frey, too, stops short of explaining adequately what this "real flaw" is.

15.   This interpretation is supported and elaborated by Lily B. Campbell's *Shakespeare's Histories: Mirrors of Elizabethan Policy* (Cambridge: Cambridge University Press, 1938) and E. M. W. Tillyard's *Shakespeare's History Plays* (New York: Collier Books, 1944) as well as by an editor of the Arden edition, Antony Hammond. Frey argues against the thesis and then, inadvertently, affirms it.

16.   See St. Thomas Aquinas *Summa Theologica* questions 75-87, especially question 75, which is a refutation of the objections that the soul is corporeal, in *Introduction to St. Thomas Aquinas*, ed. Anton C. Pegis (New York: Random House, Inc., 1948), 280-428. Also St. Augustine in *The City of God* makes a good point, pertinent to Richard's case, that the cause of evil in the fallen angels was "their turning away from him who supremely is, and their turning toward themselves, who do not exist in that supreme degree" Book XII, chapter 6, trans. Henry Bettenson (New York: Pelican Books, 1972), 477.

17.   See Matthew 16:24-25 for the biblical use of self and soul synonymously. Richard is caught between trying to escape the strong Christian division between body and soul, coyly expressed by Andrew Marvell in "A Dialogue Between Body and Soul," and recoiling from viewing himself in solely material terms. The former view he believes deluded and the latter places him in a very unattractive light (his deformity). He relies on the concept "self" to accommodate his new view of individuality.

18.   Richard refers to soul seventeen times (I.i.11, 41, 119; I.ii.180; I.iii.179; II.i.71; III.v.27; III.vii.225; IV.iv.251, 256, 263, 311, 408; V.iii.202, 204, 218, 309). The question of his soul's existence is most at issue when he tries to persuade Elizabeth (IV.iv) and then when he faces death in battle (V.iii). Clarence refers to soul eight times (I.iv.38, 44, 48, 67, 74, 240, 242, 246) as he wrestles with the issue just before his murder. Elizabeth, Anne, King Edward, and, notably, Richmond all speak of "soul." Richard's soul is referred to sixteen times in the play. The word is used sixty-one times altogether.

19.   Hammond, 287, n. 259.

20.   As the wooing scene progresses, Anne begins using Richard's syntactic constructions. Richard controls the structural power of her language, that is, her phraseology, and so controls her responses. This situation is reversed in act 4, scene 4 as Richard comes to use Elizabeth's rhetorical structures.

21.   Coppelia Kahn, *Man's Estate: Masculine Identity in Shakespeare* (Berkeley: University of California Press, 1980), 47, 63-64, 49. See also Marguerite Waller's illuminating attempt to synthesize deconstructive and feminist readings of Richard's courtship of Anne in *Rewriting the Renaissance: The Discourses of Sexual Difference in*

Early Modern Europe, eds. Margaret W. Ferguson, Maureen Quilligan, and Nancy J. Vickers (Chicago: The University of Chicago Press, 1986), 159-174.

22. Madonne M. Miner, "Neither Mother, Wife, nor England's Queen: The Role of Women in *Richard III*," Lenz, 45. One would have to except from this remark the Scrivener (III.vi), the citizens (II.iii), and even Tyrrel (IV.iii).

23. Lenz, 52.

24. Andrew S. Cairncross, ed. *King Henry VI, Parts 1, 2, and 3* (London: Methuen & Co., Ltd. [parts 1 and 2], 1962, [part 3] 1964). All citations from the plays will be taken from this edition.

25. See Whately, 125-126. John Philip Kemble responded spiritedly in defense of Macbeth in *Macbeth and King Richard III: An Essay* (London: John Murray, 1817).

26. See above, n. 15. J. Leeds Barroll in the first chapter of his book *Artificial Persons* is helpful: "Even if *Hamlet* does strike us as 'Freudian,' Shakespeare nevertheless had not read Freud; and while Shakespeare may have observed traits that modern psychology generally accepts as extant in human nature, the structure of ideas by which he sought to account for such phenomena would have been quite importantly different" (Columbia: University of South Carolina Press, 1974), 21.

27. Robert N. Watson, *The Hazards of Ambition* (Cambridge: Harvard University Press, 1984), 20.

28. Christopher Marlowe, *The Complete Plays*, ed. J. B. Steane (New York: Penguin Books, 1978), 337. Future references to this edition will be to Marlowe.

29. Richard refers to "self" generally three times (II.ii.151; III.i.63; IV.iv.425) and his "self" is referred to five times by Anne, Richard, Buckingham, and Elizabeth (I.ii.80; II.ii.151; III.vii.131; III.vii.194; IV.iv.376). But Richard speaks of "myself" twenty-seven times, far more than any other character in the play (I.ii.77, 82, 85, 190, 259, 263; I.iii.79, 319; III.i.137; III.vii.52; IV.iv.249, 376, 399 [2x], 407; V.iii.183, 186, 187 [2x], 188, 189 [2x], 190, 191, 203, 204 [2x]). It is easy to see that the question of his "selfhood" is most at issue when he faces death in act 5, scene 3. There are more references to the self in *Richard III* (85) than in any other of Shakespeare's plays.

30. Machiavelli never uses the word *anima* (soul) in either *The Prince* or *Discourses on Livy*.

31. William Shakespeare, *Hamlet*, the Arden edition, ed. Harold Jenkins (New York: Methuen, 1982).

32. This argument is made by Callicles in Plato's *Gorgias*, 482c-486c. Translated by Terrence Irwin (Oxford: Clarendon Press, 1979).

33. As Machiavelli says in the *Discourses*: "To threaten to shed blood is, in fact, extremely dangerous: whereas to shed it is attended with no danger at all, for a dead man cannot contemplate vengeance and those that remain alive usually leave you to do the contemplating" (40).

34. When Richard refers to "conscience," it has the sense of "consciousness" as well as the modern sense of "knowledge or feeling of right and wrong." Jonathan Goldberg observes with reference to the writings of King James I: "The questions raised by James's language thus bifurcate into a complex set of relationships between self-perception and other perception. In the Jacobean period the area in which these conflicts occur was conveniently housed in a single word, "conscience," a word that contains both the idea of the knowledge of self and the knowledge of others ("con-

scious" in a modern vocabulary). The unity between conscience and consciousness that the word *conscience* declares is in James's thinking divided—both in himself and his audience," *James I and the Politics of Literature* (115). Richard is profoundly aware that the word "conscience" unites a moral and a metaphysical meaning. To have a conscience is to be aware of the opinions of others, most importantly to be conscious of the opinion of God on one's actions. This "consciousness," the root of moral restraint, he believes to be wholly artificial and unnecessary. See part 3 of this chapter, "The Dregs of Conscience."

35. Niccolo Machiavelli, *The Prince*, trans. Harvey C. Mansfield (Chicago: University of Chicago Press, 1985), 71. Hereafter referred to as *Prince*. Compare this excerpt, too, with the Scrivener's speech two scenes later:

> Here is a good world the while! Who is so gross
> That cannot see this palpable device?
> Yet who's so bold but says he sees it not?
> Bad is the world and all will come to naught
> When such ill-dealing must be seen in thought.
> (III.vi.10-14)

36. Soliloquies and asides of Richard III throughout the tetralogy. Soliloquies: 2H6 V.ii.66-71; 3H6 III.ii.124-195, V.vi.61-93; R3 I.i.1-41, I.i.117-121, I.i.145-162, I.ii.232-268, I.iii.324-338, V.iii.178-207. Asides: 3H6 IV.i.82, IV.i.123, IV.vii.25-26, V.vii.21-25, V.vii.33-34; R3 I.iii.318-319, II.ii.110-111, III.i.79, III.i.82-83, III.i.94, IV.iv.431.

37. Marlowe, 347.

38. See especially *Discourses* I.27 and III.6.

39. Danby, 61-62, 66.

40. Harry V. Jaffa, "The Unity of Tragedy, Comedy, and History: An Interpretation of the Shakespearean Universe," in *Shakespeare as Political Thinker*, eds. John Alvis and Thomas G. West (Durham: Carolina Academic Press, 1981), 287.

41. Interestingly, although it is a play about the corruption of Macbeth's soul, the word "soul" is used only four times in this play. This is because the existence of soul is not in question in *Macbeth*.

42. *Prince*, 35.

43. The question of the importance of establishing reputation for a great political man is a main concern of *Julius Caesar*, a play in which the titular character has few lines and is killed a third of the way through. The play is more about the reputation of Julius Caesar than the man.

44. Again, a problem word in the play, used thirteen times, Richard himself uses it most, six times: I.i.239; III.vii.225; V.iii.179, 194, 310, 312. The word most closely associated with "conscience" in the play is "guilt," referred to seventeen times, six times by Richard: I.ii.100 (2x); II.i.137; III.v.30; V.iii.200 (2x). He is referred to as guilty six times.

45. See note 34.

46. Coleridge speaks of Richard as a man who depends on his "superiority of intellect"—who has placed "the moral in subordination to the mere intellectual being," *Lectures*, 147, 273.

47. As Jan Kott notes, "Only two people in this tragedy reflect on the order of the world: King Richard III, and a hired assassin. The one who is at the top of the feudal ladder, and one placed at its very bottom." In *Shakespeare Our Contemporary*, trans. Boleslaw Taborski (London: Methuen and Co. Ltd., 1964), 26-27. This scene in the Tower is the one in the play that comes closest to the clown scenes in the later tragedies, such as the Porter scene in *Macbeth*—grisly, comic relief.

48. "'A very bad murderer,' I said, 'like Shakespeare's Second Murderer in that scene in *King Richard III*. The fellow that had certain dregs of conscience, but still wanted the money, and in the end didn't do the job at all because he couldn't make up his mind. Such murderers are very dangerous. The have to be removed—sometimes with blackjacks.'" From *Farewell My Lovely* by Raymond Chandler.

49. H. M. Richmond in *Shakespeare's Political Plays* misreads this speech and suggests that Edward, of all the characters, comes closest to the "heroic self-recognition that is to mark such characters as Othello and Lear" (Gloucester, MA: Peter Smith, 1977), 91. This ignores the fact that Edward (portrayed as pleasure-loving and impolitic throughout the tetralogy) begins by blaming everyone but himself for Clarence's death. He fears God's wrath for his injustice to Clarence (along lines suggested to him by Richard), blames everyone in his court (except Richard), and then laments: "O God, I fear Thy justice will take hold/On me, and you, and mine and yours for this" (II.i.132-133). His deathbed remorse, given his actions earlier in the tetralogy, is hard to regard as "heroic."

50. There were many versions of Richard's reign from which Shakespeare could have chosen in constructing his villain-king. He preferred an account that included Richard's deformity, a detail introduced by St. Thomas More in his *History of King Richard III*. There is no factual evidence for it. "Richard, the third son, of whom we now entreat, was in wit and courage equal with either of them, in body and prowess far under them both; little of stature, ill-featured of limbs, crook-backed, his left shoulder much higher than his right, hard favored of visage, and such as in states called warly, in other men otherwise," ed. Richard Sylvester (New Haven: Yale University Press, 1976), 8. Shakespeare, like More, uses physical deformity to symbolize a flawed nature. See Richard's comments, especially *King Henry VI, Part 3*, III.ii.153-163, V.vi.71-80, and *Richard III*, I.i.14-27.

51. All citations to *Lear* are from the Arden edition, ed. Kenneth Muir (London: Methuen & Co. Ltd., 1975).

52. Note the classical distinction (taken from Greek philosophy) made here, between *nomos* (convention/law) and *physis* (nature). Richard makes the same distinction.

53. I follow the Quarto readings of Richard's oath as "by Saint Paul" at I.i.138, rather than the Folio "by Saint John," which is Hammond's choice in the Arden edition. Richard is very consistent in his oaths. The rare exception being his "by God's holy mother" (I.iii.306), which is spoken, appropriately enough, of a woman—Queen Margaret.

54. See also Romans 7:18-19: "For I know that in me (that is, in my flesh,) dwelleth no good thing: for to will is present with me; but how to perform that which is good I find not. For the good that I would I do not; but the evil which I would not, that I do." Richard perversely interprets Paul's teaching of the limitations of the body. All citations of the Bible are from the King James Version. For a different take on the dichotomy between soul and body which Richard, with Paul, wishes to escape, see An-

drew Marvell's poem, "A Dialogue between the Soul and Body" where the body complains: "O who shall me deliver whole,/From bonds of this tyrannic soul?" *The Poems of Andrew Marvell*, ed. Hugh Macdonald (Cambridge: Harvard University Press, 1973), 15.

55. "But, as has already been remarked, men know not how to be either wholly bad or wholly good," *Discourses*, 185.

56. See the end of *Prince*, chapter 25, "How Much Fortune Can Do in Human Affairs, and in What Mode It May Be Opposed": "I judge this indeed, that it is better to be impetuous then cautious, because fortune is a woman; and it is necessary, if one wants to hold her down, to beat her and strike her down. And one sees that she lets herself be won more by the impetuous than by those who proceed coldly. And so always, like a woman, she is the friend of the young, because they are less cautious, more ferocious, and command her with more audacity," 101.

Chapter 4

The Winter's Tale:
Leontes, a Jealous Tyrant

The Reticence of the "Romances"

In passing from *Macbeth* and *Richard III* to *The Winter's Tale* and *The Tempest*, we go from tragedy and history to something different. What are now commonly termed Shakespeare's Romances have been at the forefront of critical debate in the last forty years as the subject of genre critics.[1] John Heminge and Henry Condell originally classed *Cymbeline* as a tragedy, *The Winter's Tale* and *The Tempest* as comedies, and omitted *Pericles* altogether from the First Folio edition. Within the last hundred years of Shakespeare criticism the view that the Romances are a "new" kind of drama has come to be nearly universally accepted, and critical debate has centered on what exactly Shakespeare was trying to accomplish formally, and on the genesis of this "new" genre. Innovative critical efforts, especially those of the Marxists and New Historicists, have favored what are considered to be the more politically explicit tragedies and histories—with the notable exception of interest in "colonialism" in *The Tempest*. The Romances have, in fact, excited more commentary among feminist critics who find in the plays central, consistent concerns with such issues as father/daughter relations and the incest theme.[2]

Terry Eagleton, in his early book, *Shakespeare and Society*, sees in the Romances (he conservatively terms them "the late comedies") an early form of the nineteenth-century political/literary project to fuse "spontaneous life and social responsibility."[3] But his argument implicitly raises the question of whether the isolated worlds within the Romances offer any solution to this tension—his praise for the final Shakespearean achievement is tentative: "Shakespeare, in the Last Comedies, could reach a kind of solution, but it is achieved within a specialised context and cannot be wholly abstracted from this" (205-206).

In a later book, *William Shakespeare*, the tentative approval changes to ideological rejection. The nature of the accommodation between "spontaneous life and social responsibility" is made specific: "It is just this deconstruction of the court/country polarity which will provide Shakespeare in the last comedies with a kind of resolution to the problems we have pursued throughout his work" (91). The "crux" of this resolution is in the exploration of the inter-dependency of nature and convention during the famous exchange between Perdita and Polixenes in *The Winter's Tale* (IV.iv). Shakespeare's attempt at resolution, is, finally, a failure because, "The 'resolutions' of the late comedies thus rest not only upon a reactionary mystification of Nature but on a logical mistake. If Nature always already contains its own surplus, then it presumably contains as part of its norm that transformation of the given which is murder, as much as the various 'creative' transcendences we have examined" (93). Finally, what *The Tempest* "fails to draw attention to is the glaring contradiction on which its whole discourse effectively founders: the fact that this 'organic' restoration of a traditional social order founded upon Nature and the body rests not only on a flagrant mystification of Nature, gratuitous magical device and oppressive patriarchialism, but is actually set in the context of the very colonialism which signals the imminent victory of the exploitative, 'inorganic' mercantile bourgeoise" (96).

Eagleton sees the "late comedies," as an ideological retreat or defeat for Shakespeare, involving a "logical slide" in the articulation of the relation between nature and convention. As I hope to show, this ignores the complexity of thought and representation in the plays, ironically reducing to "ideology" plays that deliberately break apart ideologies. Finally it avoids the great difficulties of interpretation that these plays pose. We have only to glance at the circumstances of the dialogue Eagleton uses to support his contention that Shakespeare ultimately "sells out"—the famous conversation between Perdita and Polixenes on nature:

Per. For I have heard it said
There is an art which, in their piedness, shares
With great creating nature.

Pol. Say there be;
Yet nature is made better by no mean
But nature makes that mean: so, over that art,
Which you say adds to nature, is an art
That nature makes. You see, sweet maid, we marry
A gentler scion to the wildest stock,
And make conceive a bark of baser kind
By bud of nobler race. This is an art
Which does mend nature—change it rather—but
The art itself is nature.
(IV.iv.86-97)

Eagleton takes Polixenes's thesis as a cooptive ideological assertion useful in support of established authority—it provides a justification for every form of oppression, including the modern nuclear threat. Polixenes's end, however, forgets his beginning, as Antonio will say of Gonzalo in *The Tempest*. Polixenes is attracted to Perdita, to whom his son, the Prince Florizel, is illicitly allied, yet he makes an argument about nature that would seem to support that alliance. In his argument the feminine is of "baser kind" and the masculine, which makes the "bark" conceive, is "of nobler race." We are immediately invited to think of the apparent situation of Perdita and Florizel. So far as Polixenes knows, she is of base birth while his son is legitimate heir to the kingdom. But soon after, Polixenes forcefully condemns that alliance, on the surface completely contradicting his argument for seeing the natural as contained within and extending the conventional. His fury, an echo of Leontes's jealous fit in the first half of the play, is finally circumvented and Perdita and Florizel come to be married, and responsible for the reawakening of life in Sicilia. Polixenes's argument is further undercut because, as we know and relearn in the final scene of reconciliation, Perdita is, after all, not exactly of "wilder stock" but royal. It would be unwise to take as ideological conviction the words of a character who contradicts himself and whose argument is contradicted by the action of the play. The subversions of this argument point to its limitations—if nature is susceptible to endless transformation or mutilation. How can we then refer to something as natural? The action of the play would seem to suggest both the elasticity of nature and the importance of retaining some natural standard—of returning to the natural origins—the progenitors of "nature's bastards," if these are discoverable.

Eagleton's argument, it seems to me, goes directly against the movement of these plays, in particular obscuring the treatments of tyranny in *The Winter's Tale* and *The Tempest*. It is an illuminating misreading to argue that Shakespeare's Romances collapse into "reactionary mystification" in support of established modes or authority—one which suggests the centrality of questions of authority in these plays. Eagleton shares Lytton Strachey's strong and proper reaction to critical sentimentalization of these plays, though Strachey goes to a different rhetorical extreme by suggesting that they were the product of Shakespeare's aged boredom: the poet having been "urged by a general disgust to burst occasionally through his torpor into bitter and violent speech."[4] My contention is that *The Winter's Tale* and *The Tempest* are no less concerned with the dangers of tyranny than *Macbeth* or *Richard III*, but treatment of the problem is more abstract, since these fictional tyrants are to be transformed within worlds influenced or ruled by art. I wish to look first at Leontes, the "jealous tyrant" of *The Winter's Tale* and then at the fraught relation between Prospero and Caliban in *The Tempest* to explore the ways in which, far from radically "mystifying," Shakespeare offers dramatic explanations for the worst kind of political oppression—tyranny.

What Eagleton characterizes as the "ideological" component of the Romances has been variously called naturalism, symbolism, theological exploration, or political subversion.[5] For me the "so-called Romances" (I borrow this
tactful compromise from Geoffrey Hill) are better understood as reticent. Mr.
Hill offers one of the best descriptions of this quality in an essay on *Cymbeline*
in which he suggests that the elusiveness of that play cannot be simply attributed to political caution under James I:

> There is an edgy watchfulness to the play's virtuosity which might indicate
> Shakespeare's reluctance 'to commit himself wholly to the claims of his mate-
> rial'. No such reluctance need be deduced. Even so, an element of reserve
> about the claims of orthodox mystique, or about the eloquence of current
> political mythology, might be demonstrable. Imogen sees Britain's relation to
> the world's volume as being 'of it, but not in't' (III.iv.141), an enigmatic
> phrase which might equally well describe *Cymbeline's* capacity for private
> nuance in its unfolding of the supreme theme of national regeneration and
> destiny.[6]

What I term the "reticence" of the Romances, is reticence about first causes, or
motivation of action, but also especially a reticence about the nature of politics.[7] The genesis of Leontes's jealousy or Prospero's Art is not explained—so,
though we might ask where these destructive and creative forces come from,
we may more successfully ask what they represent and how they are controlled.
Eagleton describes the privileging of the individual in the last comedies: "A
society is available to us in the plays as a web of relationships which are personal, and yet point beyond themselves to a shared life not reducible to individual components."[8] The reticence that comes out of the domesticity of these
plays is most clearly represented in the sixteen-year "silence" of Hermione in
The Winter's Tale. Why is her death/absence necessary? What cannot be said or
taught to Leontes?

What I would like to illustrate in the following two chapters is that politics
do not recede, as a concern, from the Romances, nor do the Romances represent a retreat into "reactionary mystification." The last plays describe a king at
war, a self-exiled prince, a king without an heir, and a duke who wishes to
regain his dukedom. The political concerns about war, usurpation, perpetuation of a monarchy, and founding are as visible in these plays as in the tragedies
and histories, though the problems are explored in more fantastic environments.
Both plays to be discussed are profoundly concerned with the problem of tyranny. What causes tyranny? What excessive desires provoke tyranny? What
does the tyrant want? But a new question is introduced—are there remedies for
tyranny? The political situations of Leontes and Prospero are as desperate and
self-inflicted as those of Macbeth and Richard, with entirely different resolutions.

Though this treatment will not take as its focus the ways in which generic differences dictate differences in treatment of the political questions raised in the two plays, those differences in kind or tone will necessarily emerge as the political problems and their proposed solutions are discussed. Though both plays are more fairy-tale-like, they have a more natural rhythm than the tragedies or histories, because the connections between events are not articulated. Instead of sequential logic, we have events and scenes whose connections are elusive or supplied by an abstraction (for instance, Time in *The Winter's Tale*). We are not told everything: some dissatisfied critics (Johnson, Dryden, and Coleridge among them) would say we are not even told enough. Northrop Frye explains the dominance of genre criticism on the Romances by explaining such ellipses in *A Natural Perspective*: "In comedy and in romance the story seeks its own end instead of holding the mirror up to nature."[9] But I treat *The Winter's Tale* and *The Tempest* together not first because of similarities in form, but because they both propose solutions to the problem of tyranny. The question of whether this tendency towards resolution is dictated by or productive of a new and different kind of form is secondary. In moving to the more fantastic worlds of these plays, we are asked explicitly in the middle of *The Winter's Tale* and at the beginning and end of *The Tempest* to suspend our disbelief.[10] We are asked to believe that sixteen years have passed in the first play and that Prospero's plan may succeed with our approval in the second play. Such authoritative requests require our attention to differences in form that will be treated only as they concern our central question: What is tyranny?

The other unique aspect of the Romances is that the two tyrants are portrayed as educable and even benevolent. Leontes is brought to a point of faithful subjection to his wife by the end of the play. By the end of *The Tempest*, Caliban is held in check and Prospero gives up his Art. Indeed, Prospero's apparent benevolence—his "mercy"—raises the question of how he may be termed a tyrant at all. Of course, both Leontes and Prospero survive to redeem themselves, whereas Macbeth dies "bear-like" and Richard III dies divided against himself and against nature.

Unlike Shakespeare's historical tyrants, Leontes is a tyrant whose tyrannical impulses are educated or, at least, moderated in the sixteen-year course of the play. His fit of blind passion leads him to destroy all that is dear to him and, having defied the gods, he comes to believe himself punished by them. One wise woman, Paulina, seizes on the words of the Oracle and, from what we later learn, spends fifteen years educating Leontes in piety. What does an education in piety have to do with conquering a tyrannical disposition, learning how to rule one's kingdom and one's royal house well, or learning how to love? *The Winter's Tale* is Shakespeare's exploration of the intricate relations between the excesses of erotic love, and a power that is able to check it: piety. This is the only play in which the words of an Oracle determine the events of the play.[11] What releases Leontes from his tyranny has to do with his respect for the Delphic Oracle. But how does piety restrain tyranny?

If the King Had No Son

The play opens with a conversation between the two most powerful lords of Sicilia and Bohemia, Camillo and Archidamus. They discuss the "great differences betwixt" the two countries, they vie for superiority in graciousness, and they congratulate one another on the stability of their respective kingdoms. Sicilia and Bohemia appear, by their accounts, to have solved the great problem facing any established kingdom: the problem of succession—each has a male heir.

Camillo and Archidamus express themselves in prose with the cautious casualness of members of two rival, if friendly, courts. The artificialities of court speech draw our attention to the fragility of monarchic stability, suggesting how the realms may be disrupted and the alliance of friendship severed between the two monarchies. Our introduction to a play that focuses on domestic relations is through the speech of two courtiers concerned with the larger, political implications of what are to be dramatically presented as private issues: the fidelity of a wife and the loyalty of a son. How are the events in Sicilia and Bohemia related? The destruction of a royal marriage is domestic tragedy (Leontes's violation of Hermione's bedchamber and his denying her the "child-bed privileges" II.i, III.ii.103),[12] but one having drastic political consequences (as in the courtroom scene). Polixenes reaches the point where he will disown his only heir to prevent his dishonoring the Bohemian throne. Both actions of the play represent the imposition of considerations of justice on a love bond. They represent the fractures that may occur with the imposition of strict demands for justice on the bonds of love. This problem links the Sicilian and Bohemian halves of the play.

The difficulty of sustaining private relations as a public figure is discussed by the two lords. We learn that Leontes and Polixenes have, until now, had no "personal" encounters since childhood (27). Given the political consciousness of the two speakers, it is not surprising that the conversation turns on how Bohemia is to repay the "magnificence" of Sicilia's hospitality and whether it is necessary for him to do so. Archidamus talks of how they are to "be justified" in love. He speaks of the place of justice in friendship. In using such political terms for personal affairs, Camillo and Archidamus make the awkward connection between the private and public. The political strain caused by the visit between the two monarchs shows as the courtiers compete against one another for effortlessness in hospitality and effusion in gratitude.

Archidamus suggests that there is "great difference betwixt our Bohemia and your Sicilia" and dies not specify what he means by this. Does he mean the men or their realms? Does he refer to political, geographic, or temperamental differences? The persons and what they embody cannot be easily distinguished. Yet their characters are very different.[13] For instance, Leontes insists that Polixenes stay on after an already lengthy visit of nine months while Polixenes is very reluctant to do so. They also have different occasions for anger. Leontes is enraged at the idea that his wife and friend have been faithless to him in love, whereas Polixenes is enraged that his son has been unconcerned with the honor attaching to his royal status and paternity. This difference is reflected also in Archidamus's deflation of Camillo's rhetorical excess—would all Sicilians really wish to die if the king had no heir (39-45)? The difference in character exacerbates the tension created in moving from the plane of personal friendship to the plane of political allegiance—as Bohemia and Sicilia have apparently done.

Camillo and Archidamus introduce the problem of the relation between justice and friendship, which goes beyond a simple difference in character. Camillo speaks of the men: "I think, this coming summer, the King of Sicilia means to pay Bohemia the visitation which he justly owes him" (3-6). Archidamus responds by saying that "we will be justified in our loves" (9). Camillo speaks of the justice of the return visit casually, as repayment of a pleasurable favor—it is the visit that is "owed," not the love itself, but Archidamus describes it in terms of the justification of love, and he does not know how to express how this justification will be brought about. Archidamus touches on a problem that Aristotle expressed in his description of the magnanimous man, possessor of all virtues, in his *Nicomachean Ethics*:

> And he is the kind of man who does service to others but is ashamed to receive service from them; for doing a service is a mark of a superior man, but receiving it is a mark of an inferior man. And he is disposed to do a greater service in return; for thus the man who did a service first will be still indebted and will have been treated well. And he seems to call to mind those whom he has done good to, not those from whom he has received a good; for he who received a good is inferior to the man who conferred it, and a high-minded man wishes to be superior. (Book IV, 8)[14]

A genuinely magnanimous man is best satisfied by being the fount of honors, and finds difficulty in receiving them. To receive honors is to somehow to place oneself in the debt of others. The problem of the high-minded man is that he remains, somehow, dependent on the honors accorded him by others though he prides himself on being independent of them. Kings assume the role of bestowers of honor; to exchange other than ceremonial honors implies less than omnipotence. The friendship between Bohemia and Sicilia overcomes this concern to be first in honor until Leontes's excessive desires for love lead him to believe his honor in the court has been destroyed.

This question of whether two powerful men may be friends is conjoined with the question of whether it is possible to "justify" love in the sense of vindicate, or prove.[15] These complex pressures exerted on the most intimate human relations are at the core of the rupture between Hermione and Leontes. Camillo focuses on this when he lightly admonishes Archidamus, "You pay a great deal too dear for what's given freely" (17-18)—no debt should be incurred by spontaneous affection. In private affairs, there are higher concerns than concerns of justice. How can love be rationally measured and repaid? This conversation then sets up the problem of the incompatibilities between the desire to be just and receive justice, and the pleasures of friendship.

In marriage, the problem of justice enters with regard to the legitimacy of children. It is not just for a father to raise others' children. Concerns for the legitimacy of one's offspring are specific concerns for justice. One cannot demand or require fidelity on the grounds that love is just or fair; love is beyond such concerns. But one can speak of justice with respect to the legitimacy of one's offspring. The intimacy of married love makes the question of fidelity important because the question of legitimacy is important. Considerations of justice must prevail in public affairs, even if the justice is artificial or false, but such considerations find an awkward place in private affairs.

Macbeth belatedly comes to regret that he has no "troops of friends" and to see, vaguely, the connection between friendship and the honor he has fought so viciously for. Richard boasts to have abandoned these concerns, though he is finally caught in the contradictory nature of his own ambitions. But Leontes makes others' love for him his chief concern, honor secondary. He is driven by a desire to be loved absolutely and provably by Hermione and by Polixenes, though in different fashions by each. The action of *The Winter's Tale* suggests that this desire to be perfectly and unquestionably loved can be as destructive as Macbeth's desire for great honors, but its sphere of destruction is more intimate. This accounts for some of the unusual talk about Hermione's pregnancy (it is one of two plays—also *Measure for Measure*—to begin with a pregnancy which is somehow the key to a larger political problem), and the dramatic presentation of her playful relation with her son, Mamillius. Excessive desires for love or honor are not as starkly divided as this schematic comparison between Leontes and Macbeth would suggest, but the orientation of the two protagonists is different. Macbeth is excited to tyranny by thoughts of the crown and its attendant honors; to be loved more intensely is a wishful afterthought. Inversely, Leontes's concern for his honor as king is awakened by the intense desire to make certain of others' love. The different impetuses to tyranny are reflected in their stances towards the problem of procreation and self-replacement. The origins of the powerful domestic tyranny of the "jealous" tyrant, Leontes, are bound up with a concern for true progeny while the "bloody" tyrant Macbeth lives in fear of the chimera of Banquo's line, with no positive concern for his own. Leontes's actions are worked out in Archidamus's idle speculation about what would happen "If the king had no son."

The Delphic Oracle

After seeing act 1 of *The Winter's Tale*, any member of the audience must ask, what happened? We are greeted in scene 2 with the hospitable, if bullish, Leontes, pleading with his boyhood friend, Polixenes, King of Bohemia, to prolong his nine-month stay. Failing this, Leontes requests his queen, Hermione, to use her charms to win him over. It is a pleasant scene of apparent courtly graciousness and tranquility. Hermione's and Polixenes's banter is similar to that of Beatrice and Benedick in *Much Ado About Nothing*.[16] The royal playfulness that opens scene 2 is made more charming by Hermione's grace.

"Grace" is spoken of more frequently in this play than in any other, primarily with its aesthetic sense of the quality of pleasing and charming, occasionally with references to a royal personage, but also with the sense of divine grace. Hermione uses it in both the first and last scenes. When speaking ironically of Polixenes's reference to man's corruption by woman, she compliments him as having "Grace to boot!" (I.ii.80). Later when excusing her imprisonment, "this action I now go on/Is for my better grace" (II.i.121-122). The second scene of act 1 is a study in gracious behavior, as exemplified by Hermione, set next to Leontes's descent from courtly manners to vulgarity. He goes so far as to call his queen a "bed-swerver" (II.i.93). With hypocritical prudishness, he rejects the language of "vulgars" while implying that vulgar speech alone can express what she is.

Leontes's vulgarity consists partly in his undervaluing or misunderstanding Hermione's gracious manner. What is done graciously is not done out of necessity, but out of a kind of superfluity; in this sense human grace is like divine grace. It is what makes Hermione "rare" (I.ii.452). She conducts herself as a friend towards Polixenes, taking walks with him, conversing informally, and even teasing him familiarly. Hermione possesses the ultimate hostess's art: the capacity to entertain and charm others with intelligent and even mildly provocative conversation. This is intended to please rather than to be consciously admired. Her lack of ostentation has led one recent feminist critic to remark with some condescension that Hermione "expresses visually as well as in her words a dependent, sexist role."[17] Castiglione has Signor Magnifico offer a description of the woman courtier's role in *The Book of the Courtier*, which suggests the subtleties of Hermione's art:

> Leaving aside, therefore, those virtues of the mind which she must have in common with the courtier . . . I say that the lady who is at Court should properly have, before all else, a certain pleasing affability whereby she will know how to entertain graciously every kind of man with charming and honest conversation, suited to the time and the place and the rank of the person with whom she is talking. And her serene and modest behaviour, and the candour that ought to inform all her actions, should be accompanied by a quick and vivacious spirit by which she shows her freedom from boorishness;

but with such a virtuous manner that she makes herself thought no less chaste, prudent and benign than she is pleasing, witty and discreet. Thus she must observe a certain difficult mean, composed as it were of contrasting qualities, and take care not to stray beyond certain fixed limits.[18]

It is this balance of modesty and friendliness that Hermione appears to achieve to everybody's satisfaction but Leontes's.

Without obvious provocation, beyond his peculiar interpretation of the allusions and puns acceptable in court speech, Leontes orders the murder of his best friend Polixenes, the incarceration and subsequent public trial and humiliation of Hermione, the fatal separation of Mamillius from his mother, and the destruction of his infant daughter, Perdita. His final tyrannical action in this fit of rage is to blaspheme the gods: "There is no truth at all i'th'Oracle/ . . . this is mere falsehood" (III.ii.140-141). When Leontes first imprisons Hermione he meets with unlooked for resistance from his courtiers. Antigonus and another Lord argue forcefully for Hermione's chastity (II.i.126-172)—or at least for preserving court appearances. Leontes responds with the threat of his supreme power:

> Why, what need we
> Commune with you of this, but rather follow
> Our forceful instigation? Our prerogative
> Calls not your counsels, but our natural goodness
> Imparts this; which if you, or stupefied,
> Or seeming so in skill, cannot or will not
> Relish a truth, like us, inform yourselves
> We need no more of your advice: the matter,
> The loss, the gain, the ord'ring on't, is all
> Properly ours.
> (II.i.161-169)

Leontes here exemplifies the classical definition of tyrant: one who acts according to his own will, without regard to the good of his subjects.[19] But Leontes insists further that his actions not be viewed as caprice, but as emanating from his superior knowledge of the truth of the situation which, for whatever reasons of weakness, no one else chooses to face. Still he requires the approval of others. In his next response, Leontes asserts that the crime he supposes "lack'd sight only" (II.i.177), and he shows his political prudence by adding that he has already sent for word from the Delphic Oracle:

> Yet for a greater confirmation
> (For in an act of this importance, 'twere
> Most piteous to be wild), I have dispatch'd in part
> To sacred Delphos, to Apollo's temple
> Cleomenes and Dion, whom you know

Of stuff'd sufficiency: now from the Oracle
They will bring all; whose spiritual counsel had,
Shall stay or spur me. Have I done well?
(II.i.180-187)

The question is rhetorical. Leontes's view of religion is a very sophisticated one, as he reveals,

Though I am satisfied, and need no more
Than what I know, yet shall the Oracle
Give rest to th'minds of others; such as he
Whose ignorant credulity will not
Come up to th'truth.
(189-193)

The Oracle is for the court and the people who are not blessed with his level of understanding and require mystic confirmation of what he alone knows to be true. This is a quick, dense, and complete portrait of a pagan tyrant who knows how to use the gods, but does not limit himself by them. He regards the gods as instrumental to rule, for the ruled not the ruler. Religious sanction is a required formality for Leontes.

The opening scene of act 3 is one of several narrative passages in the play where a particularly profound moment is described rather than portrayed. Cleomenes and Dion describe the pagan ritual surrounding the Delphic Oracle (a description unique in Shakespeare). According to Plutarch, Cleomenes and Dion were both zealous reformers. Cleomenes, a stoic, attempted to reform the Spartan people and Dion, a member of Plato's Academy, attempted to reform the tyrant Dionysius.[20] Dion says the sacrifice was "ceremonious, solemn, and unearthly," and Cleomenes is most impressed with "the burst and ear-deaf'ning voice o'th'Oracle" (III.i.7, 8-9). Dion is impressed with the otherworldly quality of the spectacle, and Cleomenes with the fear it inspires. The ceremony and form of the Oracle make them feel their own smallness in relation to the gods. Leontes observes the proper ceremonies and has the Oracle (which has been kept sealed) read aloud, sight unseen, at the trial. He is concerned to be publicly exonerated from the charge of tyranny, not like Macbeth, for whom popular mistrust is merely incidental, or like Richard for whom the reputation of tyrant is merely politically cumbersome. He intends the proclamation to be the climax of the trial and a definitive refutation of the charge of tyranny made by Paulina:

Let us be clear'd
Of being tyrannous, since we so openly
Proceed in justice, which shall have due course,
Even to the guilt or the purgation.
(III.ii.4-7)

Hermione takes refuge in her faith, asking that the oracle be read, and Leontes commands it. His conviction is such that he views this as necessary confirmation of his private knowledge of betrayal. When it refutes him, he questions and then rejects it: "Hast thou read truth?" and then, "There is no truth at all i'th'Oracle/The sessions shall proceed: this is mere falsehood" (140-141). His true view of religion emerges: oracular pronouncements are complementary to the king's power. They are politically decorative. But Leontes, in the intensity of his own conviction of his superior private knowledge, ignores the political dangers of his public atheism. His court and subjects are caught between their loyalty to the king and their need for a higher sanction of royal infallibility. He destabilizes the court. Only when it is announced that the heir, Mamillius, has died, does Leontes retreat from his bold and destructive position. Public defiance of the gods is not acceptable, particularly when the gods appear to intervene drastically in human affairs. But Leontes's immediate self-recrimination is obviously not simple political prudence. He is shocked:

> Apollo's angry, and the heavens themselves
> Do strike at my injustice.
> (III.ii.146-7)

But this is a momentary, forced conversion to belief. Leontes accedes to a belief in the gods that he seems to have regarded as popular superstition requiring flattery. His attempt to reverse what he has said is too facile:

> Apollo, pardon
> My great profaneness 'gainst thine Oracle!
> I'll reconcile me to Polixenes,
> New woo my queen, recall the good Camillo.
> (III.i.153-6)

He interprets his son's death as punishment from the gods, acknowledges his "injustice," and tries to undo everything with words (III.ii.146-172). Significantly, he omits from this rectifying catalogue his daughter, whose recovery is essential to the restoration of public and private harmony. As the oracle says, "The king shall live without an heir, if that which is lost be not found" (III.ii.134-136). When he is told Hermione is dead, he vows daily penance at her tomb. Damage done in words cannot be as easily undone in words—this is one of the most painful observations of the play. Time must pass in order to overwhelm "custom." Leontes has been accustomed to viewing the gods in a particularly arrogant way and must be drawn into a deeper faith. The scene of tyranny concludes here and we do not see Leontes again until act 5 where, sixteen years later, he is a much humbled man, entirely under Paulina's counsel.

"A sad tale's best for winter" Mamillius says, correcting his mother when she asks for a "merry" tale unsuited to the season. He gives her a ghost story instead. Mamillius's description of the tale he begins to tell is the only direct reference to the title of the play and intimates the tone of *The Winter's Tale*. "Sad" means both sorrowful and serious.[21] The play is about death (the deaths of Mamillius, Antigonus, and the sixteen-year "death" of Hermione) and about resurrection and reunification, or the serious topic of faith. Mamillius's ghost story is interrupted by Leontes's imagination of the world around him as a world of betrayal. The harmless children's tale is usurped by the destructive adult's imposition of his own fiction on the lives of those around him. This, the most intimately domestic scene between mother and child in all of Shakespeare, is interrupted by the jealous rage of the father, Leontes, which transforms the play into a more elaborate ghost story, with real "sprites and goblins." Hermione appears to the counsellor Antigonus as a ghost and later as a statue brought to life, while the Bohemian characters disguise themselves as pagan gods and goddesses. The story is told by a child to his mother and has the private quality of a narrative—shared rather than performed—which is then brought back into the public sphere of drama by Leontes. A story is superseded by an imagined scenario. As Calvino notes in the introduction to a collection of Italian folktales, this is an all-important instance of the fictional moment "that does not deny the invention of a destiny, or the force of reality which bursts forth into fantasy. Folklore could teach us no better lesson, poetic or moral."[22]

Leontes's accusation and trial of Hermione reads like a dramatic rehearsal for King Henry VIII's trial of Queen Katherine (II.iv). In the latter play, however, there is the explanation of romantic caprice, the kings' unresisted attraction to Anne Bullen. There is no rational explanation for Leontes's actions. Tillyard remarked that the nature of Leontes's jealousy "is that of an earthquake or the loss of the 'Titanic' rather than of rational human psychology."[23] That is what makes him, like his dramatic precursor Othello (who was given much more cause to doubt), very dangerous in his tyranny: it creates its own probabilities against reason.

Every rational search for provocation is strained, which has led some readers to consider Leontes's sudden passion a major dramatic flaw. Norman Holland catalogues a few of the responses by psychoanalytic critics to the play: Otto Rank sees an "incest motif"; L. A. G. Strong suggests that Leontes feels himself inferior to Hermione; and J. I. M. Steward argues that Leontes's jealousy, in Freudian terms, "combines the projected and delusional forms."[24] The best known exponent of the last view is W. H. Auden who, in *The Dyer's Hand*, argued that "Leontes is a classical case of paranoid sexual jealousy due to repressed homosexual feelings."[25] C. L. Barber sees it as "the release of a motive which threatens a family tie with gross sexuality."[26] Marilyn French, on the other hand, sees in *The Winter's Tale*, as in all of the Romances, an effort to "rearrange" or reconcile "masculine and feminine principles." This is a structural rather than an interpretive explanation. It is for this reason, according to French, that "the feminine principle is exiled in the romances. . . . That which is precluded from active power can manifest its power only by its absence." She sees this as part of the necessary exile of the feminine principle. Shakespeare makes its power felt by its absence.[27]

Such sympathetic critical efforts tend to underemphasize the characterization of Leontes's actions by others, notably Camillo, Paulina, and Hermione, as tyrannical. More importantly, they do not account for the connection between Leontes's radical doubt of Hermione and his defiance of the oracle. Robert N. Watson in *The Hazards of Ambition* gives an alternative to the psychoanalytic approach, seeing in Leontes's actions an effort to free himself from original sin. The play is "partly a rereading of the New Testament as festive comedy." Leontes is a redeemed Shakespearean version of the prodigal son whose ambition for himself attempts to circumvent divine design.[28] This argument picks up on Leontes's disposition to internalize faith and guilt, but overlooks the movement that occurs in the play from pagan to Christian systems of belief. It does not take account of the "great difference" mentioned at the very beginning of the play between Sicilia and Bohemia. This interesting theory has the advantage of attending to the religious elements of the play, but it neglects to account for the highly confusing combination of pagan and Christian religious language and form in both Bohemia and Sicilia, reading the play as dominated solely by Christian precept. But it is, after all, Polixenes, not Leontes, who speaks of original sin, as well as Judas and Christ (I.ii.73-74, 420). Sicilians believe in the Delphic Oracle. The religious references indicate that, at the beginning of the play, Sicilia is a pagan land and Bohemia is a Christian land. In the latter, pagan gods have been demoted to the status of "parts" for a sheepshearing festival.[29] Florizel refers to them as the "petty gods" (IV.iv.3). Watson views the drama as taking place symbolically in a Christian context from beginning to end, as a celebration of "the partial benevolence of the Christian myth" (276), but without seeing how the play explores the genesis of what he terms "Christian myth." The play cannot then be a "rereading of the New Testament as festive comedy" (278), but is better described as a discovery of the principles underlying the faith advocated in the New Testament. In the course of time, however, Sicilia's paganism is refashioned to permit the resurrection that concludes the play. It is in this that the difficulty and great interest of the play lies: what sort of conversion occurs?

In the closest source for the play, Greene's *Pandosto*, Pandosto does not challenge the oracle. Greene seems more interested in showing how the king tyrannizes his subjects up until the point where he is condemned by the gods. Pandosto is impolitic: he tells the noblemen they must abide by his decision or suffer his wrath (195).[30] Bellaria (Hermione's counterpart) must insist that the Delphic Oracle be consulted. In Shakespeare's reworking of the story, Leontes, with complete confidence, orders that the Oracle be consulted to satisfy the credulity of others. Shakespeare shifts the focus then to Leontes's defiance of the Oracle, rather than his early tyrannizing of his court.

If we take the climax of the first half of the play to be Leontes's rejection of the oracle instead of his jealous outburst, we discover what permits Leontes's utter loss of faith in his wife and friend.[31] Leontes's rejection of the oracle is the source for the remaining action of the play. Hermione, who has asked the gods to reveal the truth and vindicate her, believes firmly in the oracle, and, she tells us ultimately, "I, /Knowing by Paulina that the Oracle/Gave hope thou wast in being, have preserv'd/Myself to see the issue" (V.iii.125-128). She keeps herself from her husband, which helps ensure that the oracle will be fulfilled since she will bear no more children to him. Paulina prevents his remarrying also out of respect, she argues, for the oracle. Either by divine intervention or human complicity the oracle is, by one interpretation, properly fulfilled.

When Mamillius dies, Leontes sees his death as an act of the gods' vengeance against him. But his conversion from defiant skepticism, "There is no truth at all i'th'oracle" to ardent belief, "Apollo's angry, and the heavens themselves/Do strike at my injustice" (III.ii.140, 146-7), is too rapid. This instantaneous declaration of belief needs to be tempered.

What does the Oracle mean in calling Leontes a "jealous tyrant"? He was reared royally with Polixenes and rightfully inherited his throne. The oracle, then, uses "tyranny" in a different sense, referring to Leontes's actions as a legitimate ruler. It is the more dubious Renaissance usage of the term "tyrant" against which Hobbes would later complain in his *Leviathan*: "For they that are discontented under *Monarchy*, call it *Tyranny*."[32] But the charge of tyranny is given supreme authority here because it comes from the gods. Macbeth, Richard III, and Prospero may all be considered tyrants in the strict legal sense, because they are all usurpers. Leontes is a legitimate ruler, but tyrannical because he has abused his absolute power. The Oracle introduces a higher standard of kingship, attributing his tyranny to a passion—jealousy.

So this dramatic characterization of Leontes raises again the question between Malcolm and Macduff: "What is the relation between legitimate rule and good rule? Or, is legitimacy sufficient to non-tyrannical rule? In this case it is not a mortal dispute—it is a divine pronouncement, preempting the question. Again, Shakespeare creates a dramatic situation that forces us to answer this question in the negative.

Title to the throne is not immediately at issue in *The Winter's Tale*. No one challenges Leontes's claim to rule but the gods. Leontes presents us with the problem of the instantaneous decay of an unquestioned authority based on legitimate claims to rule into a morally doubtful authority. The gods, Hermione, and Paulina, call Leontes a tyrant because he has abused his absolute authority, subverting the common good to his misperceived private good. The most glaring instance of this subversion is that he is indirectly responsible for his heir's death and he commands that his daughter be exposed to die—leaving the throne without an heir. In other words, he destroys his own line. We are prepared to be attentive to this by the conversation between Camillo and Archidamus about succession in the first scene of the play.

The oracular definition of tyranny is, then, a classical one. The tyrant is one who rules in his own interest (whether it is in the interest of a particular passion, or complex of passions, as here), regardless of legitimacy. We encountered such a definition before in *Macbeth*. Macbeth and Richard both acknowledge themselves as tyrants. Macbeth in doing so falls into despair, but Richard is coolly appreciative of his lust for power while remaining indifferent to his moral position. The latter loses his composure only once when he begins to recognize that his carefully worked out ideology of nature may have entrapped him—but the mask is quickly reassumed. Macbeth is a seeker of the highest honors; he is willing to "jump" the life to come in order to achieve the kingship he knows he deserves. Only after the suicide of his wife does he fully articulate the nihilistic view of this world that he has created by his actions and the rejection of the afterlife. His clearest expression of what he has lost comes in act 5, scene 3 where he speaks of what he will never have: "honors, troops of friends." Taking the "nearer" way to the honors he knows he deserves, he has unthinkingly lost the respect of all the Scottish thanes. Macbeth's self-refutation is painfully foretold. He is knowingly unjust, believing it will not matter, while Richard is willfully unjust, believing that that is the only way to be politically successful.

But in *The Winter's Tale*, Leontes, King of Sicilia, does not view himself as a tyrant at all. Hermione and Paulina charge him with tyranny at the trial he stages to "prove" Hermione's treachery. He denies it repeatedly: "Were I a tyrant, where were her life?" he says—meaning the gadfly Paulina (II.iii.122). His conviction of his own justice extends so far that when the oracle from Delphos is read and he is named by the gods "a jealous tyrant" he rejects it: "There is no truth at all i'th'Oracle" (III.ii.140). At the height of moral indignation, he cannot conceive that he is in the wrong. The gods must lie.

What sets Leontes apart from the two previous Shakespearean tyrants we have looked at is that he is susceptible to education. Leontes, having defied the gods does not, like Macbeth, conclude in nihilism, nor, like Richard, does he brazen it out gambling on the last "hazard of the die." He interprets his misfortunes in a religious light—they are the punishment of the gods. He has blasphemed, and so he has been deprived of what is most precious to him. He submits to a charismatic person of apparently superior wisdom, Paulina—whom he has called a "mankind witch" (II.iii.67). The oracle is not explicit enough, as Coleridge notes, to explain the miracle-like ending of the play, but Paulina's interpretation of the oracle explains, or even produces, the final events. That Leontes has been educated is proved by his final act of faith in the statue scene. *The Winter's Tale* brings to the fore a most powerful check on tyranny—religious belief—and, more than any other of Shakespeare's plays, proves both Santayana and Tolstoy wrong in insisting on the absence of religion in Shakespeare.[33]

Severance

In the final speech of the play, Leontes concludes by asking that what happened "since first/We were dissever'd" be recounted (V.iii.154-155). Sixteen years earlier bonds were broken between husband and wife, mother and child, friend and friend, and counselor and king. "Dissever'd" means primarily physical separateness that is irreversible in some way, but refers in this instance to several levels of separation.[34] What generates this separation is Leontes's recognition of his separateness from those he loves and those he wishes to love him, and his tyrannical attempt to overcome this separation? The integrity of individuals prevents his certain knowledge of their feelings for him and throws him into radical doubt. This severance is also the frustration of the separation between lover and beloved—the fact that two can never be permanently one—the discovery that what is most desired, erotic love, complete union with the beloved, is not in all ways possible. Hermione's pregnancy emphasizes the separateness between herself and her husband by emphasizing their physical difference.

Severance also occurs on the level of language. Leontes begins to use a language that is exclusively his own, as Hermione says in the trial, "You speak a language I understand not" (III.ii.80). Leontes becomes a prisoner of his own meanings and interpretations. These severances are bound up with Leontes's defiance of the gods, his radical faithlessness.

The fantasy quality of *The Winter's Tale*, a quality emphasized by the title, implies associative as well as sequential connections between characters and events. This is the only play whose title refers to a season. The word "tale" draws attention to the fictional and narrative qualities of the play itself. What I wish to show is what connections are drawn, not on the level of plot, between the loss of elasticity in Leontes's language, his loss of faith in his wife's fidelity, and his defiance of the Oracle. The play makes the connections between these three levels of language, relations between persons, and relations between men and gods, both thematically and structurally.

The story of Leontes's fall from domestic bliss—his erroneous and unjustifiable rejection of the Queen, Hermione, his loss of his heirs (Mamillius and Perdita), and his penitence—is compressed into the first half of the play (through III.ii).[35] This unusual dramatic form struck Coleridge, who made an imitation of it in *Zapolya: A Christmas Tale in Two Parts:*

> The form of the following dramatic poem is in humble imitation of *The Winter's Tale* of Shakspeare, except that I have called the first part a Prelude instead of

a first Act, as a somewhat nearer resemblance to the plan of the ancients. . . .
This is, however, in mere obedience to custom. The effect does not, in reality,
at all depend on the Time of the interval; but on a very different principle.[36]

The different principle that Coleridge depends on is the principle of parataxis.
The two actions are aligned and comment on each other.

In the final scene of the third act we are abruptly transported with Perdita,
to Bohemia, the kingdom of Leontes's boyhood friend and supposed betrayer,
Polixenes. Time gives the prologue to act 4, explaining why we do not need to
know how Leontes, Perdita, Hermione, or Polixenes, have spent the succeeding sixteen years. This transitional chorus reminds us of the tyrant Time of the
Sonnets, dramatized. Greene's subtitle for *Pandosto*, "The Triumph of Time,"
suggests, among other things, the power of Time to uncover injustices and right
wrongs. In sonnet 16 "that bloody tyrant Time" limits the possibilities for the
writer's beloved to immortalize himself through generation. In Sonnet 115 Time's

> . . . million'd accidents
> Creep in 'twixt vows, and change decrees of kings,
> Tan sacred beauty, blunt the sharpest intents,
> Divert strong minds to th'course of alt'ring things:
> Alas, why fearing of Time's tyranny,
> Might I not then say, "Now I love you best,"
> When I was certain o'er incertainty,
> Crowning the present, doubting of the rest?[37]

Time draws out attention to his ability to "o'erthrow law, and in one self-
born hour/To plant and o'erwhelm custom" (8-9). Time suggests we anticipate
changes and tells us that the focus of the play, having been Leontes, will now
be Perdita. Time summarizes from "Leontes leaving" to "A shepherd's daughter, /And what to her adheres, which follows after, /Is th'argument of Time."
This chorus if different from the chorus of *Henry V*, which narrates the geo-
graphical scene changes, defusing dramatic improbability and theorizing on the
inadequacies of drama that retells history. Time in *The Winter's Tale* does not
appeal to "your fancies" to imagine the physical transport of an army from
England to France (giving the drama an epic atmosphere). Instead it asks the
audience to imagine the passage of time and consider future consequences of
past actions. Unlike the chronicler/narrator of *Henry V*, this speaker interjects
himself only once, and warns of his own unreliability: just as he "unfolds"
error, he also creates it. Time is not a truth-teller.

This observation about the power of time calls to mind young Prince
Edward's questioning of his uncle on the subject of Caesar's Tower in *Richard
III*,[38] where a similar point was made. Time creates and preserves fame and
legend, but not necessarily truth. The good are not always vindicated, just as
the bad are not always punished. That scene is particularly ironic, since the

play itself uses the myth of Richard's deformity rather than simple historical fact—an example of the effect of time. In *The Winter's Tale*, as time passes the dramatic focus must change: Leontes has gone through the most significant moment and error of his life, and Perdita's great moment is about to happen. As the quote from Calvino, which begins the chapter says, a tale speaks of "the potential destinies of men and women, especially that stage in life when destiny is formed, i.e., youth, beginning with birth." Leontes is abandoned by the storyteller just after a moment of apparent choice, of potential destiny, to move to another moment of potential destiny, Perdita's maidenhood.

Why does Time break apart the play? The speech suggests that, because of this interruption, we cannot view the play as a chronological sequence of events. Instead we see the actions of time itself on character. Not only has the time frame changed, but the dramatic focus on person has changed. We are asked to view the play paratactically. We are invited to view the first and second halves of the play as two separate stories connected by Time. It is, after all, a "tale," which not only does not preserve the unities (whose technical "flaw" this speech excuses), but it violates our sense of how a play is meant to happen. In act 4, scene 1 we are asked to consider the play in another light, as a description, in part, of the powers of time. Time may even make this "tale" itself grow "stale."

On the dramatic level, then, the plot is severed; lives intimately bound up are separated from one another—the result of Leontes's refusal to acknowledge his true progeny. Language, too, is no longer held in common. The rupture that occurs first manifests itself in Leontes's withdrawal into his own private language and meaning. He loses consciousness of any decorum: he no longer cares to whom or in front of whom he speaks, only that he speaks the truth. This is most obvious in his bedchamber accusation of Hermione in front of their son, Mamillius. Later, it is suggested that this destructive moment may have precipitated his son's death (III.ii.143-144). Leontes moves from being lost in the ambiguities of court speech (the exchange between Hermione and Polixenes), to imposing his private meaning onto the words of others. Leontes demands that others believe him unconditionally. This insistence leads, in the case of his most trusted adviser, Camillo, to the suppression of wise counsel. The culmination of this is his defiance of the oracle.

In the first and second scenes our attention is drawn to language, to its unreliability, to its ambiguities, as Leontes becomes obsessively concerned with narrowing down meaning. In the second scene of act 1 the language ambiguities are foregrounded. This is prepared for in the first scene where the courtiers, Archidamus and Camillo each vie to outdo one another in rhetorical exchanges and comment on the resulting rhetorical excesses. There is a strange combination in this prose dialogue of expected formality, and comic appreciation of the pomposity of such formality between two counselors who, having spent nine months together, are well aware of the comic exaggerations that courtly speech necessitates.

In the next scene, Leontes moves away from an acceptance of the playful-ness of language (in the scene with Polixenes and Hermione), towards a dark literalization of language—the self-conscious attempt to draw out every linguis-tic ambiguity severely. The courtly pun, with which Hermione freely plays, becomes a dangerous hidden code for Leontes, a code in which he discovers his betrayal by Hermione and Polixenes.[39] As Camillo emphasizes to Polixenes at the end of the scene, Leontes acts "as he had seen't" (415). Shadows of mean-ing are literalized into reality—Leontes's use of language changes as he be-comes a tyrant. The penumbra of meaning that each word has, and its depen-dence on context, has been eliminated. Two passages bring out Leontes's changing conception of court jargon in particular. There is the early speech indicating his jealous passion:

> Affection? thy intention stabs the centre:
> Thou dost make possible things not so held,
> Communicat'st with dreams;—how can this be?—
> With what's unreal thou coactive art,
> And fellow'st nothing: then 'tis very credent
> Thou may'st cojoin with something; and thou dost,
> (And that beyond commission) and I find it,
> (And that to the infection of my brains
> And hard'ning of my brows).
> (138-145)

This speech suggests that Leontes is half-conscious of his lack of proof in the matter. He pushes an interpretation into certain fact. Strong doubt becomes strong belief.

This passage recalls Theseus's reflection on imagination from *A Midsummer Night's Dream*:

> Lovers and madmen have such seething brains,
> Such shaping fantasies, that apprehend
> More than cool reason ever comprehends.
> The lunatic, the lover, and the poet
> Are of imagination all compact:
> One sees more devils than vast hell can hold;
> That is the madman: the lover, all as frantic,
> Sees Helen's beauty in a brow of Egypt:
> The poet's eye, in a fine frenzy rolling,
> Doth glance from heaven to earth, from earth to heaven;
> And as imagination bodies forth
> The forms of things unknown, the poet's pen
> Turns them to shapes, and gives to airy nothing
> A local habitation and a name.
> Such tricks hath strong imagination,

That if it would but apprehend some joy:
It comprehends some bringer of that joy,
Or, in the night, imagining some fear,
How easy is a bush suppose'd a bear!
(V.i.4-22)[40]

Where Theseus argues from the improbable to the probable, Leontes argues from the probable towards the improbable. Theseus is trying to explain the "tricks" of imagination, all of which are experienced by "the lunatic, the lover, and the poet." He concludes that wishing may make things appear. Leontes says of the intention of affection, "with what's unreal thou coactive art"—that is, he begins by acknowledging that strong feelings may act with the "unreal" to make it appear real, but he concludes by analogy that they may equally act with what is real.

The speech of Leontes is very difficult to understand, attracting nearly three pages of commentary in the Furness Variorum.[41] What does it mean to speak of the "intention" of "affection"? In what sense do affections have intentions? It is interesting that five of the commentators cited in the Variorum assert that "affection" is "imagination" (Steevens, Malone, Collier, Staunton, and Keightley), the only proof offered being *Merchant of Venice* (IV.i.50): "Affection, mistress of passions, sways it." Not one cites the passage above from *A Midsummer Night's Dream*, though they incline to the definition of "affection" as "imagination," I would suggest, because of the similarities of the two passages. Their vocabularies are similar. Pafford's suggestion that "affection" means "lustful passion" in the New Arden edition is based on a reading of Montaigne's essay "Our affections are transported beyond ourselves" (165-167), and is, I believe, closer to the mark. Montaigne's examples of affections are those things that cause us to believe in predictions, which take us beyond ourselves and underpin belief in an afterlife. Affection is linked to superstition and faith. What is the relation between faith in one's intimates and religious faith? One is an immediate enactment of the other. One cannot perfectly know the mind and heart of another person. The source of his fractured speech is Leontes's conviction that he is not loved, or not loved sufficiently, or exclusively. It is an extreme of disappointed expectation much like Lear's when Cordelia speaks bluntly of her filial love. The coolness of Hermione's courtly banter gives Leontes reason to think back on those "three crabbed months" it took to win her hand: a bitter memory, distorted by new suspicions.

This is a speech that resists a philologically correct reading. Leontes uses no concrete terms, no object nouns. His analogical argument is not rational; because affections can make us believe things that are not true to be true, it can make us understand the truth of true things. What is most striking in the speech is that Leontes attributes "intention" to affection, and yet, by any definition we take of affection, it has to do with the passions rather than with reason. It is a movement based on feeling, not reason. If we replaced "affection" with "imagination" as the Variorum commentators suggest, we would have something very close to an inversion of Theseus's speech, with an opposite conclusion. This gives added irony to Florizel's insistence that he is "heir" to his "affection" (IV.iv.481-482). The romantic power of the statement is strongly undercut by Leontes's experience of "affection."

Leontes believes in the likely truth of his intuitions without the necessity of any visual proof. To support them, he infuses language with his own deeply felt meanings—the attribution of "intention" to "affection," the personification of "intention," the unlocated "centre." The disruptive, rhetorical "how can this be?"—the two final parenthetical digressions. What does it mean to be "beyond commission"? How can the act he imagines Hermione and Polixenes to have committed be "beyond commission"?

The speech is not incoherent, as many critics suggest, but a precise description of the feelings of one consumed by a passion with no rational foundation. It is not a logical argument, but it is comprehensible. Leontes describes how passions are experienced by an intensely passionate man. It is as though he were being acted on by a purposeful force external to him. Because passions have their own beautiful rhetorical expression, because they are capable of shaping powerful arguments to their ends, a rational speech is not an effective "antidote." Leontes cannot be reasoned with. Camillus immediately realizes this, but Paulina does not and risks the royal princess. From his threats to burn her, and Perdita, Paulina apparently learns that a passionate nature must be reformed, not by dialectic, but by a rhetoric suited to the passions.[42]

The later instance of Leontes's linguistic confusion comes when he begins to literalize the courtly repartee of Hermione and Polixenes. He seizes on unintended secondary meanings that he brings out—the dark side of the pun. This is parodied in the second half of the play by the sexual innuendo of Autolycus.[43] The early exchanges are full of Hermione's wit (her pretense not to know that Leontes refers to her consenting to marry him, I.ii.100, her seizing on Polixenes's words as impugning herself and his queen). The most serious matters, marriage, heredity, fidelity, and sin are spoken of in a playful, licensed fashion, and Hermione as well as Polixenes flirt with carefully chosen ambiguities of meaning. Language is bent to express and support the logic of Leontes's feeling rather than there being any accommodation between the logic of language and feeling. Further, Leontes removes from his language any sense of its playfulness, of its comic potential, since ambiguity can disguise betrayal. He sticks on words: "neat" (123-5), "play" (187-90), "good" (220-222), "satisfy" (223-5), "nothing" (292-6), and separates their various meanings in order to choose one authentic meaning. Language loses all its flexibility for him.

Puns represent the unstable margins of language that Leontes wishes to fix. A pun depends as much on the stability of the common sense meaning of a word as on the unlikeliness (in context) of the alternative meaning. In comedy the pun, to achieve its effect, brings all meanings to the same level. Leontes worries about the dignity of language "lest a like language use to all degrees" (II.i.85). He won't refer to her as queen but as "thing" so language itself is not debased. He is trying to concretize language. Leontes wants an unambiguous one-to-one correspondence between word and thing that will morally elevate language. From this perspective, what prevents language from constantly slipping into senselessness is the received, expected meanings of words, stable without regard to context. Leontes no longer trusts what he does not see with his own eyes, and imagining that he might see what does not exist, no longer respects the received meanings, no longer tries to give hierarchical order to the several meanings a word may have, but imposes meanings on words that accord with his own feelings, or emotions. It is as though Leontes suddenly explores every sentence for the Freudian slip that might betray the truth about his marriage and/or his masculinity.

Leontes becomes a prisoner of his own interpretation of the world around him. He founds this interpretation on his language. It provides what is necessary for the emotion he experiences or desires to experience. It creates the particular circumstance to accompany an emotion. Leontes says the exact opposite in his "affection" speech, that circumstances create feeling. Leontes's tyranny is that he insists that everyone else, including the gods, not only accept but vindicate his interpretation.

Camillo recognizes the absence of a necessary connection between truth and language or language and provability. He assents, perhaps too readily, to Leontes's plan, concluding that Leontes has gone mad. His proof: Leontes may not be reasoned with, he is "in rebellion with himself" (I.ii.355). This superficial pliability might be explained by the fact of his base birth, of which both Leontes and Polixenes remind him at critical moments. As he explains in the most political speech of the play, he is governed by enlightened self-interest: "Let villainy itself forswear't" (I.ii.361).

What Leontes fears is that Hermione and Polixenes "would unseen be wicked" (I.ii.292). What he requires is something like the ancient Ring of Gyges, which would make him invisible and able to watch everything, like a god. He must be allowed to observe everyone's actions to make sure they are not being unfaithful to him. He must have the power and omniscience of a god in order to be certain of his family, friends, and followers. His actions presume such knowledge. Leontes moves from suspicion towards imagining not just the actions but the wishes or thoughts of his wife and Polixenes—something that implies the most intimate knowledge of another human being. He comes up against the inviolability of other beings.

Tyranny in this case is the presumption to know the other and judge the other on their innermost thoughts and feelings. Leontes requires satisfaction of that desire for such perfect knowledge. Faith will supply that certainty for Leontes, and allow him to act without a certain knowledge that it is impossible for him to have.

Leontes, in his accusation, asks Camillo if he has not seen or heard or thought anything wrong—three different ways of knowing. He admits later that his own suspicions "lack'd sight only." Leontes proclaims himself both blessed and cursed by what others of "lesser knowledge" do not have—knowledge of his cuckoldry.

Hermione's response is curious because she does not outright deny the charge but uses indirection to preserve both her honor and his. She speaks indirectly not because she is in fact guilty, but because she does not deem it proper to stoop to denying such an accusation publicly. Only when on trial does she do it for honor's sake. To respond directly to such a charge is to place questions of love and respect on the low level of "just" dealings involving equal exchange. Hermione regards this as a denigration of married love. At all costs she wishes to maintain friendship and love on the high ground of generosity and faith (and its counterpart, grace), above the level of provability where such emotions are too elusive or frail. Leontes insists on proof she cannot provide. He has become a materialist of feeling. She attempts to keep the level of debate high—matters of love may only be debated ironically on a witty level, never spoken of too seriously. In *Pandosto* her counterpart, Bellaria, says, "what hath passed between him and me the gods only know, and I hope will presently reveal" (197). Leontes excuses the incredulity of the nobles by referring to her "without-door form"—people have their appearance, but they also have an inner reality, to which Leontes claims to have access. Hermione concludes by suggesting that Leontes needs "clearer knowledge" (II.i.97). During the trial she acknowledges his withdrawal into his own world of meaning (III.ii.80).

Leontes speaks of "those foundations which I build upon" (II.i.101). He has created his own metaphysical scheme, his own assumptions, his own view of the world, as this phrasing suggests. Antigonus echoes the kind of knowledge Leontes strives for and claims. In defending Hermione, he says that if she is proved false, he will disbelieve his own wife, and trust her no further, "Than when I feel and see her" (II.i.136). This is the ultimate end towards which Leontes's argument tends, but tangible proofs are not available to him. As Leontes becomes more beset, he makes further claims for his knowledge. The act of treachery has become so real for him that he asserts, "I do see't and feel't, /As you feel doing thus," with a pinch for Antigonus (II.i.152-3).

From an act that "lack'd sight only" he has come to "feel't and see't." He accuses his counselors of refusing to "relish a truth" (II.i.167). They aren't strong enough to enjoy the truth of Hermione's infidelity. But Leontes claims to prefer truth to all else. He thinks the solution to his pain at the truth is to eliminate its cause. Leontes acknowledges he cannot move against Polixenes because he is too powerful. Still, vengeance is somehow important to make him feel better. He must have the crime proved publicly and then somehow punished; for this he requires public support of his own interpretation. Leontes is very afraid of a comic response—something Camillo knows about him, but

Antigonus does not. His tragic view of the world would be violated by such a response to his beliefs. Comedy gets at unpleasant or embarrassing truths, without necessarily showing them corrected. It undermines myth, power, prestige, aura of authority, and fear. A king must play on all these things. Leontes persists in his theme that not to believe the truth, however awful, "is but weakness" (II.iii.1). He asserts a moral pride in being able to face brutal facts—it is this self-flagellating tendency that makes him very ripe for the harsh penance Paulina imposes. As Howard Felperin says of *The Winter's Tale*, Leontes's jealousy is not "the absence, but the dark side of his faith."[44] Plutarch draws this connection in his "Life of Alexander" where he gives detailed accounts of the oracles. When he is young, Alexander acts with contempt towards the Delphic Oracle, but later

> Now after that Alexander had left his trust and confidence in the gods, his mind was so troubled and afraid that no strange thing happened unto him (how little soever it was) but he took it straight for a sign and prediction from the gods; so that his tent was always full of priests and soothsayers that did nothing but sacrifice and purify and tend unto divinements. So horrible a thing is the mistrust and contempt of the gods when it is begotten in the hearts of men, and superstition also, so dreadful that it filleth the guilty consciences and fearful hearts like water distilling from above; as at that time it filled Alexander with all folly, after that fear had once possessed him.[45]

Leontes's defiance of the Oracle expresses a desire for godlike knowledge, a claim to rival knowledge or knowledge superior to that of the gods. Leontes sets his own perception of the truth against what the Oracle proclaims. He seeks a deeper security than proofs and reassurances can afford him—that Hermione loves him and only him best. Camillo's betrayal only confirms Leontes's doubts about those closest to him and his final desire to return to Sicilia suggests how much he regrets what appeared to him a necessary decision (I.ii.313-314). Camillo concludes that Leontes is "in rebellion with himself"—passion has usurped reason (355) and it is an insurrection that he cannot quell, because its foundation "Is pil'd upon his faith" (430). It is a matter of belief, rather than reasoned conclusion. Leontes's skepticism has found an anchor in an utter conviction of his own interpretative powers.

Leontes demands public vindication of his tyranny. He insists that Hermione be given a public trial, in which her infidelity may be proved. He calls also for the approval of the gods—by sending to the Delphic Oracle. Once Hermione has been jailed, Paulina imprudently approaches the king with his new daughter, and accuses him, by suggestion, of tyranny: "I'll not call you tyrant; /But this most cruel usage of your queen . . . something savours of tyranny," (II.iii.115-119). He responds by demanding, "Were I a tyrant, /Where were her life?" The reference is unclear. He could mean either, "if I were a tyrant, I would already have had Hermione killed on mere suspicion of infidelity," or, since he speaks to Paulina in the third person, he could mean, "if I were a tyrant, you would be killed for even daring to challenge my suspicion." It is to this accusation Leontes refers in the courtroom scene in act 3: "Let us be clear'd/ Of being tyrannous, since we so openly/Proceed in justice, which shall have due course, /Even to the guilt or purgation" (III.ii.4-7).

What complicates our approach to understanding the figure of Leontes is that we must connect his insistence on the truth of his own passionate belief in his betrayal and his equal insistence on maintaining the high regard of those around him. He is dependent on the respect of his courtiers and their support of his belief to sustain it. He steps beyond the bounds of such public belief only briefly, when he defies the Oracle, and that is his moment of collapse. It is not enough that he know the truth; his truth must be publicly approved. This insistence that the hearts and minds of others be in exact accord with one's own is part of Leontes's tyranny.

What Leontes experiences in a momentary flash in act 1 is the gulf between the love that he believes, or has been led to believe, that others have for him, and the unprovability of such love. In Xenophon's *Hiero*, a dialogue between a poet and a tyrant, the tyrant Hiero expresses this profound uncertainty in ironic fashion, detailing to the impoverished poet Simonides, the disadvantages of his luxurious, omnipotent life:

> The fact is, a private citizen has instant proof that any act of compliance on the part of his beloved is prompted by affection, since he knows that the service rendered is due to no compulsion; but the despot can never feel sure that he is loved. For we know that acts of service prompted by fear copy as closely as possible the ministrations of affection.[46]

Stanley Cavell speaks of Leontes's uncertainty in terms of "skepticism":

> If *The Winter's Tale* is understandable as a study of skepticism—that is, as a response to what skepticism is a response to—then its second half must be understandable as a study of its search for recovery (after Leontes, for example, and before him, Othello, have done their worst).[47]

Leontes's jealousy is a violent desire to be loved exclusively and provably by Hermione. In *Pandosto*, Greene describes the hero, "thinking that love was above all laws and therefore, to be stayed with no laws," and killing Bellaria with his cruelty.[48] This is an essential part of the "jealous tyrant." What produces this domestic strain of tyranny is the uncontrollable desire to be loved absolutely and provably by another being, in Leontes's case the desire to be loved exclusively by both Hermione and Polixenes. Language is inadequate to convey certainty about another's feelings, even dangerously ambiguous. Doubt afflicts Leontes and what he wants is not susceptible of ocular proof. Living in domestic harmony requires that emotions and passions be taken for granted in part, rather than be subject to the damage of vigorous, rational proof.

Cavell suggests that Leontes doubts his own convictions just after he learns of Mamillius's death, and not until then, because he may be tricking the gods into taking revenge for him against a "usurping heir" (195). It is another instance of the Shakespearean tyrant's lack of concern for progeny. We have seen how Macbeth seems to forget that he has no heir of his own to supplant Banquo's, whom he is concerned to kill at all costs. And Richard marries to legitimize his own claims, without reference to establishing a line.[49] Cavell describes Leontes's skepticism during his jealous fit:

> Chaos seems to have come again; and what chaos looks like is the inability to say what exists; to say whether, so to speak, language applies to anything.

In this sense it is "a response to what skepticism is a response to" (197-198). The "is whisp'ring nothing?" speech portrays "the skeptic at the moment of the world's withdrawal from his grasp . . . the skeptic as fanatic" (206). Fanaticism is an integral part of tyranny for Shakespeare: it is complete confidence in an idea or passion. The tyrant, unlike the common fanatic, is in a position to impose this idea or passion on others.

Playing with Mamillius, Leontes tries to prove to himself, by visual comparisons, that his son is his own. This uncertainty is an expression of radical skepticism about knowing the external world. Part of this skepticism, which Cavell does not mention, is the immediate uncertainty—does his wife love him alone? This most intimate doubt represents the general, philosophical problem posed by skepticism. Cavell points out, rightly, that what Leontes requires is the experience of seeing something (204), rather than being told something. We hear about the gods, but only when they reveal themselves do we see them act. Paulina's presentation of Hermione resurrected is such a revelation.

In the tragedy, *Richard III*, Richard's self-enclosed intelligence dominates the play unchallenged, but here two intelligences stand opposed to Leontes: Camillo and Paulina. Camillo keeps his own counsel (I.ii.351-364), but Paulina first calls him tyrannous (II.iii.28). She provokes the ugly side of his ruthless passion for justice, which shows itself when he insists twice that the infant be burned (II.iii.94-95, 134). Paulina has overlooked the force of his passion, or has underestimated the seriousness of his conviction and fear of ridicule.

In the trial scene (III.ii), Hermione knows that her "life stands in the level of your dreams" (81), and refers to his pronouncements and threatened punishments as "rigour and not law" (112). Leontes opens the trial with reference to himself, as though he were being tried rather than Hermione: "Let us be clear'd of being tyrannous" (5). Hermione's whole defense rests on reference to the gods—they alone know what passed between her and Polixenes and they alone know why Camillo left. The gods alone (divine knowledge) can persuade Leontes that he is wrong. It is his moral pleasure as opposed to strict legal justice: the king's will as opposed to the king's law, which James I (echoing Aristotle) warns against.[50] Acting solely on grounds of moral satisfaction causes him to be a tyrant. This sense of offended justice he shares with the immoralist Richard, who wants vengeance against Nature, and the immoral Macbeth, who want the crown that is rightly his. Hermione appeals against his self-constituted morality to the higher authority of the god Apollo.

Leontes's immediate response to the oracle suggests his casual dependence on Hermione's resilience. He will undo the libel with words, but language is too powerful. He considers, with respect, Camillo's "piety." Camillo somehow must have known when the king did not, that the oracle was true. His defiance of the king's orders was in fact an act of piety.

Leontes's desire for certainty in love comes together with his concern for honor in his fear of cuckoldry. What he comes to believe is that, without some superior intercession against the limits of human knowledge, you can never be quite sure. The acceptance of this uncertainty in affairs of the heart is difficult, because married infidelity is not the same as infidelity between lovers. Concerns of justice enter with concerns for the legitimacy of children. Leontes's doubts are more profound than superficial concern for the purity of his line. To forestall the ambiguities of language he reinvents his own meanings, and his own readings of those around him. It is his capacity for powerful and passionate belief that makes him susceptible of having this belief, or faith, refashioned and then reawakened by Paulina in the final scene of the play.

It Is Requir'd You Do Awake Your Faith

At the end of the play Paulina says to her audience, "It is requir'd/You do awake your faith" (V.iii.94-95). Leontes, his desire to recapture what he has destroyed renewed on his encounter with Perdita, commands that she proceed. What has transmuted his radical skepticism at the beginning of the play into his strong desire to believe? In the beginning he imposes a rational construct on a world with which he cannot satisfactorily connect. In the end, he accepts a healing force external to himself. We know that Leontes's character does not fundamentally change. With greater self-understanding, he acknowledges that Hermione's ghost, if he took a new wife, "would incense me/To murder her I married" (V.i.61-61). Leontes is still less concerned with any conventional impediments to desire, but he is now aware and able to articulate the destructive passions he is capable of. Unlike Pandosto, he has not killed himself; he has been kept in check by religious observances imposed by Paulina.

Leontes's tyrannical outburst, though the damage he seeks to do is partly forestalled by Camillo and Paulina, leaves him with the greatest crisis of any legitimately established king—the crisis of succession. He has no heir to the throne and cannot produce one without remarrying, yet he accepts Paulina's admonition not to remarry without her permission.

As many different critics have noted, the ending of The Winter's Tale is Shakespeare's greatest dramatic deception. For those seeing or reading it for the first time, there is no indication at any point in the play that Hermione is not dead or that she will be brought back at the end of the play. There is only one reference to the fact that Paulina has spent a good part of her days in a removed cottage supervising work on the statue (V.ii.93-103). Dramatically, we are taken by surprise. Coleridge found that the oracle was implausible, because not specific enough, and that it did not prepare the audience adequately for the "*deus ex machina*" at the end of the play:

> Altho' on the whole exquisitely respondent to its title, and even in the fault I am about to mention, still a winter's tale, yet it seems a mere indolence of the great bard not to have in the oracle provided some ground for Hermione's seeming death and fifteen years concealment, voluntary concealment. This might have been easily affected by some obscure sentence of the oracle, as e.g., "Nor shall he ever recover an heir if he have a wife before that recovery."[51]

This complaint draws attention to the unusual dramatic effect the play has. The last scene is, literally, a revelation onstage. Who causes Leontes to adhere to so strict an interpretation of the oracle that he never remarries, though he is tempted? Paulina. We are given an indication of how she has kept him in line in act 5 when she blames him for admiring Perdita and reminds him of his terrible responsibility for the uncertainty around Sicilia's throne. It is important that the oracle be open to interpretation because the play is very much about the interpretation of events and words of whose meaning we cannot know enough to be entirely certain. Paulina acts as interpreter of the oracle and by the final act occupies the most powerful position in the Sicilian court, as Leontes's spiritual counselor (like Camillo before her). As we learn later, it is she who is mainly responsible for the fulfillment of the oracle in the way it is fulfilled. She keeps Hermione alive and hidden for sixteen years, she prevents the king from remarrying, and keeps him mindful of his "sin," and "penitent." This play corresponds more closely to its source, *Pandosto*, than any other nonhistorical play by Shakespeare. But there is one major character in the play who has no counterpart in its source: Paulina. She serves as a religious conduit. Her name, of course, is a reminder of Paul—perhaps the most famous early Christian proselytizer.

Cleomenes and Dion, the messengers who brought the oracle, have risen to power in the court, constant reminders to the king of the gods' powers. At the opening of the last act in Bohemia, Cleomenes's language is surprisingly anachronistic for a pagan society:

Sir, you have done enough, and have perform'd
A saint-like sorrow: no fault could you make
Which you have not redeem'd; indeed, paid down
More penitence than done trespass: at the last
Do as the heavens have done, forget your evil,
With them, forgive yourself.
(V.i.1-6)

Cleomenes explains that Leontes has done enough "penitence" and performed
a "saint-like sorrow." He has "redeemed" every fault and has done more "penitence" than "trespass." All these are Christian concepts. It cannot be dismissed
as simply a concession to contemporary religious thought, since Shakespeare
has characters speak of pagan religion earlier in the play with great eloquence.
Cleomenes has adopted the language of the New Testament to describe Leontes's
expiation of his guilt. For the first time, Leontes refers to what he has done as
a sin (V.i.167). With Paulina reminding him, he meditates on his guilt.

Hermione's self-exile (encouraged by Paulina) has a disturbing cruelty about
it. Why do Paulina and Hermione keep Leontes and the Sicilian kingdom itself
in a dangerous state of abeyance for sixteen years? Hermione's first public
words are a prayer to the gods in which she explains

. . . I,
Knowing by Paulina that the Oracle
Gave hope thou wast in being, have preserv'd
Myself to see the issue.
(V.iii.125-128)

Hermione's self-preservation was an act of faith, spurred by Paulina's account
of the oracle. Paulina could not permit him to remarry and violate the oracle
without betraying Hermione. Instead she kept him from remarrying by reminding him always of his guilt in his son's and wife's death—by keeping him
penitent. In this way the oracle is not violated. Hermione accounts for her own
conduct by saying that she acted out of faith (V.iii.126-128). But Paulina keeps
Leontes in a state of penitence for a crime he did not commit: the murder of his
wife. Her pretence is reminiscent of the Genesis account of original sin, which
burdens all human beings. From a pagan perspective, man is originally innocent. Paulina's lie points to the intractability of some human passions. Certain
passions are powerful enough, such as those at the core of Leontes's tyranny, to
be controlled only through contrived guilt. This is not to say that Leontes is not
guilty; he bears responsibility in his son's death, but he is not as guilty as he is
made to believe. Cleomenes points this out (V.i.5), and Dion asks Leontes to
act out of concern for the good of the state (V.i.24-34). Paulina resists both
Cleomenes's appeal to the individual desire to be happy, and Dion's appeal to

disinterested desire for the good of Sicilia. Neither of these concerns provides sufficient check on Leontes's still passionate nature.

The Oracle is hard to make out: "the king shall live without an heir, if that which is lost be not found" (III.ii.135-136). What has been lost? Love, faith, honor, life, a child. The only remaining legitimate heir to the throne, Perdita, has been exposed, Mamillius has died, but the origin of these tragedies is in Leontes's loss of faith. His blasphemy against the Oracle is at the center of the play. Leontes's actions are all based on the conviction that Hermione and Polixenes have betrayed him, that his line has been polluted. What is the basis of his belief? Leontes has lost all faith in the honesty of his wife and of his friend. He believes Polixenes has committed the most perfect sort of usurpation: the invasion of his hereditary line. He does not believe the Delphic Oracle: "There is no truth at all i'th'Oracle." His son dies.

Time interrupts the story to emphasize his ability to "plant and o'erwhelm custom." By instating new customs it extirpates old ones. This we see clearly when the dramatic action returns, with Perdita, to Sicilia. Paulina is no longer an obnoxious and disgraced woman, but an intimate counselor to Leontes, replacing Camillo as the king's "priest." The country to which we were introduced in the opening scene of the play was there described as providing hospitality that could not be equaled, which could be requited only with drugs ("sleepy drinks"). Now it is a country in a suspended state of mourning, a "country for old men" ruled by a king past his prime, with no successor, or hope of a successor, for the crown. On a dramatic level, the potential for regeneration is found again in Bohemia, only to be exiled as quickly. Perdita in the sheepshearing festival is the embodiment of spring.

Paulina brings to life her statue with a warning, "those that think it is unlawful business/I am about, let them depart" (V.iii.96-97). No one leaves. It is belief that allows Paulina to reconcile Hermione with her husband. What "awakes" this faith? For sixteen years, Leontes has worshipped every day at the tomb of Hermione, has done his penance, has reached the point where he is able to wish to marry again, but is too surrounded by the guilt of his earlier actions (with Paulina as constant reminder) to do so. Perdita awakens this urge in him, as Paulina is quick to note and oppose. Why should Leontes spend sixteen years in meditation on a past crime, without an heir, keeping his kingdom in suspense as to the succession (the concern of the opening scene)?

The words of the Oracle taken literally and seriously serve to help move the pagan Sicilia towards something like the Christian concept of faith in a personal god of revelation. Ideas of penitence, redemption, saintedness, and guilt separate the Judeo-Christian tradition from the Greek pagan tradition. What is being described, indirectly in the play, is the transformation from paganism to Christianity. (Historically accomplished in part by Paul, whose namesake plays a similar role in the play.) We see what human passions prompt the transformation, what circumstances permit it, and what makes a society susceptible to such a transformation. It is to some extent a sketched, anthropological history of the genesis of Christianity which also characterizes those passions to which Christianity most appeals. What passions does it satisfy? What in human nature does it restrain or moderate? What may it distort? There is no Faustian compact with the devil as in Marlowe, and no focused parody of hypocritical piety as in Jonson. The interest here is in the fundamental impetus to faith. What drives man to believe in gods or God? And what characterizes the difference between pagan and Christian belief? In this play, something that approaches, or looks like, Christian belief is able, over time, to contain Leontes's unchanging passionate nature, to restrain his tyrannic impulse.

If we look back to Leontes in the first half of the play, before Time leaves him to his cloistered existence, we have a portrait of a strong pagan king. Convinced of his wife's guilt and the complicity of those around him, he consults the gods to satisfy the nobles and the people of his superior conviction. In the final scene he desires "the pleasure of that madness" which he rejected earlier—a living statue—and bows to belief in something unlooked for, which he cannot explain: "If this be magic, let it be an art/Lawful as eating" (V.iii.73,110-111).

Tzvetan Todorov defines the fantastic as that which holds the reader in an uncertainty between belief and disbelief:

> "I nearly reached the point of believing": that is the formula which sums up the spirit of the fantastic. Either total faith or total incredulity would lead us beyond the fantastic: it is hesitation which sustains its life.[52]

The final act of *The Winter's Tale* creates such an uncertainty when Hermione's statue is unveiled, only to upset the balance of the fantastic and impel its audience towards "total faith." Todorov's description of the fantastic helps us to recapture the moment of the unveiling, the dramatic moment in which Leontes and his courtiers "nearly reached the point of believing." At this moment Paulina insists on going beyond the fantastic (what are seen as the limits of Julio Romano's art), to the realm of belief: "it is requir'd you do awake your faith." Why cast Hermione, at the end, as a work of art? Art impels its audience into the realm of faith. Paulina's actions and Hermione's seclusion hover near vengeance. But their technique responds to the difficult and long task of reshaping human passions.

The resolution of the play rests finally on Leontes's will to believe. The statue is so lifelike, the desire is so strong; he obeys Paulina's command, does not condemn her as a necromancer (as before), but believes that there are powers he cannot understand. It is precisely this faith that he loses at the beginning of the play. He loses faith in his wife's fidelity, in his friend's loyalty, and in his counselor's wisdom; he loses faith in the apparent reality presented to him in court (as Lear does). His ultimate act of faithlessness is to blaspheme the

Oracle. And his son dies for it, so he believes. This is the first element of what would fulfill Todorov's requirements for the "fantastic" in the play—the timely death of Mamillius. We may devise rational explanations for the coincidence of Mamillius's death with the condemnation of his mother and the rejection of the Delphic Oracle. In fact, the courtier who reports it does just this: "The prince your son, with mere conceit and fear/Of the queen's speed is gone" (III.ii.143-144). But Leontes reinterprets the event: "Apollo's angry, and the heavens themselves/Do strike at my injustice" (146-7). We are left with this dual possibility until the end of the play, when Leontes reasserts the interpretation dictated by belief in omnipotent and punitive gods.

Does this mean that this is a play simply about faith and its moderating influences? The explanation is not so easy—Leontes believes, but what does Paulina or Hermione believe? What is the audience to believe? To get at an answer we have to ask why Shakespeare sets the development of faith and belief in the context of a play about the destruction and recovery of a royal family. Leontes defies the gods out of too great a belief in his own knowledge; he immediately repents when he believes the gods have killed his son; he reaffirms his faith when he believes he has a chance to regain his wife. Why is the connection of erotic love between man and woman the appropriate setting for an exploration of the problems of faith? Because it is not susceptible to tests and proofs as other associations are.

What Santayana and Tolstoy looked for and could not find in Shakespeare was evidence of some "system," an organized religious account of the ends of human life. But their suggestive condemnations point to Shakespeare's consistent concern, fully expressed in the last plays, with the origins of belief. And, because of the world he found himself in, this is a concern with the origins, specifically, of Christian belief. The action of *The Winter's Tale*, as we have seen, ultimately depends on Leontes's defiance and acceptance of the Oracle.

The tragic action of the play (in Sicilia) pits man against gods; the comic action of the play (in Bohemia) pits nature against convention. The two actions are joined over the divide of Time. The question of whether natural or human law is superior emerges in Bohemia between Perdita and Polixenes. It is fundamentally the same philosophic problem that Leontes comes up against when he tests the limits to his knowledge of another being. How may we satisfy our desires for exclusive love or honor from others without being able to overcome the separation between individuals that prevents absolute knowledge? If there is no natural or divine law, then such an overcoming would have to be a human construct, with all the frailties that implies. Leontes is rescued from the ultimate consequences of his tyrannical desire to retreat into his own world of meaning (and his insistence on imposing that world on those within his power), by death and Time, which enforce his recognition of his own will to believe. His capacity for belief is sustained by Paulina's spiritual instruction and finally realized in his willing the statue of his dead wife to come alive. The desired effect of the final recognition scenes is, we are told, as though we "had heard of a world ransomed or one destroyed" (V.ii.14-15): the act of gods or God. We are also, of course, told by the Gentleman narrating events that the story itself is so "like an old tale" that it is called strongly into suspicion. This secondary reflection points up the fragile quality and groundlessness of Leontes's moment of belief; like his accusation of Hermione, it is a fantastic phenomenon to others. But these moments of intense belief both give him stature and make him a tyrant.

In Leontes we see that the tyrant, for Shakespeare, need not necessarily be one thwarted by nature (Richard III) or by historical circumstance (Macbeth). Leontes is the source of his own destruction. Like Macbeth and Richard, his first concern is not the perpetuation of his line; rather he is willing to sacrifice that to the satisfaction of his own, time-bound desire. Where Macbeth was most concerned with receiving the honors due him, Leontes is most concerned with receiving the love (and consequent honor) due him, and further with proving that love, beyond what can be proved. Richard uses the rhetoric of Christianity, while Leontes defies the gods. Faith is never a possibility for the active intelligence of Richard. Leontes's character is such that it insists on belief, even if that belief has as its source radical doubt. *The Winter's Tale* elusively presents the potential which Christian belief holds for satisfying the erotic demands of highly passionate natures such as Leontes's. His tyranny is defeated rather than played out because he believes the gods oppose him, and because Paulina assists him in converting his horror at unanchored existence into a will to believe.

This play is another level of response to Machiavelli's critique of Christianity, the core of which was examined in chapter 3. Machiavelli lays bare the new kind of tyranny introduced by Christianity, while Shakespeare reflects on how elements of Christianity may be used to master tyranny itself. Leontes, once a tyrant, is always a tyrant. But what makes him a tyrant are intensely felt passions that can be turned against themselves. Properly worked on, skepticism changes to belief, anger changes to guilt. This is Paulina's magic, which, like Perdita's gardening, relies on an understanding of how human nature may be changed and how it may not be changed. Even this high art is surpassed by that of Prospero, Shakespeare's greatest necromancer, also called a tyrant.

Notes

1. For arguments about the romances as a new genre, see Northrop Frye's *A Natural Perspective: The Development of Shakespearean Comedy and Romance* (New York: Columbia University Press, 1965), C. L. Barber's *Shakespeare's Festive Comedies* (Princeton: Princeton University Press, 1959), Cyrus Hoy's *The Hyacinth Room* (New York: Knopf, 1964), Leo Salinger's *Shakespeare and the Traditions of Comedy* (Cambridge: Cambridge University Press, 1974), Muriel C. Bradbrook's *The Growth*

and Structure of Elizabethan Comedy (London: Chatto and Windus, 1955), Hallett Smith's *Shakespeare's Romances* (San Marino, CA: The Huntington Library, 1972), H. B. Charlton's *Shakespearian Comedy* (New York: Macmillan Company, 1938)— Charlton omits the romances from his study because "as comedies, they are of little account" (269)—Rosalie Colie's *The Resources of Kind: Genre Theory in the Renaissance* (ed. Barbara L. Lewalski [Berkeley: University of California Press, 1973]), John Dean's *Restless Wonders: Shakespeare and the Pattern of Romance* (Salzburg: Institut fur Anglistik und Amerikanistik, University of Salzburg, 1979), E. M. W. Tillyard's *Shakespeare's Last Plays* (London: Chatto and Windus, 1954). E. C. Pettet's *Shakespeare and the Romance Tradition* (Brooklyn: Haskell House Publishers, 1976) tries to straddle the fence on the issue of whether the romances actually constitute a genre different from comedy. E. C. Wilson's *Shakespeare, Santayana, and the Comic* (University, AL: University of Alabama Press, 1973) dismisses the generic question on the first page by asserting that "Shakespeare did not respect genres." On the other hand, Thomas Allen Nelson in *Shakespeare's Comic Theory* (The Hague: Mouton, 1972) views the Romances as the culmination of Shakespeare's comic achievement, Prospero's design being "the design of Shakespearean comic art: to transform the dissolving society of Alonso's ship, by immersing it in the magic of his art and then to send it back to the real world, not as it was before, but enlightened with a new vision to counteract and make 'unnatural' the evils of all the Antonios" (81). Coleridge takes his cue from the Player scene in *Hamlet* and asserts that "Shakespeare, though he had produced comedy in tragedy, had never produced tragi-comedy," in *Lectures*, 486.

2. See, for example, French and Lenz.

3. Terry Eagleton, *Shakespeare and Society* (New York: Schocken Books, 1967), 205.

4. Lytton Strachey, *The Shorter Strachey*, eds. Michael Holroyd and Paul Levy (Oxford: Oxford University Press, 1980), 131.

5. For examples see works by Frye and Tillyard cited in footnote 1 above, and Stephen Greenblatt's *Shakespearean Negotiations* (Berkeley: University of California Press, 1988).

6. Geoffrey Hill, *The Lords of Limit* (London: Andre Deutsch, 1984), 55-56.

7. In *Julius Caesar* for instance we are told and we know that Caesar aspires to be a god. In *Henry V* we are told that Henry claims to be "no tyrant, but a Christian king" (I.ii.241). In *Macbeth*, Macbeth's motivation is completely on the surface; *Richard III* begins with an opening soliloquy giving us a window into the thinking and causes behind the most Machiavellian of Shakespeare's protagonists. In *The Winter's Tale* and *The Tempest* there are fewer explanatory soliloquies. The relation between cause and effect is less clear, which is part of what makes the plays so difficult and fascinating.

8. Eagleton, *Shakespeare and Society*, 141.

9. Frye, 8.

10. Italo Calvino offers a description of what he finds compelling about fantasy in the introduction to his collection of *Italian Folktales*, which could serve as an introduction to reading the Romances: "these folk stories are the catalog of the potential destinies of men and women, especially that stage in life when destiny is formed, i.e., youth, beginning with birth, which itself often foreshadows the future; then the departure from home and, finally through the trials of growing up, the attainment of maturity and the proof of one's humanity. This sketch, although summary, encompasses everything: the arbitrary division of humans, albeit in essence equal, into kings and poor people; the

persecution of the innocent and their subsequent vindication, which are the terms inherent in every life; love unrecognized when first encountered and then no sooner experienced than lost; the common fate of subjection to spells, or having one's existence predetermined by complex and unknown forces. This complexity pervades one's entire existence and forces one to struggle to free oneself, to determine one's own fate; at the same time we can liberate ourselves only if we liberate other people, for this is the *sine qua non* of one's own liberation." Trans. George Martin (New York: Pantheon Books, 1980), xviii-xix.

11. In *Cymbeline*, an oracle is given to Posthumus in the penultimate scene and reveals his salvation, but it does not influence him to particular action. An interest in religion unites the four last plays to which their unusual formal qualities are suited. It is this shared question of man's relations to the divine that provides the strongest argument for grouping the plays together.

12. All citations from this play are taken from *The Winter's Tale*, ed. J. H. P. Pafford, *The Arden Shakespeare* (London: Methuen, 1982). Hereafter referred to as Pafford.

13. Mary Nichols interprets this scene as primarily a description of the destructive difference in character between the two friends, and extrapolates: "In Sicily desires are indulged and to some extent satisfied, while in Bohemia they are moderated, or perhaps dulled." It is this difference in moderation, she argues, in which the original tragic accusation is rooted. "*The Winter's Tale*: The Triumph of Comedy Over Tragedy," *Interpretation* 9.2-3 (1981): 169.

14. Aristotle, *Nicomachean Ethics*, trans. Hippocrates G. Apostle (Grinnell, IA: Peripatetic Press, 1984), 67-68.

15. In Shakespeare "justify" is used with the sense of proved or set right, see *Tempest*, V.i.128, *Henry VIII*, II.iv.163, and *The Winter's Tale*, V.iii.145.

16. These two plays are similar in other ways: the comedy is also about the destructiveness of unfounded jealousy, and it is the only other Shakespeare play set in Sicily (specifically in the capital of its province, Messina). As in *The Tempest* other comedies and tragedies are being dramatically reworked here.

17. Irene G. Dash, "A Penchant for Perdita on the Eighteenth-Century Stage," in Lenz, 277.

18. Baldesar Castiglione, *The Book of the Courtier*, trans. George Bull (New York: Penguin Books, 1986), 212.

19. According to Aristotle, "Tyranny is monarchy with a view to the advantage of the monarch," *Politics*, 1279b5-6.

20. Cleomenes was distressed at "the manner of the citizens of Sparta, giving themselves over to idleness and pleasure . . . ; insomuch—no man regarding the profit of the commonwealth—every man was for himself and his family" (6:161). First he purged the city, then divested the monarchy of its royal trappings, then set the Spartans at war to keep them tough. Plutarch opens his "Lives of Agis and Cleomenes" (told together in North's version) by cautioning that "they that govern the commonwealth for honor's sake, are no better than honorable slaves of the people" (6:137). It is, finally, Cleomenes's love of honor that destroys him. In exile from Sparta, he starts a riot against the licentious King Ptolemy in the streets of Alexandria and, disgusted with the slavishness of the Egyptians, he kills himself. Dion (compared by Plutarch with Brutus), a Sicilian, was a favorite student of Plato and first tried to reform, then eventually overthrew, the tyrant Dionysius. Dion tries to educate Dionysius out of tyranny: "supposing that igno-

rance and want of knowledge in Dionysius was the cause, he devised to put him into some honest trade or exercise, and to teach him the liberal sciences, to frame him to a civil life, that thenceforth he should no more be afraid of virtue and should also take pleasure and delight in honest things" (7:245). Having overthrown the tyrant, Dion is eventually killed by his own brother, Callipus. *Plutarch's Lives of the Noble Grecians and Romans*, trans. Sir Thomas North (New York: Limited Editions Club, 1941), 6:137-205, 7:237-302.

21. The *OED* cites Bacon's use of the word with its latter meaning in *The Advancement of Learning* (II.xxiii): "Of this wisedome it seemeth some of the auncient Romanes in the saddest and wisest times were professors." The *OED* also records the meaning, "settled, firmly established in purpose or condition," as having currency at this time.

22. Calvino, *Italian Folktales*, xxxii.

23. Tillyard, *Shakespeare's Last Plays*, 41.

24. Norman N. Holland, *Psychoanalysis and Shakespeare* (New York: Farrar, Straus and Giroux, 1979), 279-280.

25. W. H. Auden, *The Dyer's Hand* (New York: Vintage Books, 1968), 264.

26. C. L. Barber, "'Thou That Beget'st Him That Did Thee Beget': Transformation in 'Pericles' and 'The Winter's Tale,'" *Shakespeare Survey* 22 (1969), 66.

27. French 286, 290.

28. Robert N. Watson, *Shakespeare and the Hazards of Ambition* (Cambridge: Harvard University Press, 1984), 278. See the final chapter (222-279) for a complete interpretation of the play along these lines.

29. The only objections that might be raised to Sicilia's paganism are Leontes's reference to Camillo as being "priest-like" and to himself as "thy penitent" (I.ii.237, 239). But these are highly ambiguous statements, which could as easily refer to pagan priests (see III.i). The beginning of Mamillius's tale refers to a "churchyard," which seems the one misplaced religious reference in the pagan world, but then he is telling a ghost story. Paulina's early reference to Leontes as "an heretic" (II.iii.114) is in keeping with her transitional religious character, discussed in the final section of this chapter. In Bohemia, there is the simple superstition of the shepherd who believes in fairies (III.iii.116, 121), but this is not at all incompatible with Christian belief. Autolycus, also a transitional character, is of indeterminate religious affiliation. He speaks of himself both as "littered under Mercury" and as compassing a "motion of the Prodigal Son" (IV.ii.25, 93).

30. Pafford, 195.

31. Only a few critics are interested in explaining why this point would be the climax of the first part. J. M. Gregson, for instance, notes it, but only in passing in *Public and Private Man in Shakespeare* (Totowa, NJ: Barnes and Noble Books, 1983), 245.

32. Thomas Hobbes, *Leviathan* (London: Penguin, 1968), 240.

33. George Santayana, "The Absence of Religion in Shakespeare," Kermode 158-169. The following is an example of how far Santayana's criticism extends: "for Shakespeare, in the matter of religion, the choice lay between Christianity and nothing. He chose nothing; he chose to leave his heroes and himself in the presence of life and death with no other philosophy than that which the profane world can suggest and understand" (162). Further he intimates his suspicions of Shakespeare's true religious affinities hidden by temporal circumstance: "If the Christian in him was not the real man, at least the Pagan would have spoken frankly" (169). Tolstoy is Shakespeare's

other great (and less charitable) accuser: "people when they are freed from this falsehood will come to understand that a drama which has no religious basis is not only not an important or good thing, as is now supposed, but is most trivial and contemptible." From "Shakespeare and the Drama" in *Recollections and Essays*, trans. Aylmer Maude (London: Oxford University Press, 1961), 382.

34. It is used two other times in Shakespeare, in *All's Well That Ends Well* when the king speaks of discrediting himself by severing himself from his reputation for sagacity and in *King John*, II.i.388 when the breaking up of the troops is commanded. Chaucer used it earlier in the second sense, when lovers lament their parting, "That I was born allas what me is wo, /That day of us mot make desseueraunce" (*Troilus and Criseyde*, III.1375).

35. Time's interlude in act 4, scene 1 divides the play in two parts. The first part follows through the consequences of Leontes's jealousy and is 1382 lines long. The second part introduces another plot, Florizel's love for Perdita and is two hundred lines longer. These two "halves" of the play occur in Sicilia and Bohemia respectively, with the final scenes of reunion in Sicilia. This stark division allowed for the eighteenth-century dismemberment of the play in which the more cheerful second half of the play was performed. One aspect of this is described by Dash in "A Penchant for Perdita on the Eighteenth-Century Stage," Lenz, 271-284.

36. Samuel Taylor Coleridge, *Complete Poetical Works*, 2 vols. (Oxford: The Clarendon Press, 1912), 2: 883. Coleridge subtitles the two parts of the play respectively, "The Usurper's Fortune" and "The Usurper's Fate." The play is named after Hermione's counterpart, the virtuous Queen of Illyria, and the character of Leontes is, roughly speaking, divided in two: King Emerick and the dying King of Illyria, perhaps for dramatic clarity.

37. Sonnet 16 reads,

> But wherefore do not you a mightier way
> Make war upon this bloody tyrant Time?
> And fortify yourself in your decay
> With means more blessed than my barren rhyme?
> Now stand you on the top of happy hours,
> And many maiden gardens, yet unset,
> With virtuous wish would bear your living flowers,
> Much liker than your painted counterfeit:
> So should the lines of life that life repair
> Which this time's pencil, or my pupil pen,
> Neither in inward worth nor outward fair
> Can make you live yourself in eyes of men.
> To give away yourself keeps yourself still,
> And you must live drawn by your own sweet skill.

The Riverside Shakespeare, ed. G. Blakemore Evans (Boston: Houghton Mifflin Company, 1974), 1770, 1752.

38. See page 50, "Thy Self is Self-Misus'd" above.

39. For an excellent depiction of the sort of breakdown of language Leontes believes he experiences see Thucydides's account of the Corcyrean sedition in his

Peloponnesian War: "The received value of names imposed for signification of things, was changed into arbitrary . . . The cause of all this is *desire of rule* out of *avarice* and *ambition*; and the zeal of contention from those two proceeding." *Hobbes's Thucydides*, ed. Richard Schlatter (New Brunswick, NJ: Rutgers University Press, 1975), 222-223.

40. Harold F. Brooks, ed., *A Midsummer Night's Dream* by William Shakespeare, the New Arden Shakespeare (London: Methuen, 1979).

41. Horace Howard Furness, ed. *The Winter's Tale*, a New Variorum edition, fourth edition (Philadelphia: J. G. Lippincott Co., 1898), 27-30.

42. In Plutarch's "Life of Dion" he describes how the tyrant Dionysius reacts to Dion's and Plato's attempts to moderate him with philosophy: "And to say truly, he had a marvelous desire to hear Plato's philosophy, but on the other side, he reverenced them that did dissuade him from it, and told him that he would spoil himself, if he entered over-deeply into it" (7:253).

43. I am indebted for this observation to Jane Rebecca Oliensis's "The Winter's Tale and Alcestis," thesis, Harvard University, 1979, 73. Autolycus also satirizes the tragic language of *Macbeth* in one of Shakespeare's many Romance reworkings of great tragic moments, "for the life to come, I sleep out the thought of it" (IV.iii.30). Macbeth has offered to "jump the life to come" for the crown (I.vii.7).

44. Felperin notes further on Leontes's refusal to accept the "ultimate subjectivity of all interpretation," "'Tongue-Tied Our Queen?'" The Deconstruction of Presence in *The Winter's Tale*" in *Shakespeare and the Question of Theory*, eds. Patricia Parker and Geoffrey Hartman (New York: Methuen, 1985), 16.

45. Plutarch, 5:358.

46. Xenophon, *Scripta Minora*, trans. E. C. Marchant and G. W. Bowersock, the Loeb Classical Library, 7 vols. (Cambridge: Harvard University Press, 1968), 7:14-17.

47. Stanley Cavell, "Recounting Gains, Showing Losses: Reading *The Winter's Tale*," in *Disowning Knowledge* (Cambridge: Cambridge University Press, 1987), 198.

48. Pafford, 186.

49. W. H. Auden's poem, "Epitaph on a Tyrant" alludes to this.

> Perfection of a kind, was what he was after,
> And the poetry he invented was easy to understand;
> He knew human folly like the back of his hand,
> And was greatly interested in armies and fleets;
> When he laughed, respectable senators burst with laughter,
> And when he cried the little children died in the streets.

In *Selected Poetry of W. H. Auden*, 2nd ed. (New York: Vintage Books, 1970), 51-52. Elise Partridge called this poem to my attention.

50. See page 22.

51. Coleridge, *Lectures*, 380.

52. Tzvetan Todorov, *The Fantastic: A Structural Approach to a Literary Genre*, trans. Richard Howard (Cleveland: Case Western Reserve University), 31. My attention was drawn to Todorov's exploratory definition of fantasy by Calvino's response to it in his essay, "Definitions of Territories: Fantasy" in *The Uses of Literature*, 71-74. Calvino points out the narrowness of Todorov's definition.

Chapter 5

The Tempest: A Plague Upon the Tyrant That I Serve

Where's the Master?

I n *Macbeth* and *The Winter's Tale* there is no single governing intelligence. Macbeth advances by brute strength of will and passion for honor, believing himself dependent on the Witches rather than on his own imperfect calculation. Leontes follows his "affections" and eventually places himself under the direction of Paulina and the gods. Richard III determines the events of his play but only until he confronts his self-contradiction. He performs and directs those around him, most obviously in the balcony scene where he accepts the crown (III.vii), but he is not able to sustain the performance. Prospero's directorial control, however, extends through to his abnegation of power in the epilogue of the play. His "project" is the plot of the play, a play in which nothing happens. There are no deaths and no marriages, even the guilty are not adequately punished. His project unites three rebellions, two conspiracies, and one romance to preserve the classical unity of action that Aristotle had praised.[1]

But in the exercise of his Art to complete his project, there are apparent points of strain, signaled by Prospero's moments of anger. To understand better what insight Prospero provides into Shakespeare's exploration of tyranny, I wish especially to examine those points of strain. This interest I share with several new historicist and Marxist critics of the play. Francis Baker and Peter Hulme point to Prospero's "well-known irascibility"[2] to counter Frank Kermode's portrait of the coolly controlled white magician in his introduction to the Arden edition of *The Tempest*.[3] Any critical approach that tries to understand the politics of the play must be drawn to these taut moments because Prospero is there shown to be exercising rule—rule particular to his servant, slave, or other temporary subjects.

The question of who rules and how is advanced in the first scene. "Boatswain" is the first word of the play, spoken by the master of a ship about to go down in a storm. He orders the Boatswain to "speak to th'mariners," and then is silent for the rest of the play (I.i.3). This prompts King Alonso and Duke Antonio, the two figures of civil authority aboard the ship, to question: "Where's the master?" (I.i.9, 12) But the Boatswain addresses his sovereign ambiguously as well as defiantly: "Do you not hear him? You mar our labour: keep your cabins, you do assist the storm" I.i.13-14). The Boatswain implies that it is the one speaking to them; it is he who is "master" of the situation, not the boat's captain, not the legitimate authority, but the one most competent to save them.

In the midst of disaster, the king and duke look for a figure of conventional authority, but find instead one whom they conceive to be merely the instrument of power. In the presence of the force of the elements, those who command under normal circumstances are reduced to subjects—they must obey the Boatswain to save themselves, or so they believe. Alonso, King of Naples, has no power over Nature, and no skill as a mariner, but he attempts to reassert his legitimate authority: "Good boatswain, have care. Where's the master? Play the men" (I.i.9-10). He makes a superfluous command undermined with an unintentional suggestion of the mariners as players in a tragedy—a word-play recalled when we discover who has truly created the drama (Prospero). The irony of the moment is further reinforced as we are invited to reconsider Alonso's challenge to the Boatswain's rule as a repetition of his usurpation of Prospero, the proper ruler of Milan.

Natural necessity deprives men of their right to rule unless, as the Boatswain sardonically suggests, they can "command these elements to silence, and work the peace of the presence" (I.i.21-22).[4] But the "roarers" care nothing for the "name of King" (I.i.16-17). The Boatswain dismisses these figures of conventional authority and continues to command since he values his life. His competence combines with his strong self-interest. In response to Gonzalo, who reprimands his impudence, he asserts there are "none that I more love than myself" (I.i.20). Gonzalo points to the Boatswain's essentially criminal nature when he comforts himself with a piece of proverbial wisdom: "Methinks he hath no drowning mark upon him; his complexion is perfect gallows. Stand fast, good Fate, to his hanging" (I.i.28-30). The proverb he refers to states: "He that is born to be hanged will never be drowned."[5] The overriding self-interest that the Boatswain displays qualifies him to command skillfully, if unsuccessfully during the storm, while the tempest is master. When the order that man assumes during "calm seas and auspicious gales" (V.i.314) is upset, the civilized veneer that disguises individual self-interest drops away.

With characteristic dramatic economy, Shakespeare's first scene lays out the central concerns of the play: legitimate and illegitimate rule and the relation of self-interest to the common interest. It also brings out the essential elements of the main characters in the drama when they are faced with sudden death.

Alonso becomes powerless, Gonzalo conciliatory but skeptical, while Antonio and Sebastian comfort themselves with Caliban-like cursing: "A pox o'your throat, you bawling, blasphemous, incharitable dog!" (I.i.40-41) The Boatswain's vital self-love comes through: "What, must our mouths be cold?" (I.i.52)

The opening sixty-six lines of the play have all the makings of a tragedy. But the second scene reframes the drama and has an immediately softening, restorative effect. Miranda pleads for the lives that she supposes lost, and alludes to a higher power than that of nature controlling events:

> If by your Art, my dearest father, you have
> Set the wild waters in this roar, allay them.
> (I.ii.1-2)

By contrast with the hierarchical confusion of the first scene, the opening lines of the second scene immediately establish an order, of familial relation and of power.

Miranda's opening speech puts all that has gone before in an entirely new light—the magic "charm" that pervades the play is introduced, though it is not named until the last act (V.i.54). Miranda narrates what we have just seen:

> The sky, it seems, would pour down stinking pitch,
> But that the sea, mounting to th'welkin's cheek,
> Dashes the fire out. O, I have suffered
> With those that I saw suffer!
> (I.ii.3-6)

She offers the perfect audience reaction to a tragedy—so caught up in it as to believe it real. But her distress turns our attention from the shipwreck: she believes it to be the product of her father's Art and so remediable. She instinctively sympathizes with the "noble creature" she presumes is aboard the ship (because it is a "brave vessel" she infers there are "souls" on it.) She exemplifies the experience of catharsis that Aristotle says tragedy awakens.[6] Hers is the immediate, unreflective response to tragedy: compassion for the sufferers.

Prospero is another master. He may be a magician, but his magic bears a complex relation to human powers. It includes the power to create a "spectacle," which he uses to educate his daughter.[7] As Rosalie Colie points out, "Prospero's art is not anti-natural, but works from well within the natural processes."[8] Prospero uses a natural phenomenon rather than a blink of the eye to transport his enemies to the island. When he questions Ariel about the shipwreck he speaks directorially: "Hast thou, spirit, /Perform'd to point the tempest that I bade thee? (I.ii.193-194), and Ariel details his performance proudly.

Once the spectacle is concluded and Miranda's first apprehensions allayed, Prospero removes his "magic garment" and puts his magic at a distance: "Lie there, my Art" (I.ii.24-25), in order to explain what has happened. He will do this once again, in the final scene, when he resumes his ducal robes (V.i.85-94). Both times he tells a story of injustice done him. Why does he lay aside his Art to do this? To tell the story of how he lost his dukedom (which he recites to Miranda and then to King Alonso and his courtiers) does not require Art. It is as though the tale of the injustice done him required no other dimension, no dramatic context. Prospero prefaces his exposition by saying, "I have done nothing but in care of thee/Of thee my dear one, thee my daughter" (I.ii.16-17). This is the most explicit statement of his motive that Prospero gives to any "audience" within the play. When he addresses an audience beyond the play in the epilogue, he says his aim is "to please." Its most immediate sense is that the shipwreck, which has disturbed Miranda so greatly, has been entirely for her benefit. Prospero insists twice that Miranda learn of her history just after the tempest. First he notes, "'Tis time/I should inform thee farther," and then, "The very minute bids thee ope thine ear" (I.ii.23, 37).

His concern with the timing of his tale implies that his staged tragedy has in some way prepared his daughter for the story of her true identity. The "very virtue of compassion" in her has just been touched. She has "suffer'd with those" she saw suffer (I.ii.26, 5-6). Compassion is a virtue made possible for Miranda only by a belief in the existence of creatures like herself. It takes her out of herself, and this self-forgetting prepares her to hear her father's misfortunes and her own true history, to acquire self-knowledge. Prospero prefaces his story to her by calling her one who is "ignorant of what thou art" (I.ii.18).

What does compassion have to do with self-knowledge? Later in the same scene we learn that Miranda has experienced pity, for the creature Caliban:

> I pitied thee,
> Took pains to make thee speak, taught thee each hour
> One thing or other . . .
> But thy vile race,
> Though thou didst learn, had that in't which good natures
> Could not abide to be with. . . .
> (I.ii.355-362)[9]

Her pity and careful teaching were wasted on Caliban, through whom she came to learn that compassion has its bounds, for Caliban is: "A devil, a born devil, on whose nature/Nurture can never stick" (IV.i.188-189). Pity causes her to reflect on her differences as well as her similarities with others. As Rousseau observes in Emile, "Do you wish, then, to excite and nourish in the heart of a young man the first movements of nascent sensibility and turn his character toward beneficence and goodness? Do not put the seeds of pride, vanity, and envy I him by the deceptive image of the happiness of men. Do not expose his eyes at the outset to the pomp of courts, the splendor of palaces, or the appeal of the theater. Do not take him to the circles of the great, to brilliant assemblies

. . . To show him the world before he knows men is not to form him, it is to corrupt him; it is not to instruct him, it is to deceive him."[10] As Prospero notes, his private education of Miranda has "made thee more profit/Than other princess' can, that have more time/For vainer hours and tutors not so careful" (I.ii.172-4). In his *Second Discourse*, Rousseau briefly gives the origins of compassion: "There is, besides, another principle which Hobbes did not notice . . . I speak of pity, a disposition that is appropriate to beings as weak and subject to as many ills as we are; a virtue all the more universal and useful to man because it precedes in him the use of all reflection; and so natural that even beasts sometimes give perceptible signs of it."[11]

Miranda's education is part of Prospero's "project," and he recalls her apparently wandering attention to the story of her birth three times. She is far more enthralled by the spectacle of the wreck than by her father's prosaic explanation of it: an early intimation in the play of both the power and the necessity of Art. By telling her the story of their banishment from Milan, he gives Miranda a sense of her own position in the world, but this is a preparatory aspect of her introduction to the "brave new world" brought to the island with the "brave vessel."

It is not enough that Miranda honor her father and come to know Caliban for a "villain" (I.ii.312). She must see a "third man" (I.ii.448), Ferdinand, in order to gauge how far her father's nature surpasses that of Caliban. Her experience of pity also prepares her for romantic love. An indication of her changed understanding (brought on by the shipwreck, the recounting of her father's misfortune, her meeting with Ferdinand) is that in her second interview with Ferdinand she speaks of knowing only two men: "nor have I seen/more that I may call men than you, good friend, /And my dear father" (III.i.50-52). This time, Caliban is left out of her catalogue of men, since, having met Ferdinand, she no longer counts Caliban a man.[12] Miranda requires a fuller understanding of what separates the human from the bestial (Prospero from Caliban) than the understanding she has acquired on the island.[13]

Through intense pursuit of the "liberal Arts" Prospero has lost his realm. But after twelve years, fortune is kind and he takes advantage of an "auspicious star" to correct his mistake. After telling his story, Prospero gently commands Miranda to sleep: "'tis a good dulness, /And give it way: I know thou canst not choose" (I.ii.185-6).

Alonso and his party are similarly lulled to sleep at the end of act 2, scene 1, this time by Prospero's minister, Ariel. In both cases the sleep of others allows Prospero to further his "project." At this point he has opportunity for a conference with Ariel (a character seen in his true form only by Prospero in the play). In the second instance sleep precipitates the conspiracy against the king between Antonio and Sebastian, which will permit Prospero to keep them in check later (V.i.127-129).

The question of where power is vested in the play is elaborated by Prospero's narrative. The Boatswain assumes the power of the Master, and it is implied, he usurps the power of the King of Naples, who has no control over the elements (although he tries to usurp the Boatswain's authority on board ship), therefore, according to the Boatswain, no legitimate power in a tempest. But when we are offered a more comprehensive view, we recognize that the Boatswain's exercise of power is ineffectual against a higher master: Prospero, who, his daughter believes, can command the elements. There is a claim to power that can be made based on more than technical competence—a claim based on knowledge.[14]

In explaining the tempest to Miranda, though, Prospero appears to acknowledge a limitation to his power:

> By accident most strange, bountiful Fortune,
> (Now my dear lady) hath mine enemies
> Brought to this shore; and by my prescience
> I find my zenith doth depend upon
> A most auspicious star, whose influence
> If now I court not, but omit, my fortunes
> Will ever after droop.
> (I.ii.178-184)

Prospero's claim to power is his knowledge which guides his Art, and this in turn enables him to use nature. But his powers are useless without the assistance of fortune.[15] Part of the knowledge Prospero has is of how and when to practice his magic Art. The Master of the ship possesses the legitimate authority and power to save or wreck the ship, but he relinquishes it to the Boatswain who knows how to exercise it and rules the ship during the tempest. The true master is one who is capable of using power for the common good, legitimately or illegitimately, and during the tempest the Boatswain serves the common interest by serving his own.

Where is the master? Is it he who legitimately possesses power or he who knows how to use it? The first scene offers the second view. But the simple moral of Prospero's own history is that the master is he who legitimately rules. We return to the question that stood between Malcolm and Macduff. Is tyranny simply illegitimate rule, or is it bad rule?

Servant and Slave

Tolstoy condemns Shakespeare for *The Tempest* among other "absurd, dramatized tales" not only because of his atheism, but because of his anti-democratic sentiments, unsuited to an age of liberalism.[16] Shakespeare's great hero/magician, perhaps his autobiographical persona, is, after all, a slave-keeper. It is his back-talking slave, Caliban, who alone calls him a tyrant (II.ii.163; III.ii.40).

Prospero plays magic with the elements, but the beings he commands on the island have needs and desires and can speak. He has a "slave," Caliban, who believes himself Prospero's only subject, and a "servant," Ariel, visible only to him (I.ii.187, 315). Both demand freedom. Prospero's ability to contain the energies of both Caliban and Ariel shows that he has learned something about the art of rule. He acknowledges his earlier mistake when

> . . . neglecting worldly ends, all dedicated
> To closeness and the bettering of my mind
> With that which, but by being to retir'd,
> O'erpriz'd all popular rate, in my false brother
> Awak'd an evil nature; and my trust,
> Like a good parent, did beget of him
> A falsehood in its contrary. . . .
> (I.ii.89-95)

He accepts blame for his own overthrow. This does not deny the honor of pursuing the "liberal Arts" (I.ii.73), which study, "O'erpriz'd all popular rate," but Prospero now knows the perils incurred "by being so retir'd." A ruler must exercise rule in order to maintain his power. Prospero's analysis of his overthrow displays a self-examination that Shakespeare's tragic heroes do not arrive at.

These two new creatures are opposites and require very different sorts of rule: Ariel is of the air, a "tricksy spirit," and Caliban (imperfect anagram of cannibal) is of the earth and called "earth," "tortoise," "savage," "hagseed," and "fish." The symbolic element of the characters is underscored by Ben Jonson who criticized the unnaturalness of Caliban in his introduction to *Bartholomew Fair* and accused Shakespeare of pandering to the audience's taste for the grotesque.[17] Prospero exercises a different power over each being, expressed by different manners of address. He summons Ariel: "Come away servant, come. I am ready now" (I.ii.187), and, after this interview, calls Caliban, "What, ho! Slave! Caliban: /Thou earth, thou speak!" (I.ii.315-316) Through Ariel he rules the "sprites" that torment Caliban and enchant Ferdinand, but he rules Ariel through speech, with alternate praises and threats. It is in his rule of Caliban through physical punishment and threats that he appears most unsteady of temperament.

Prospero's power is effective because he understands the different natures of the creatures he controls. He appeals to the desires and fears of each. For each of them, he provides an explanation of why they must serve him. For Caliban, it is punishment for his attempted rape of Miranda, for Ariel it is an appeal to gratitude and fear. As Caliban is quick to point out, in neither case can he claim that his power is legitimate, only that it is backed by the compulsion of his Art: "I must obey: his Art is of such pow'r/It would control my dam's god, Setebos" (I.ii.374-375).

In the case of Ariel, Prospero works on the spirit's love of liberty (which he presumably enjoyed before Sycorax came), his gratitude, and his fear of imprisonment. Monthly, he reminds the spirit of how he set him free from a "torment to lay upon the damned" (261-263). When Ariel finds that there is "more toil" after the tempest, he asks for his liberty, and Prospero shows anger for the first time in the play:

> Dost thou forget
> From what a torment I did free thee?
> . . . Hast thou forgot
> The foul witch Sycorax . . . ?
> . . . she did confine thee,
> By help of her more potent ministers,
> And in her most unmitigable rage,
> Into a cloven pine; within which rift
> Imprison'd thou didst painfully remain
> A dozen years; within which space she died,
> And left thee there; where thou dist vent thy groans
> As fast as mill-wheels strike.
> (I.ii.250-281)

Sycorax could not undo this spell, but Prospero's "Art" set Ariel free (290). He completes his lesson with a threat, to "peg" him in an "oak" twelve years (294-296) if he further disobeys. Ariel excuses himself (297-298), and Prospero promises him liberty again. After this harsh rebuke he has nothing but praise, and Ariel alludes to Prospero's promise only once more, in the "sixth hour; at which time, my lord/You said our work should cease" (V.i.3-4).

Ariel's power to transform himself and to call up spirits is to be the instrument of Prospero's liberation from a twelve-year banishment (as he set Ariel free from a twelve-year imprisonment). For this reason Ariel must not only be kept in mind of his debt of gratitude to his master, but must also be kept hopeful by promises of freedom (I.ii.298, 423, 445, 502; IV.i.265; V.i.96, 241, 318).

Ariel's power is transformative; he appears as the elements water and fire, as a harpy, and as a goddess. This power is most like the power of the dramatist's imagination, which makes the unreal appear real, and may influence an audience's understanding with costumed morality. Ariel performs small morality plays in the banquet/harpy and goddess scenes. But he plays to select audiences. Three characters who prove redeemable (within Prospero's "project") are allowed to hear Ariel privately: Ferdinand, Alonso, and Gonzalo; he sings and speaks to them. Ferdinand hears Ariel's music, but it is clear he does not see the figure of the "nymph o'th'sea" since he cannot tell whether the music is "i'th'air or th' 'arth" (I.ii.390). Yet Prospero has been specific as to how Ariel should appear:

Go make thyself like a nymph o'th'sea:
Be subject to
No sight but thine and mine; invisible
To every eyeball else. Go take this shape . . .
(I.ii.301-304)

Prospero tells Ariel to transform himself and then to be invisible to all but him, perhaps in order that he may enjoy his own imaginative conception to the fullest without overpowering Ferdinand.

Ariel enters in act 3, scene 3, dressed as a harpy but apparently invisible to all but Alonso, Antonio, and Sebastian, to whom his accusation is addressed. Alonso, most affected by the performance Prospero has arranged, thinks the elements have spoken to him:

Methought the billows spoke and told me of it;
The winds did sing it to me; and the thunder,
That deep and dreadful organ-pipe, pronounc'd
The name of Prosper: it did bass my trespass.
(III.iii.96-99)

Sebastian and Antonio imagine that they face "legions" of fiends rather than one spirit (103). Gonzalo and the rest of the King's company do not see the anti-masque and are utterly confounded by the distraction of the King and Duke and attribute their seeming madness to "their great guilt" (104).

This is a remarkable presentation of the different effects of Art on different natures; some are susceptible to tragedy (Miranda, I.i), some to revenge tragedy (Alonso, III.iii), some to music (Ferdinand, I.ii; Alonso, Gonzalo, III.ii; and Caliban, III.ii), and some to comedy (Gonzalo, I.i). While Ariel presents a spectacle to Alonso, Sebastian, and Antonio, in their responses they present a spectacle to Gonzalo who interprets their distraction as guilt. Spectacle has a multiplied effect, as those who watch are watched. Audience reaction is presented as spectacle repeatedly in the play; first Miranda is watched viewing the tempest, then as she watches Ferdinand; they are both watched watching the masque of goddesses; the King and his co-conspirators are watched watching the anti-masque; and the King and his party are watched as they see the unveiling of Ferdinand and Miranda at chess. The audience is invited continually to observe, along with Prospero, how Art charms, frightens, saddens, and teaches.

After the banquet has disappeared and the villains have been accused, Prospero commends Ariel on his performance much as he did after Ariel "perform'd" the tempest (I.ii.237-78):

Bravely the figure of this harpy hast thou
Perform'd, my Ariel, a grace it had devouring;
Of my instruction hast thou nothing bated

In what thou hadst to say. . . .
(83-86)

Prospero stresses careful attention to aesthetic detail and in particular the exact repetition of speeches. The audience, with Prospero, occupies the privileged position of seeing the whole spectacle of Ariel even when he is only a sound: song or voice. As the dramatic horizon is finally expanded at the end of the play, we are made aware of Prospero's consciousness of us, his immediate audience, to whom he has in part addressed his "tricksy spirit." To those accused, Ariel's words are real; the threat of "heart-sorrow" is potent. Only Prospero can appreciate the "baseless fabric of this vision" since he has created it (IV.i.151). Through his instruction of Ariel, the audience is kept aware of how the drama is made up.

His stance as an observer in this scene may be likened to his stance in act 3, scene 1, referred to wrongly by one critic as "voyeurism."[18] Though the lovers are ignorant of the repercussions of their romance, Prospero looks on the love scene knowing fully the political significance of the union of Milan and Naples.

Ariel performs imaginative services. He strikes guilt into Alonso and fear into Sebastian and Antonio. He charms Ferdinand and at times, it is suggested, Caliban as well (III.ii). He performs as Prospero's "soul prompts" him (I.ii.423). The affinity between Ariel and Prospero is emphasized both by their twelve-year imprisonment (I.ii.53, 279), and their desire for freedom (I.ii.245, Epilogue.20). To the extent Ariel is emblematic of the dramatist's imagination, he is visible only to the dramatist, and to others only as the dramatist wishes him to be. The imaginative appeal to a character susceptible to suggestion may be as brief as the song Ariel sings to lure Ferdinand to Miranda, "Full fathom five." As Prospero has taken pains to learn from Ariel, Ferdinand is suggestible; he was the first to jump ship, completely taken in by the performance of the tempest (I.ii.212-215). Stephano and Trinculo hear Ariel as a tune, and see him as the dogs hunt them. For Alonso, a godlike reprimand and mention of his crime are adequate to awaken his guilt. For Sebastian and Antonio (who do not possess the "deity" of conscience), he excites fear and is perceived as "legions" of fiends, whereas the honest counselor Gonzalo is so sensitive, he may be awakened by a mere whisper. Ariel, instructed by Prospero, works on each being according to his nature.

The complex variety of Ariel's powers, kept prisoner by Sycorax, is freed only by Prospero's imagination; his capacity to conceive how Ariel may be used as harpy, spirit, sea nymph, or goddess. Through this imaginative process, Ariel is the instrument of Prospero's rule over others. Though he does not serve freely, he serves with hope of reward, and with some pleasure in his artistic tasks.

More than the servant, the slave, Caliban, has excited most contemporary critical interest in the play. The suggestion for this focus comes from outside the field, with the publication in 1956 of a translation of Dominique Mannoni's book *Prospero and Caliban: The Psychology of Colonization*. Mannoni saw in the Prospero/Caliban relation a paradigm for English colonial experience. He discusses the colonial drive to master and colonize, how it is also a drive to repress what are considered undesirable elements in the colonizer, by projecting them onto the colonized culture. This creates in its turn a "dependency complex" in the colonized culture that prevents the colonized freeing themselves from illegitimate domination. One chapter of the book is devoted to the title characters in whom he sees a psychologically realistic portrait of the colonial experience.[19] One contemporary critic, Paul Brown, argues that the play tries to offer a utopic perspective on colonial politics.[20] He sees *The Tempest* as a "radically ambivalent text" (48) that attempts intervention in a colonialist discourse emerging in contemporary England with the discovery of the New World. He argues that the oppression masked in colonization is accidentally brought forward in the play. I would suggest, however, that this oppression is not simply a reflection on particular historical circumstances so much as a reflection on the nature of tyranny and politics generally.

Recent criticism has fortunately moved away from simple allegorizing of Caliban and Ariel as versions of the vulgar and the noble, to shed light on how the problem of "colonialism" and, consequently, the problem of a particular form of tyranny is addressed in the play. But the new historicist and Marxist critics have tended to constrain their discussions by surrounding the text with contemporary historical anecdote.[21] What Brown objects to is the "mystification" of colonial rule that he believes occurs in the play (48). A healthy condemnation of the injustice of such rule appears, inadvertently, because of Shakespeare's honest representation of discourse (63, passim). This constitutes the play's "political unconscious" (69). But it is important, in this play, to sort out what is being mystified, to whom, and by whom, and what is simply hard to understand. After all, unlike the *dramatis personae*, we have the advantage of seeing Prospero wave his magic staff, put on and take off his cloak of Art. *The Tempest*, as I have indicated, far from being an "unconscious" commentary on the politics of colonialism, is one of Shakespeare's most politically sophisticated plays. It picks apart rather than obfuscates the components of rule.

Ariel is essential to the realization of Prospero's "project," but why is Caliban necessary? As Prospero reminds Miranda: "We cannot miss him: he does make our fire, /Fetch our wood, and serves in offices/That profit us" (I.ii.313015). He is like Aristotle's "natural slaves" in *Politics I, Book I*, who are necessary to free men for higher pursuits. The perfect natural slave is one of

> those who are as different [from other men] as the soul from the body or man from beast—and they are in this state if their work is the use of the body, and if this is the best that can come from them—[they] are slaves by nature. For

them it is better to be ruled in accordance with this sort of rule . . . Moreover, the need for them differs only slightly: bodily assistance in the necessary things is forthcoming from both, from slaves and from tame animals alike. (1245b16-26)[22]

Prospero identifies Caliban as a "slave" (I.ii.344-8), who, despite generosity and education, is unable to overcome his inferior nature. Caliban's defiance and the poetry of his speeches indicate how this designation of "natural slave" does not satisfactorily justify the enslavement of another being. Prospero's final plea for forgiveness, as I argue, recalls the unsettling nature of his rule on the island, insisted on by Caliban.

"A plague upon the tyrant that I serve!" This is Caliban's call to revolution against Prospero (II.ii.162). He justifies his complaint to Stephano and Trinculo:

> As I told thee before, I am subject to a tyrant, a sorcerer, that by his cunning hath cheated me of the island. (III.ii.42)

After his opening curse, Caliban's first complaint when he enters is against Prospero's illegitimacy: "This island's mine by Sycorax my mother/Which thou tak'st from me" (I.ii.333). He inherited the island from his exiled mother, a witch, but was seduced into allowing Prospero to rule because of his impressive powers (language, knowledge of the sun and moon). Prospero and Miranda were affectionate with him, fed him, and taught him, only to enslave him. Caliban's expression of this fury gives away his own dilemma. How is one "subject" to a tyrant? To a tyrant, all subjects are slaves.

In his first rebellion against Prospero, Caliban rejects Prospero's sovereign language:

> You taught me language; and my profit on't
> Is, I know how to curse. The red plague rid you
> For learning me your language.
> (I.ii.365-7)

The curse turns back on itself. Caliban doesn't express himself with a sequential, non-contradictory logic, but reduces language to the way he feels. The beautiful dream soliloquy comes out of this intuitive use of language. But when up against Prospero's words, Caliban is enslaved by the very language he disdains: "I needs must curse" (II.ii.4). It has enabled him to articulate and better understand his world, but with language an alien system of significations was imposed. Speech is the first level of compulsion Prospero exercises against Ariel and Caliban. Language gives material form to Prospero's power. And he uses it with a versatility (to equivocate, to disguise meaning or intention; I.ii.456-57, 345; V.i.142-3) that Caliban does not have.

Caliban's soliloquy in the play provides one of the few insights into exactly how he perceives Prospero's Art, and the speech begins with two curses:

> All the infections that the sun sucks up
> From bogs, fens, flats on Prospero fall, and make him
> By inch-meal a disease!
> (II.ii.1-3)

Caliban wishes on his enemy the worst he can conceive. Unlike Prospero, he cannot call on the supernatural to aid him because his imagination does not reach beyond the natural and material; it is not clear he even remembers how to name the "bigger" light and the "lesser." Prospero, on the other hand, threatens his slave with harms that surpass natural disaster. His threats, or his poetic expressions, are stronger. There are two striking examples of this in act 1, scene 2, where Prospero threatens Caliban to make him perform his duties:

> . . . thou shalt be pinch'd
> As thick as honeycomb, each pinch more stinging
> Than bees that made 'em

and

> . . . I'll rack thee with old cramps,
> Fill all thy bones with aches, make thee roar,
> That beasts shall tremble at thy din.
> (330-332, 371-3)

This last threat is the one that convinces Caliban that he "must obey: his [Prospero's] Art is of such pow'r, /It would control my dam's god, Setebos, / And make a vassal of him" (372-376). Caliban states plainly his reason for obedience—superior force. This superior force is contained within Prospero's imagery, the strength of which is that it exceeds the bounds of the natural. The pinches that Caliban will have are worse "than bees that made 'em." The cramps and aches will cause such painful cries that "beasts shall tremble." This latter image is, in the exact sense, an unnatural one. It is much like the image Prospero uses to describe the horrors of Ariel's imprisonment: his howls penetrated the "breasts of ever-angry bears" (288-289).

To Caliban, Prospero's images are frightening because they come from outside his realm of imagery. He understands "bogs," "fens," and "flats." But Prospero describes supernatural pain, which encourages Caliban to consider it superior to the highest power he has known—that of Setebos, his "dam's god."

When he meets Stephano, he believes he has found another creature more powerful than Setebos, and possibly Prospero, so he asks Stephano (master of the bottle) to be his new "god" (II.ii.149). When Caliban takes a new master, he receives a second language as well. Stephano has him drink: "Come on your ways; open your mouth; here is that will give language to you, cat" (II.ii.84-85). Having opened the scene with a lengthy and imaginative curse on Prospero, he ends with a burst of song, celebrating himself: "'Ban, 'Ban, Cacaliban/Has a new master:—get a new man" (184-5). Part of the sense of this song is that Caliban wants procreative rights, he wants to "beget" more of his kind.[23] As the conspiracy against his former "tyrant" builds (II.ii.162), Caliban leaves off cursing, believing that the brave language of drunken revelry, and the celestial liquor, which gives him song, releases him from Prospero's Art and from his bondage to cursing (II.ii.4). When he believes he has found a new god, with "celestial liquor," he believes he has a potent weapon against Prospero's spirits.[24] And when the conspiracy begins to fail, Caliban returns to cursing with Prospero's language: "The dropsy drown this fool" (IV.i.230).

Caliban chooses to trade bondage for bondage. He asks Stephano, "I prithee be my god" (II.ii.49) and offers to perform those services for him that he once performed as Prospero's slave:

> I'll show thee the best springs; I'll pluck thee berries;
> I'll fish for thee, and get thee wood enough.
> A plague upon the tyrant that I serve!
> I'll bear him no more sticks, but follow thee,
> Thou wondrous man.
> (II.ii.160-164)

Caliban has replaced one "tyrant" with another, of lesser capacity—a "dull fool" as he calls him at the end of the play (V.i.197). Caliban never reconciles his desire for freedom with his apparent desire to be ruled; one cannot "serve" a tyrant, since service implies some willingness or hope of reward.

Caliban was the occasion of Prospero's second serious misjudgment after the one that led to his banishment from Milan:

> *Pros.* . . . I have us'd thee,
> Filth as thou art, with human care; and lodg'd thee
> In mine own cell, till thou didst seek to violate
> The honour of my child.
> *Cal.* O ho, O ho! would't had been done!
> Thou didst prevent me; I had peopled else
> This isle with Calibans.
> (I.ii.347-353)

He misjudged the nature of Caliban, trusting him as he trusted his brother Antonio. Prospero's explanation of why Caliban is enslaved is lost on a creature to whom honor is unimportant. To say Caliban is not a noble creature, however, is not to say that he is inferior in power. We know from Prospero's interruption of the wedding masque that Caliban poses the greatest danger to him and to his project. This seems strange since it is Ariel who performs the most impressive tricks: tempest, songs, masque, anti-masque. Ariel has far greater powers than Caliban, but Caliban, powerless against physical "pricks," is more to be feared. The slave is more dangerous than the servant.

What has Prospero learned on the island? He has learned, literally, to "see" Ariel and to recognize Caliban for what he is. Only Prospero can "see" and communicate with Ariel. No one else is able to recognize that component of human nature that desires freedom at all costs, and responds to shame and praise. Everyone can see Caliban, but no one appreciates his necessity as Prospero does. Miranda hates him for his attack on her, though, as her father says, "we cannot miss him." It is his labors that allow Prospero his afternoon studies and Miranda her education. Stephano and Trinculo first regard him as a curiosity, then as a tool to satisfy their desires (for "trumpery"), which are lower than Caliban's. For Antonio and Sebastian he is a commodity (V.i.264-266), and Alonso cannot place him at all. For Prospero: "this thing of darkness I/Acknowledge mine" (V.i.275-6).

Prospero was exiled and marooned with his precious books, which somehow enabled him (through magic) to provide for all his wants and those of his daughter. As before in Milan, he was dedicated to the "closeness and bettering" of his mind. What attractions could the outside world hold for someone of contemplative temperament? In his exile, Prospero finds Caliban and Ariel and in recognizing and learning how to rule them, he recognizes hidden parts of human nature. He is more in sympathy with Ariel, who responds to the promptings of his soul, and more at odds with Caliban towards whom he adopts a constantly threatening posture. Ariel, an embodiment of the will to be free, enables Prospero to muster enough moral indignation to act against those who did him injustice.

If we were to read *The Tempest* as paradigmatic of political rule, we would have to explain why Shakespeare chooses to divide the elements to be ruled into the creatures Ariel and Caliban. What aspects of human beings or peoples do they represent? If it is correct that, on one level, Ariel and Caliban represent two distinct impulses within human beings, why would Caliban be visible as a monster, but Ariel invisible altogether? If Caliban represents the desires that enslave human beings, then Antonio and Sebastian are more familiar with him because both are usurpers: their allegiance to authority is easily overcome by a desire for self-aggrandizement. And Prospero would have come to know him through his experience with his "unnatural" brother.

Ariel is ruled by a sense of gratitude, fear of imprisonment, and a delight in praise. Caliban is ruled by threats of physical violence. Both are ruled by Prospero's anger. At the end of the play, Ariel is promised freedom within two days (after taking the ship back to Milan), but Caliban is left unaccounted for.

This is an expression of Prospero's difficulty in mastering the slavish aspect of human nature, and in the end he abandons the task.

Any close examination of the charge of tyranny Caliban brings against Prospero must acknowledge its merit. Prospero controls Caliban's island and has enslaved its legitimate ruler. This play also presents the dilemma of rule over an unwilling subject. Caliban says he want freedom, but this freedom is the freedom to choose a new, and perhaps more lenient master. He makes a poor choice in Stephano, which causes him to reconsider how "fine" Prospero is (V.i.262). One way of defining tyranny is to say, with Aristotle, that it is rule against the common good. Caliban believes that Prospero's rule is for himself, since he sees no benefit for him. Another way to define tyranny is as rule over an unwilling individual, whether in that individual's interest or not. There is no question that Caliban is unwilling to be ruled by Prospero. By both definitions then, for Caliban, Prospero is a tyrant. But this tyrant/slave relation points up how improbable any form of non-tyrannic rule is. How does one rule a subject whose interest is against, or has no connection with, the common interest? Caliban wishes to breed with Miranda, and Prospero will never permit it. Caliban wishes to roam freely: Prospero needs menial duties performed. There is no common good between them. The other part of this question is whether rule over the unwilling, in their own best interest, constitutes tyranny. If one believes oneself tyrannized over, however much one's interest is served, it is tyranny. The only solution to the latter problem is Gonzalo's republic, whose ruler, having established a common good, disappears. The passion for freedom that Caliban imperfectly embodies is, of course, connected with the question of what legitimizes rule. If there is no common good and no legitimacy, can even a wise man such as Prospero avoid the just charge of tyranny?

Willing Bondage

Terry Eagleton starkly divides Caliban and Ariel into language and body, seeing the project of the play as follows:

> For the body to take on the universal availability of a language, and for language to become a kind of physical gesture, is to heal the cleavage between signs and things, created and inherent values, freedom and body.[25]

Rosalie Colie writes of the "emblematically represented" human beings in *The Tempest*. This "bracketing"

> Between the passionate, brutal Caliban on the earthy side and the supersubtle Ariel on the elevated side, stresses the problematical within the human condition: as Pico della Mirandola put it, a man can become all air, to forget other

human beings altogether (Prospero in Milan), or he can sink to bestial level, either from high place (Antonio, Alonso, Sebastian) or from high place parodied (Stephano, Trinculo).[26]

Paul Cantor sees Caliban and Ariel as "abstraction from human nature" offering Prospero an "enlightening lesson in government."[27] And Lionel Trilling sees the play's division of Ariel and Caliban as Hegelian:

> If we speak of *The Tempest* in the context of a discussion of the *Phenomenology*, we can scarcely fail to remark other elements of the play which bear in a striking way on Hegel's formulations—the 'baseness' of Caliban which commands the sympathy of the modern audience not merely for its pathos but for what is implied of its 'nobility' by its resistance to servitude, and the achieved aspiration of Ariel to be Spirit fully realized in autonomy.[28]

Do these creatures represent ends of the spectrum of human behavior (Colie and Eagleton) or are they distillations of human inclinations (Cantor)? The question of how to regard these characters is answered in looking at how Prospero puts his two different techniques of rule to use against other characters in the play. Just after quelling the rebellions of Ariel and Caliban, Prospero must master Ferdinand. His first political gesture in the play is against Ariel, an obliging creature, "correspondent to command" (I.ii.297), his next against Caliban, a creature intimidated by force who "must obey" superior power (I.ii.374), but finally he moves against "a goodly person" (I.ii.418), Ferdinand. Prospero tries him by first shaming him as he did Ariel—accusing him of being a usurper, a "spy" and a "traitor" (456, 458, 463). Next Prospero threatens him with superior force and vows to enslave him as he did Caliban (463-476).

Prospero's comic perspective mediates the exhilarated perspective of the young lovers. When they first meet, in a state of quieted confusion, Ferdinand gives way to wonder as he beholds Miranda: "most sure the goddess / On whom these airs attend!" (I.ii.424-5) His mistake directly follows Miranda's similar misapprehension: "I might call him [Ferdinand]/A thing divine; for nothing natural/I ever saw so noble" (I.ii.420-22). Miranda goes on in this vein, speaking of Ferdinand as a "brave form," a "temple where nothing ill can dwell" (I.ii.460). She has spoken in the same fashion of the ship (I.ii.5-6). Each lover idealizes the other from the first.

Prospero's three asides during the first encounter of the lovers indicate that his unjust charges of treason against Ferdinand are part of a larger design. It is clear from the first that he controls the budding romance and intends that his daughter and the Prince of Naples change "eyes" (I.ii.444). He praises Ariel for this:

> It goes on, I see,
> As my soul prompts it. Spirit, fine spirit! I'll free thee

Within two days for this.
(I.ii.421-424)

Miranda judges Ferdinand, whom she takes first for "a thing divine," according to his "brave form," rather than by any certain knowledge of his nature
(I.ii.421, 414). Since Miranda's un-courtly education has not taught her the
sexual politics of coyness, Prospero tests the mettle of her prospective husband:

> . . . this swift business
> I must uneasy make, lest too light winning
> Make the prize light.
> (I.ii.453-55)

To this end he charges Ferdinand with usurpation—angering him to rebellion—
and puts him in servitude. The ostensible provocation is Ferdinand's claim to
the title, King of Naples, which Prospero knows to be false, an example of his
powers of equivocation. With the audience, Prospero appreciates his own dramatic irony. Yet Ferdinand has good reason to believe his father dead:

> *Pros.* What wert thou if the king of Naples heard thee?
> *Ferd.* . . . He does hear me;
> And that he does I weep, myself am Naples.
> (I.ii.434-7)

Ferdinand's line strangely echoes the Boatswain's impudent retort. When asked
"Where's the Master?" (I.i.9), he rejoins: "Do you not hear him?" (I.i.13). In
both cases the speaker does in fact "usurp the name" that belongs to another.
This is a parodic reflection on Prospero's usurpation by Antonio, and his own
usurpation of Caliban. What power inheres in the title to power?
    Prospero tests Ferdinand by treating him as though he were all Caliban so
that Miranda may better understand what elevates him above the servant-monster:

> I'll manacle thy neck and feet together:
> Sea-water shalt thou drink; thy food shall be
> The fresh-brook mussels, wither'd roots, and husks
> Wherein the acorn cradled. . . .
> (I.ii.465-7)

The physical state he describes approaches that of Caliban, who subsists on
such nourishment and is "not honour'd with a human shape" (I.ii.283). Ferdinand
is compelled to assume the place of Caliban, carrying wood, a slave, at the
beginning of act 3, while Caliban wanders off to instigate tyrannicide. Prospero
emphasizes to her the comparison she should make:

To th'most of men this is a Caliban
And they to him are angels.
(I.ii.483-4)

The juxtaposition of Caliban's recalcitrance and Ferdinand's quick submission begs a comparison of their characters. Each finds himself under the rule of Prospero and wishes to escape it. They are both set to the menial task of carrying wood. Each feels treated unjustly—Caliban is deprived of an island and Ferdinand of his status as King of Naples. Caliban turns to cursing, but Ferdinand finds an object of admiration and praise. They each seek to escape their bondage, neither one knowing how to challenge Prospero's Art, or, indeed, of what it consists.

What preserves Ferdinand from becoming a Caliban? He reasons: "some kinds of baseness / Are nobly undergone" (III.i.1-2). He fashions his slavery to Prospero into service to Miranda, speaking of Miranda as "the mistress which I serve" who "quickens what's dead" (III.i.6). That which prevents him from cursing his circumstances, as Caliban does, is his capacity for viewing his slavery as having a higher end—love of Miranda (III.i.64-67). Ferdinand's relinquishing of "all corners else o'th'earth" replaces Caliban's complaint that "the rest o'th island" is kept from him by Prospero (I.ii.494, 346). He ennobles his slavery:

There be some sports are painful, and their labour
Delight in them sets off: some kinds of baseness
Are nobly undergone; and most poor matters
Point to rich ends. . . .
(III.i.1-4)

Ferdinand lives out the fantastic love trials of courtly love poetry. There is "space enough . . . in such a prison" as Caliban's rock, Prospero's cell, or Ferdinand's manacles, so long as contemplation—the admiration of something higher than present circumstances—is possible (I.ii.495-96). Ariel is kept in willing obedience by promises of freedom; Caliban is subjugated by promises of physical pain; but Ferdinand resigns himself to his fate without promise of freedom or pardon. Miranda pledges herself Ferdinand's servant (III.i.83-86). The desire for freedom is overcome by love which transforms itself into the desire to serve another. As Ferdinand puts it, "with a heart as willing / As bondage e'er of freedom: here's my hand!" (III.i.88-89) Miranda disobeys her father for the first time and tells Ferdinand her name. This is according to Prospero's project (III.i.36); his "prescience" permits him to foresee how those who will deceive him will deceive him.

His magic brings Ferdinand, his third subject, under control, but as he acknowledges, it is as much Miranda's power as his own that makes Ferdinand obedient (441-443). He is led to the cell by Ariel's music, confused: "Where should this music be? i'th'air or th'earth" (I.ii.390-2). The first of Ariel's songs pictures the dance concluding a masque, the second, a peculiar transformation in death "Nothing of him that doth fade, / But doth suffer a sea-change" (I.ii.402-403), broken off by an anti-masque of frightened dogs and a cock, herald of dawn. These songs, and Prospero's charge that Ferdinand is powerless because of a guilty conscience, foreshadow the full anti-masque and masque, also performed by Ariel, in the fourth act (the harpy scene and the conversation of the goddesses). But all these charges and punishments are manifestly unjust. Ferdinand is not a usurper, traitor, or spy, nor is he full Caliban. Prospero's project requires that he treat him as such in order to bring him under his and Miranda's control. He must enslave Ferdinand in order to test him and inspire his gratitude for earned freedom. The slavishness that is ugly in Caliban, is attractive in Ferdinand, because that element, which is so willing to "bondage," brings him into the service of romantic love.

Prospero explains on releasing him: "all thy vexations/Were but my trials of thy love, and thou / Hast strangely stood the test" (IV.i.5-7). From this point, Ferdinand is treated with respect, and entertained as royalty. He is rewarded, as Ariel is throughout the play, with praise for his nobility, and with freedom. Unlike Ariel's promised freedom, however, Ferdinand's is partial, since he remains obedient to his beloved Miranda.

Ferdinand is the third example of Prospero's rule (after Ariel and Caliban), and the fourth example of his attempt to educate (after Miranda, Ariel, and Caliban). Prospero treats him first as a Caliban, a being unable to rule himself, who is naturally suited to slavery, and then as a being part-Ariel, a free being who can appreciate the high aesthetic pleasures of a masque of goddesses, and who can be trusted not to "violate" Miranda's honor.

Prospero's rule of Ferdinand, combining as it does his rule of slave and servant, suggests that Ferdinand like any "goodly person" has both elements in him and so requires both sorts of rule. Prospero's control of Ferdinand, like his control of Ariel and Caliban, though, is founded on manifest injustice. The mutual subjection pledged by the lovers shows vividly the inadequacies of political rule that requires subjection of both willing and unwilling subjects (Ariel and Caliban). In political rule, outside of Gonzalo's utopic commonwealth, those who are being ruled are feelingly aware of the constraints on them, and to the extent these are believed unjust, a tyranny exists.

Open-Ey'd Conspiracy

At the end of the love scene, Prospero speaks of resolving "business appertaining." This "business" is that of Alonso's repentance and the rendering of Antonio and Sebastian powerless to protest this royal match. Ariel induces all but these two to sleep in order to permit an attempt on the crown, a repetition of Antonio's usurpation of Prospero.

Antonio corrupts Sebastian, who uses him as "precedent" (II.i.286), advising him with metaphorical language of sleep and dream, which reminds us of Caliban's dream-lust for the treasure-giving heavens (III.ii.137-141). Antonio, like Richard III, does not feel the "deity" of conscience (II.i.272-3), but sees how he may free Milan from paying tribute to Naples by this murder, and gain the new King of Naples as an instrument of power. Antonio's conspiratorial art has elements in common with Prospero's Art, as he disguises the conspiracy poetically, using supernatural imagery (II.i.309-310). Alonso's sleep is like Prospero's when, "being transported and rapt in secret studies," he "awak'd an evil nature" in Antonio (I.ii.76-77, 93). Forgetting his political responsibilities to Milan, he "grew stranger" to his state (II.i.76), leaving Antonio the power. Finally he found himself in Caliban's position, that of a legitimate ruler without the power to rule. A ruler who does not rule (who appears asleep) is no longer a ruler. The master is he who acts as master.

Gonzalo evinces what appears to be the same sort of "sleepy" rule in his description of a utopia. He reminds us of the difficulties of perfect political rule when he envisions his choice commonwealth:

> I' th'commonwealth I would by contraries
> Execute all things; for no kind of traffic
> Would I admit; no name of magistrate;
> Letters should not be known; riches, poverty,
> And use of service, none; contract, succession,
> Bourn, bound of land, tilth, vineyard, none;
> No use of metal, corn, or wine, or oil
> No occupation; all men idle, all;
> And women too, but innocent and pure:
> No sovereignty. . . .
> (II.i.143-151)

The speech is taken from Montaigne's essay (translated by John Florio). "Of the Caniballes."[29] He would have his subjects served by nature as Adam and Eve were: "All things in common Nature should produce" (II.i.155). The unlikeliness of Gonzalo's proposal is suggested by the disappearance of the sovereign power. This is now King Alonso's problem, as it was Prospero's. In his grief, he leaves rule aside and he does not exercise his authority. Gonzalo's state, where the "latter end of his commonwealth forgets the beginning," as Antonio points out sharply (II.i.154), shows the necessity of active, visible leadership. Gonzalo's unintentional irony extends further when he banishes "sword, pike, knife, gun, or need of any engine" (II.i.156-7), an addition to the passage from Montaigne, which might alert a wakeful Alonso to the danger he faces from the ambitious members of his party. As Harry Epstein says of Gonzalo's prediction of rescue from the tempest in the first scene,

> In so calling our attention to Gonzalo's correct perception in the face of common sense reasoning, Shakespeare's intention can only be to establish Gonzalo's reliability as witness capable of perceiving truths which escape more cynical and worldly wise observers.[30]

Gonzalo is also right in calling Dido a widow and in identifying Carthage and Tunis. An ear attuned to Lear's Fool would recognize in him a counselor whose wisdom hides itself in the ridiculous.[31] Like other royal fools, he is a survivor. (This he has in common with Rosse in *Macbeth*, Stanley in *Richard III*, and Camillo in *The Winter's Tale*. It requires great discretion or apparent foolishness to remain below suspicion under a tyrant.)

While Gonzalo draws attention to the need for kingliness, however, Antonio and Sebastian urge Alonso to sleep (II.i.189-192). All the King's company, except for Antonio and Sebastian, succumb to Ariel's "solemn music" and sleep, at which point Antonio counsels Sebastian to follow his own "precedent." Ariel intervenes to awaken Gonzalo, or else Prospero's "project dies" (294).

Having foiled the open-ey'd conspiracy of Sebastian and Antonio, Ariel is sent by Prospero as a delegate of the moral imagination to enact poetic vengeance. Alonso, Sebastian, and Antonio each react differently to the charge of "sin." Alonso immediately accepts the explanation of the loss of his son as his just punishment, but Antonio and Sebastian (like Macbeth who wishes to do battle with a "bear" rather than with the supernatural) vow to fight these Fates down. This performance shames Alonso into "heart-sorrow," but produces only a Caliban-like belligerence in Antonio and Sebastian. There is something in them permanently resistant to any appeal to conscience, so they must be controlled by being kept sharply aware of the inferiority of their power, and as a consequence fearful.

The anti-masque is followed immediately by the masque for Ferdinand and Miranda, which Prospero terms a "vanity of mine Art" (IV.i.141). This implies that the Art is intended for more serious purposes, but he is just as attentive to detail in this performance ("bring a corollary, / Rather than want a spirit" IV.i.57-58). The poet, through his Art, is able to bring the gentler divines (Iris, divine messenger; Ceres, harvest goddess; and Juno, goddess of married love) closer to the couple to ensure they will keep their oaths of chastity.

In this masque celebrating "a contract of true love," for a moment, it seems, he loses his artistic distance. He becomes engrossed in the conversation of the goddesses "by Art/ . . . call'd to enact" his "present fancies" (IV.i.120-

22), and enjoins the young couple to silence (as he called for Miranda's attention in act 1, scene 2) to preserve the spell:

Sweet now, silence!
Juno and Ceres whisper seriously
There's something else to do: hush, and be mute,
Or else our spell is marr'd.
(IV.i.124-6)

Without attention an audience cannot fall under the spell of a dramatic performance and have it achieve its effects.

Stephen Orgel remarks in his discussion of the Jonsonian masque: "Every masque concluded by merging spectator with masquer, in effect transforming the courtly audience into the idealized world of the poet's vision."[32] The final resolution is prevented in this masque scene. The poet's vision is interrupted, as was the king's banquet, by remembrance of a harsh political necessity. For the first time in the play, Prospero admits an error, "I had forgot" (IV.i.139).

Antonio's and Sebastian's plot does not upset Prospero, because, as Ariel says, his master "foresees" it (II.i.292). Like the romance it turns out to be part of the master plot, giving him power over the villains later. But Caliban, whom wisdom cannot tame and can only barely control, disturbs him so greatly that Miranda remarks at this point:

Never till this day
Saw I him touch'd with anger, so distemper'd.
(IV.i.144-5)

He concludes with a reflection on the insubstantiality of theatrical revels and of the world, eliding art and life (IV.i.148-58). When he is called back from his momentary and complete absorption in the masque to the necessities of political life, he also recalls his deceptive absorption in life itself (to be remedied when "every third thought" becomes his grave, V.i.311). Wakened from his benediction, Prospero reminds his audience of the precarious status of Art. He is above his creatures in this; Ariel desires freely to inhabit the margins of this illusory world ("where the bee sucks"), while Caliban begs for more such dreams and illusions (III.i.135-41). His expressed detachment borders on a nihilism, a cosmic reflection, which Prospero is compelled to excuse to the young lovers as the product of an "infirmity" (IV.i.151). But it is this infirmity that has also led him to ignore the final threat to his "project"—in his delight with the vanities of Art he has forgotten Caliban.

Caliban believes Prospero to be asleep—a master who is not actively oppressing, must be asleep:

> . . . 'tis a custom with him
> I'th'afternoon, to sleep: there thou mayst brain him,
> Having first seiz'd his books. . . .
> (III.ii.85-86)

But in the preceding scene we learn from Miranda that Prospero usually spends these hours of the afternoon in study:

> . . . My father
> Is hard at study; pray, now, rest yourself:
> He's safe for these three hours.
> (III.i.19-21)

Caliban's plot, too, recalls the event that originally cost Prospero his dukedom. To a usurper, whether the ruler sleep or pursue high ends (studies) makes little difference; both these employments absent a prince from his duties and so make him invisible to his subjects. Power, to be visible, must be seen and felt.

This material understanding of power is emblematically presented in Prospero's books, which are, to the uninitiate Caliban, no more than "brave utensils" of his Art. For Caliban (whose own leisure is spent in dreamful sleep), as for Antonio, studying is a kind of sleep. He believes that once these books are destroyed, Prospero will be impotent. This perfectly captures what the power of "intellectual" knowledge means to an intuitive being:[33]

> Remember
> First to posses his books; for without them
> He's but a sot, as I am, nor hath not
> One spirit to command: they all do hate him
> As rootedly as I. Burn but his books.
> (III.ii.89-93)[34]

Antonio looks on Prospero's "secret studies" in the same way, judging Prospero "incapable" of "temporal royalties" because of them (I.ii.110-111). Prospero's studies and creativity require a self-forgetting and seclusion that make him vulnerable.

Prospero on the island has acquired as part of his Art a "prescience" (I.ii.181-2) that allows him to judge how others will act in a particular context through an understanding of character. This prescience is connected with memory and it serves him for Antonio and Sebastian, but nearly fails him for Caliban, whom he seems to wish to forget (as he does during the masque and at the end of the play). This forgetting is even more curious since Caliban, unlike the others, intends to kill Prospero.

Prospero is, of course, the ultimate conspirator in this play. As Caliban points out, he is, among other things, a usurping tyrant: "This island's mine, by Sycorax my mother" (I.ii.333). He complains to Stephano and Trinculo:

As I told thee before, I am subject to a tyrant, a sorcerer, that by his cunning hath cheated me of the island. (III.ii.40-42)

Caliban is justified in insisting that Prospero illegitimately rules the island he inherited.

Why should Prospero be most apt, then, to forget Caliban, the slave, the only one of those he controls who is dauntless enough to call him tyrant? Caliban is necessary but unattractive to Prospero: he represents the part of human beings from which Prospero wishes to be furthest. And it is only Caliban over whom he must permanently tyrannize. Calling himself back from his created world, Prospero is able to boast finally, "My charms crack not, my spirits obey" (V.i.2), while Caliban, far from obeying, still plots tyrannicide. Prospero's survival and his "project" originate in an injustice much like the injustice done to him by Antonio. Is his forgetfulness of Caliban a forgetfulness of the unjust foundations of his own power?

What Is Prospero's Art?

Prospero's Art consists partly in a political understanding, but also in his dramatic skill or poetry. He orchestrates the tragedy of the first scene in the play and later directs the performances of an anti-masque and masque in the third and fourth acts. These scenes provide a mode in which to look at Shakespeare's hero. The question of the first scene—Where's the master? —keeps us looking for who controls events in the play. Watching Prospero at work staging dramas within the play causes us to consider how he is responsible for controlling all action, as he claims in the epilogue. For this reason, the preeminently popular interpretation of Prospero's Art was, from the nineteenth century until the 1960s, that it represented Shakespeare's dramatic art.[35]

The Tempest opens in the midst of a tragedy, yet it ends quietly with the promise of "calm seas and auspicious gales." The opening chaos emphasizes the tragic potential in the play, which appears frustrated by the ordering force of Prospero's Art, a creation of Shakespeare's art. This Art is exemplary of a process or of a stand towards experience. Prospero possesses a moral wisdom which, he claims, enables him to give his daughter an education superior to a court education. This moral wisdom is part of a larger political wisdom that enables him to frustrate the usurpers, Caliban, Antonio, and Sebastian. Dramatic poetry is an instrument of this wisdom. Prospero keeps Ariel obedient until the completion of his unknown "project"; he keeps Caliban a slave performing necessary tasks that free him for his afternoon studies, he subjugates Ferdinand, he frightens Antonio and Sebastian, and he makes Alonso penitent, all with the help of dramatic art. Shakespeare shows us how poetry may be used to moral and political ends, and this commences in the first scene, where Prospero creates a "tragedy" to educate his daughter, to prepare her for her introduction into the "brave new world" of which she must become a part.

Prospero's "project" most obviously consists in his reinstatement as Duke of Milan, confirmed by the expected marriage of his daughter Miranda to the heir of Naples (to which Milan is now subject). He ensures his progeny control of Naples, and in doing so assures control of Milan. He cannot create the circumstances that bring his enemies within his power (I.ii.178-184). For this he is dependent on "bountiful Fortune," of which he (like Machiavelli's prince) knows how to take advantage. This exercise of power is parodied in Caliban and Antonio, who try to take advantage of those who sleep.

Prospero says he does nothing except for Miranda's benefit. Prospero is the Italian of Faustus, and Miranda derives from the Latin for "wonder." In his *Metaphysics*, Aristotle comments on the power of wonder to induce men to reflection on themselves and the world around them, or philosophy:

> for it is because of wondering that men began to philosophize and do so now. . . . Now a man who is perplexed and wonders considers himself ignorant (whence a lover of myth, too, is in a sense a philosopher, for a myth is composed of wonders).[34]

"Wonder" is one of the refrains of *The Tempest* (mentioned ten times). Prospero's project is to preserve wonder and to permit it continuously to renew itself. The preservation of and acting upon wonder is Prospero's most important activity in the play, for which he is willing to tyrannize over Caliban. It is by making others wonder that he causes them to reflect on themselves—to the extent each is capable. Gonzalo's pious-sounding summary of events concludes with mention of this induced reflection:

> O, rejoice
> Beyond a common joy! and set it down
> With gold on lasting pillars: in one voyage
> Did Claribel her husband find at Tunis,
> And Ferdinand, her brother, found a wife
> Where he himself was lost, Prospero his dukedom
> In a poor isle, and all of us ourselves
> When no man was his own.
> (V.i.206-213)

Prospero causes this reflection by manifestations of his Art, which sadden, amuse, and frighten. All Prospero's magic feats have been performed by means of others. Jove's "own bolt" has split the "oak." The tempest was the work of nature, dramatically enhanced by Ariel. Prospero's Art consists in knowing how to take advantage of the powers of others: Ariel, Caliban, and Jove. He controls these "weak masters" (V.i.41) by knowing how to rule them according to their particular natures, which he does through creating dramatic situations. When he speaks of "graves" that have opened at his "command" to let forth their "sleepers," for instance, he may be taken to mean his reuniting of Ferdinand, the king's party, and the boat crew. Or, less literally, his power to make the writers of the books from which he has learned speak anew.

Prospero's history parallels that of Caliban's mother, the sorceress Sycorax, who,

> For mischiefs manifold, and sorceries terrible
> To enter human hearing, from Argier
> . . . was banish'd, for one thing she did
> They would not take her life. . . .
> (I.ii.264-67)

She

> . . . was a witch; and one so strong
> That could control the moon, make flows and ebbs
> And deal in her command without her power.
> (V.i.269-71)

Prospero, too, was spared death and brought with him his only child. Both are magicians who act with the powers of others, like the Boatswain. Prospero commands Ariel, but does not have his power; he rules the island, but with Caliban's usurped authority. He is also connected with Ovid's mythic evildoer, Medea. Just after the last group of conspirators has been routed, he marks his triumph: "At this hour/Lies at my mercy all mine enemies" (IV.i.262-3). He next pledges to abjure his Art in a speech that is a transformation of Medea's invocation of the gods in Book 7 of Ovid's *Metamorphoses*. She describes her powers and then asks the gods to extend them so that she may preserve her husband's father from death.[35] Once she obtains the power to confer immortality she wreaks vengeance on her enemies. But Prospero does not ask for the power to delay death; he relinquishes it instead (V.i.41-51). He dismisses all the instruments of his power in favor of life in Milan where, "Every third thought shall be my grave" (V.i.311). Prospero's wisdom recognizes its own limits. Unlike his archetypal predecessor, Medea, he refrains from seeking power over mortality, but submits to the tyranny of time.[36] His only frivolity (unlike Marlowe's Faustus) is the wedding masque for Ferdinand and Miranda, and even that serves the purpose of reinforcing the coming nuptial vows. He is able to call up anger, and to restrain it. He is most angry with Caliban because the monster responds only to anger, until the very end of the play. Having experienced another type of master (Stephano), Caliban is now impressed with Prospero's dignity (V.i.262). Prospero exacts penitence from those who are capable of it (Alonso, V.i.197-99, and Ariel, II.i.293-99) and constrains the ambitions of those who cannot feel shame or pangs of conscience (Antonio, Sebastian, Stephano, Trinculo, and Caliban). His Art punishes unjustly (Ariel, Caliban, Ferdinand) as well as justly (Caliban, Alonso, Antonio, Sebastian). But he uses his "magical" powers no further than to restore himself to his place as "Absolute Milan" (I.ii.109), and to assure his "only heir and princess" (I.ii.58-59) the throne of Naples and possession of Milan.

Those who wish to view *The Tempest* as a simply utopic vision have difficulty in accommodating Prospero's anger in this scheme. From Caliban's perspective it makes him a truly fearful tyrant. This injustice in the play produces the greatest strains on Prospero's Art, as recent critics have emphasized, and mars the spell. This flaw in the comic texture comments on the optimistic vision of the rule of a wise man, expressed by a young Milton:

> almost nothing can happen without warning or by accident to a man who is in possession of the stronghold of wisdom. Truly he will seem to have the stars under his control and dominion, land and sea at his command, and the winds and storms submissive to his will. Mother Nature herself has surrendered to him. It is as if some god had abdicated the government of the world and committed its justice, laws, and administration to him as a ruler.[37]

Expectation of "calm seas" makes us forget the tempest required to make Prospero's political project successful. It is, after all, Prospero's tyranny over Caliban that permits him to regain his political fortunes and to insure his progeny the thrones of Naples and Milan. Prospero never manages to get Caliban to serve his "project"; he is only able to keep him from destroying it, and it is for this defiance in spirit that Caliban is now found admirable. He is a slave, but he is a rebellious and belligerent slave, a constant reminder of the one injustice on which Prospero's project rests.

From the first scene on, power belongs to those who know how to exercise it and do so in the play: the Boatswain, Antonio, Sebastian, Stephano, Sycorax, and Prospero. There are many powerless masters in the play: Prospero (as Duke of Milan), the Master of the boat, Caliban, and Alonso. And there is the alternative fostered by romantic love, where lovers exchange power over one another, represented by Ferdinand and Miranda.

One traditional critical school of thought on this play views Prospero's Art as morally ameliorative, so Robert Egan argues:

> Thus Prospero has employed his art to expose and chastise Caliban's faults, lead him to goodness, and depict images of what he should be. This specifically moral function is the basic pattern of almost all his artistic endeavors . . . Prospero's project, then, is no less than to purge the evil from the inhabitants of his world and restore them to goodness. . . . His faulty moral perception will not permit him to acknowledge as natural and human any being with the least taint of evil.[38]

But the distinction between Caliban and Ariel is not a simple moral one; Egan's argument misses the point of Prospero's rhetoric. He does not wish, nor is he able, to eradicate Caliban or Caliban-like creatures, because slaves are "necessary" on the island to his leisured existence. The similarities between the conspiracies draw our attention to similarities between the conspirators: Antonio and Caliban have in common the fact that they both are made to serve Prospero. From Prospero's point of view, Antonio's rule of Milan was a kind of enslavement though it initially freed Antonio from subservience, since it caused his banishment. The conspiracy that such slavery encourages is a necessary part of rule, then. Rather than acknowledge that force alone keeps such beings in check, Prospero acts and speaks as though all conspirators may be made penitent rather than acknowledge openly that some have no such "deity" as conscience.

A wise man, Prospero, accomplishes his ends by disguising his intentions: like the sovereign in Gonzalo's commonwealth, he disappears. By dissembling, he is able to arrange matters such that, even when others are most disobedient to him, they serve his ends: Miranda's rebellious love for Ferdinand is at the heart of Prospero's "project." He arranges the "business" of love so that the "third man" Miranda sees is at once the most eligible and the most worthy of her affections. Their budding romance does not surprise him, "So glad of this as they I cannot be / Who are surpris'd by all" (III.i.92-93). Shakespeare's tragic heroes lack this range of understanding that would permit them to foresee and use the resistance of others. Prospero again makes another person voice his own intentions when, in act 5, scene 1, Alonso (thinking Ferdinand dead and Prospero's daughter lost) wishes exactly what Prospero has designed all along:

> O heavens, that they were living in Naples,
> The King and Queen there! that they were, I wish
> Myself were muddied in that oozy bed
> Where my son lies. . . .
> (V.i.149-152)

Alonso, before "an enemy . . . inveterate" to Prospero (I.ii.121-22), has been brought to this point by events that Prospero has orchestrated. The King is now willing to give his life for a marriage he might once have prevented at all costs.

Prospero's Art is like that of the successful dramatist; those on whom it acts are not aware of being controlled. To the extent Prospero's Art is dramatic art, it provides a catalogue of responses to drama, which intimates Shakespearean self-portraiture or self-reflection. If we look at the various performances put on within the play we see that tragedy requires a close engagement or absorption (like that of the stage audiences for the tempest, anti-masque, and masque), while comedy requires a certain self-consciousness, or awareness of the illusory quality of what is being seen. Always in the play we are watching someone reacting to a composed action, a drama: Ariel, constrained, still delights in performing to the "syllable" Prospero's scenes and attending to aesthetic detail; Caliban, who hears beautiful noises that lead him to dream and feels punishments that make him fearful; Ferdinand, who is charmed by Ariel's music and the presentation of Miranda; the young couple, capable of complete absorption in Prospero's illusions of shipwreck and goddesses; and the King's company. Alonso succumbs to a tragic presentation of life as one great sin followed with just punishment by the gods, while Antonio and Sebastian are persuaded they are attacked by fiends, and Gonzalo admires the novelty of the banquet and spirits. All are charmed by the final presentation of the tableau of Ferdinand and Miranda at chess. Art affects everyone in the play according to his or her nature, even Prospero, whose absorption in his own illusion causes him to forget Caliban's conspiracy. In this sense, then, the play not only describes differences between comedy and tragedy, but how the audience is affected differently by each.

The comic scenes in the play are comic because there is always present an audience aware of their artificiality: Prospero. We share Prospero's comic perspective only to the extent we are able to understand how he exercises his power.

His epilogue, which takes us outside the action of the play, asks for our reflection of and comprehension of his Art. Prospero's wisdom consists in knowing other human beings; he acts in their passions and desires, preventing or permitting their realization, and the instrument he uses is his poetry. As we know from Sycorax's experience with Ariel, force alone cannot achieve every "project": Ariel will not obey "earthy and abhorr'd" commands.

Prospero takes the self-interest and the moral interest of others and brings them into service of his own good. As Stephen Orgel puts it, *The Tempest* is "a fantasy about controlling other people's minds" (225).[39] This is a chilling conclusion, since this talent is also the mark of some of Shakespeare's greatest villains, including Richard III, Iago, and Edmund. They succeed because they know their victims. But is Prospero, like Macbeth, Richard, or Leontes, a true tyrant? Orgel's insight notwithstanding, Prospero is not a progenitor of Big Brother.

Is J. M. Gregson correct in seeing the final plays as an experience of Shakespeare's skepticism about power, a "divine resignation"?[40] I think *The Tempest* alone would suggest Shakespeare's insistence on the importance of understanding power and how to use it, rather than resigning oneself to its perpetual abuse. Marilyn French sees the subject of the Romances as sex and power, with power being the masculine principle whose ascendancy necessarily devalues the feminine principle of sex. To this extent *The Tempest* is, for her, the most sexually progressive of the plays, because Prospero, in giving up his powers, shows that he values the feminine.[41] These critical responses share a reluctance to acknowledge that Prospero's power, what he calls his Art, was necessary to the accomplishment of his "project," which is what generates the play itself. Prospero's magic is necessarily "rough" since he desires to be included back in the civilized world.

To regain his political position, Prospero learns how to rule by learning to control Ariel and Caliban, a slavish creature and an imaginative one. As a result of this political wisdom, no action is accomplished within the play: no one dies, no one marries. Prospero has shown himself to be wise by seizing opportunity and averting disaster, by preventing the potential tragedies that arise in the course of the three hours he has (V.i.136). As Jean-Paul Teytaud argues, the activity of wisdom is commended in *The Tempest*, while Prospero's former seclusion is rejected as immoderate: "Shakespeare rejette par deux fois la vie contemplative isolée, bien que (pour lui comme pour Aristotle) ce soit par elle que l'homme devient semblable aux dieux. . . . C'est donc moins l'idéalisme qui est condamné dans La Tempête que la tentation de l'exces."[42]

We are invited in the epilogue to consider whether Prospero's promise of "calm seas and auspicious gales" can be accepted as feasible moral procedure in our own imagination. At the end of the play, Prospero asks the audience for "indulgence"; structurally, the decorum of the theater arising from the audience's expectation of a comedy has been violated. This final speech has elements of Prospero's first admonishment to Ariel as well as Ariel's Harpy speech to the conspirators. Prospero has "pardon'd all deceivers" (Epilogue, 7) and strict justice has not been done:

> And my ending is despair,
> Unless I be reliev'd by prayer,
> Which pierces so that it assaults
> Mercy itself and frees all faults.
> As you from crimes would pardon'd be
> Let your indulgence set me free.
> (15-20)

Prospero disappoints the expectation of revenge tragedy. He takes part with his "nobler reason" against his "fury" (V.i.26) and is able to restore himself to his rightful political sphere using the techniques he has acquired on the island. But in order to do this he must, himself, commit injustices, for which he requires "mercy" and "indulgence"; his reference to "all deceivers" is self-reflexive.

The audience shares Prospero's dramatic perspective, as we are allowed to see the otherwise invisible Ariel, and watch him direct the masque, anti-masque, and dramatic scenes. This perspective is explained in the epilogue. Of the nine of Shakespeare's epilogues, this is closest to Puck's at the end of *A Midsummer Night's Dream*. Robin Goodfellow makes a plaudite:

> If we shadows have offended,
> Think but this and all is mended—
> That you have but slumb'red here

While these visions did appear.
(V.i.430-433)

But Prospero directly requires that the audience comprehend as well as enjoy the play in order to applaud him:

Now my charms are all o'erthrown
And what strength I have's my own,
Which is most faint: now, 'tis true,
I must be here confin'd by you,
Or sent to Naples. Let me not
Since I have my dukedom got,
And pardon'd the deceiver, dwell
In this bare island by your spell
But release me from my bands
With the help of your good hands.
(Ep. 1-10)

Prospero speaks as if his powers had been taken from him ("o'erthrown") though he claims earlier to have buried them. This draws our attention further behind the scenes to the only one now able to overthrow Prospero—Shakespeare. With the end of the play, the spells cast by the dramatist, and by his creations, are undone in the loss of the audience's attention. Prospero's plea for appreciation requires an interpretation of what he has been able to accomplish, so that his dramatic wisdom may be approved. His final couplet asks for something more than passing praise:

As you from crimes would pardon'd be
Let your indulgence set me free.

This is the last spell cast by Prospero, asking for a thoughtful appraisal of the play, which throws us back to the admonishment of John Heminge and Henrie Condell in their preface to the First Folio, which opens with *The Tempest*: "Reade him, therfore; and againe, and againe: And if then you doe not like him, surely you are in some manifest danger, not to understand him."[43] The understanding this play requires hinges on the question: What is Prospero's Art?

Like Ariel, Caliban, and Ferdinand, Prospero desires to be set free. On the simplest level this freedom will come from the audience's belief in the power of his poetry. The play has ended, not in Naples, but on the island. The return to Naples depends on Prospero's promise to the King's party of "calm seas and auspicious gales" (V.i.314), which Ariel will provide. In order for this voyage to be accomplished in the imagination of the audience, they must convince themselves that Prospero has provided for the safe return of all to Naples and that he has successfully reinstated himself as Duke of Milan. If the audience remains unconvinced that all his stratagems have sufficiently quelled the ambitions of Antonio, Sebastian, and Caliban, and kept Ariel obedient until the return to Naples, Prospero's "project" (and Shakespeare's) will have failed.

In order for the audience to approve, they must understand how Prospero, in his twelve years on the island, has better learned to rule and safeguard his dukedom. They must comprehend how the knowledge he has acquired from study has enabled him to regain and ensure his rightful place in the political sphere. This requires understanding the play to reveal that Prospero's original intention, his "project," was exactly this and that it has been successfully accomplished. The audience, for one, must appreciate why vengeance was not necessary and pierce "Mercy itself" (Ep., 18), in order to understand that mercy is no longer required. They must be convinced that the threat from Antonio and Sebastian has been controlled. More than this, they must go beyond mercy to understand Prospero's own form of tyranny. If they remain unconvinced of the success of Prospero's political project or unpersuaded of his dramatic effectiveness, Prospero remains, imaginatively, on the island and the play fails.

Prospero may be considered a true tyrant insofar as he compels everyone to act as he wants them to act, by his Art. This compulsion is not experienced as force (with the important exception of Caliban who believes he has been usurped), but as poetry. In several cases, Prospero compels others towards their own enlightened self-interest or he causes their interests to coincide with his own (Ferdinand, Miranda, Alonso). There are two definitions of tyranny that compete in the play. In the first, every kind of rule that forces us to do something against our will is tyranny: Caliban knows himself subject to this kind of tyranny by Prospero. A second kind of tyranny is a tyranny that forces us to do something against our self-interest (Sebastian, Antonio, Stephano, and Trinculo).

Does Shakespeare perceive a kind of rule that would not suffer from either of these forms of tyranny? Is there a real common good, or will there always be an odd Caliban out? After all, Caliban is the only creature unaccounted for at the end of the play; Prospero's last act is to free Ariel. What happens to the "slave"? This forgetfulness, and Prospero's plea for "indulgence," suggest that Shakespeare understood the unjust treatment of Caliban as an ugly political necessity. Aristotle begins his *Politics* with a discussion of natural slavery, drawing attention to the injustice that underlies politics. Every political community must, by necessity he argues, have slavish activities performed by those who are better than the work they do. Shakespeare, in creating Caliban, appears to agree with this assessment of what brings about slavery. Caliban is presented as better than a slave by virtue of his dreams and hopes. He aspires to higher things, wishing to "people" the island with Calibans, by breeding with Miranda, a being of superior intellect and beauty. And Caliban has highly articulate speeches explaining how he has been moved by beautiful images so much that he "cried to dream again" (III.ii.141).

It seems, then, for Shakespeare there is no rule that is not, in some important way, unjust, and on this point there might be grounds for agreement between his presentation of the tyrant and those of classical and modern theorists of tyranny, especially Aristotle and Machiavelli. A perfect justice would see to the common good, satisfying the individual goods of everyone. Genuine common goods may be based on the bodies we hold in common, but bodily desires are such that they cannot always be satisfied for everyone in a just way. Caliban's desire to rape Miranda represents this acute problem in the play. Any political attempt to achieve a common good is, then, necessarily approximate. Human beings are a mix of Calibans and Ariels: individuals incline towards one or the other. Some, like Ariel, will value freedom or beautiful action above many things. Some, like Caliban, will value gratification of the senses in a beautiful way above freedom and honor. The two kinds of beings cannot be ruled in the same way.

Any political entity, like Prospero's island, is composed of high and low, rich and poor, conflicting interests that are constantly being sacrificed for one another. Ruling well is a very particular art, as Prospero's experience shows. He appears to consider in what combinations the elements of Caliban and Ariel exist in each human being. The individual attentiveness of Prospero's Art, which permits him to make a theoretical success of his "project," is utopic because this Art cannot be generalized. In moving from the world of the stage to the world of the audience, we move from the particular to the general. On the island, Prospero has only to rule a few conspirators for three hours. He is most successful with Ferdinand, but then he has the advantage of focusing on one "goodly being" whose particular desires he can encourage and gratify, rather than on a full dukedom.

Finally, there are the forgotten Caliban and the "rabble" who compose Prospero's happy vision. In the case of *The Tempest*, the sacrifices of Caliban are made for Prospero's good, in obedience to his Art, which makes for spellbinding drama, but which must ask the audience's forgiveness for the necessary injustice on which it is built. The unsentimentalized Caliban instigates Prospero's plea for indulgence and is a reminder that in any political project there is something to forgive. According to Caliban, tyranny is still tyranny, even when practiced by a wise man, and Prospero does not defend himself against this charge.

The Tempest points towards the conclusion that Shakespeare believed tyranny to be an essential part of politics and so offered no solutions. If Ariel and Caliban are fanciful distillations of what it is that enables human beings to be guided, educated, and ruled, then indignation, shame, praise, punishment, and fear would seem to be the only effective methods of a successful ruler. There are those who wish to be free and there are those susceptible to many sorts of enslavements. Those who desire freedom are always more manageable because they may be shamed into submission or reminded of past benefits. But those whose desires (like Caliban's) overlook the boundary between dream and reality, require constant vigilance, since they are always open to the bribes of a new master or god to guide and satisfy them. A creature with no sense of honor, no shame (unlike a "goodly being," who is, like Ferdinand, in love), is capable of anything. Shakespeare, a dramatist capable of showing the tragic depths of love, presents, in Caliban, the degraded version of this passion, demonstrating further why it cannot be ruled rationally. Caliban's recalcitrance is also reflected in the persistent malignancy of Sebastian and Antonio, who invite tyranny. Shakespeare does not justify tyranny, but he shows that the tendency is an ever-present danger in rule, and at the core of politics. Prospero's silence on the fate of Caliban suggests why it is that the ends of a community of abundance, as Gonzalo speculates, invite forgetfulness of its unattractive beginnings with the disappearance of authority and its implements, "treason, felon/ Sword, pike knife, gun" (II.i.156-157).

Notes

1. It is Shakespeare's only play to observe all three dramatic unities, of time, place, and action.

2. Francis Barker and Peter Hulme, "Nymphs and Reapers Heavily Vanish: the Discursive Contexts of *The Tempest*," Drakakis, 196. Paul Brown also looks to these points of strain as indicative of the ambivalence of the play towards colonialism, in "'This Thing of Darkness I Acknowledge Mine': *The Tempest* and the Discourse of Colonialism," Dollimore, *Political Shakespeare*, 61.

3. Frank Kermode, ed., *The Tempest*, the Arden edition (London: Methuen, 1977). All citations from the play are taken from this edition and noted in the text. Hereafter referred to as Kermode.

4. Kermode glosses this line: "The Boatswain is ironically asking Gonzalo to exercise his authority as a court official ('you are a councillor') and enforce the peace appropriate to the king's presence, or his presence-chamber," Kermode, commentary to I.i.22, 166.

5. Kermode, 5, n. to I.i.29-30.

6. "Tragedy is, then, a representation of an action that is heroic and complete and of a certain magnitude—by means of language enriched with all kinds of ornament, each used separately in the different parts of the play: it represents men in action and does not use narrative, and through pity and fear it effects relief [catharsis] to these and similar emotions." Aristotle, *Poetics*, The Loeb Classical Library, 23 vols., trans. W. Hamilton Fyfe (Cambridge: Harvard University Press, 1973), 23: 23.

7. Shakespeare frequently uses the word when speaking of a moving sight, an event that elicits wonder or grief from the beholder (cf. 1H6.I.iv.41; 2H6.IV.i.44; 3H6.II.i.67; II.iv.73; JC.III.i.223; III.ii.198). Line numbers refer to *The Riverside Shakespeare*.

8. Rosalie Colie, *Shakespeare's Living Art* (Princeton: Princeton University Press, 1974), 289. Colie goes on to describe the play as a distillation of the pastoral genre itself: "From this very strategy, we may take it that the poet had thoroughly understood another aspect of the pastoral fiction, by which the poet controls the pastoral nature he makes up, by which nature is entirely plastic to the poet's imagination" (290).

9. These lines have been attributed to Prospero but I would argue, going beyond Kermode's editorial defense (in which Hallett Smith and G. B. Evans, editor of the Riverside edition, concur), that they elucidate an important part of Miranda's character. She is capable of moral indignation and even hatred. This argues against a reading of her as a weak character. For an example of such criticism see Lorrie Jerrell Leininger's "The Miranda Trap: Sexism and Racism in *The Tempest*," in Lenz, 185-294. Leininger argues that Miranda is used by her father as an excuse for enslaving Caliban, and that this is all part of the play's white male "power dynamics" (289). This obfuscates the complex sentimental education she undergoes in the play and does not square with her marriage proposal to Ferdinand, or her breaking faith with her father.

10. Jean-Jacques Rousseau emphasizes the importance of compassion to education in his *Emile or On Education*: "It follows from this that we are attached to our fellows less by the sentiment of their pleasures than by the sentiment of their pains, for we see far better in the latter the identity of our natures with theirs and the guarantees of their attachment to us. If our common needs unite us by interest, our common miseries unite us by affection. Trans. Alan Bloom (New York: Basic Books, 1979), 221-222.

11. *The First and Second Discourses*, trans. Roger and Judith D. Master (New York: St. Martin's Press, 1964), 130.

12. Miranda's confusion is echoed by Caliban, who tries to describe Miranda:

> . . . I never saw a woman,
> But only Sycorax my dam and she;
> But she as far surpasses Sycorax
> As great'st does the least.
> (III.ii.98-101)

13. The concept that the human soul contained higher and lower faculties was held by many Elizabethans, and is clearly articulated by Richard Hooker, in the first book of his *Of the Laws of Ecclesiastical Polity*, ed. R. W. Church (Oxford: Clarendon Press, 1888): 24-25. "Beasts are in sensible capacity as ripe even as men themselves, perhaps more ripe. For as stones, though in dignity of nature inferior unto plants, yet exceed them in firmness of strength or durability of being; and plants, though beneath the excellency of creatures endued with sense, yet exceed them in the faculty of vegetation and fertility: so beasts, though otherwise behind men, may notwithstanding in actions of sense and fancy go beyond them; because the endeavors of nature, when it hath a higher perfection to seek, are in lower the more remiss, not esteeming thereof so much as those things do, which have no better proposed unto them.

"The soul of man therefore being capable of a more divine perfection, hath (besides the faculties of growing unto sensible knowledge which is common unto us with beasts) a further ability, whereof in them there is no shew at all, the ability of reaching higher than unto sensible things."

14. Xenophon in his *Oeconomicus* reports that Socrates claimed he was rich because "the same things are wealth and not wealth according as one understands or does

not understand how to use them. A flute, for example, is wealth to one who is competent to play it, but to an incompetent person it is no better than useless." *Memorabilia, Oeconomicus, Apology, Symposium*, Loeb Classical Library, 7 vols., trans. E. C. Marchant (Cambridge: Harvard University Press, 1979), 366-367. One does not truly possess something that one does not know how to use.

15. This is one of several affinities Prospero has with Machiavelli's ideal prince, whom the Florentine advises: "I judge this indeed, that it is better to be impetuous than cautious, because fortune is a woman; and it is necessary, if one wants to hold her down, to beat her and strike her down. And one sees that she lets herself be won more by the impetuous than by those who proceed coldly. And so always, like a woman, she is the friend of the young, because they are less cautious, more ferocious, and command her with audacity," *Prince*, 101.

16. *The Winter's Tale* is exempted perhaps because Tolstoy sensed its religious undercurrent, Tolstoy, 335. He explains his objection to Shakespeare's elitism: "The content of Shakespeare's plays, as is seen by the explanations of his greatest admirers, is the lowest, most vulgar view of life which regards the external elevation of the great ones of the earth as a genuine superiority; despises the crowd, that is to say, the working classes; and repudiates not only religious, but even any humanitarian, efforts directed towards the alteration of the existing order of society," 364. This criticism is made again by Eagleton in *William Shakespeare*.

17. "If there bee neuer a *Servant-monster* i'the Fayre; who can helpe it? he sayes; nor a nest of *Antiques*? Hee is loth to make Nature afraid in his *Playes*, like those that beget *Tales, Tempests*, and such like *Drolleries*, to mixe his head with other mens heeles, let the concupiscence of Iigges and Dances, raigne as strong as it will amongst you." As quoted in Harry Levin's *Shakespeare and the Revolution of the Times: Perspectives and Commentaries* (Oxford: Oxford University Press, 1976), 212.

18. David Sundelson, "So Rare a Wonder'd Father: Prospero's *Tempest*," in *Representing Shakespeare: New Psychoanalytic Essays*, eds. Murray M. Schwartz and Coppelia Kahn (Baltimore: The Johns Hopkins University Press, 1980), 43.

19. Dominique O. Mannoni, *Prospero and Caliban: The Psychology of Colonization*, trans. Pamela Powesland (New York: Frederick A. Praeger, 1956). See also K. M. Abenheimer, "Shakespeare's 'Tempest,' A Psychological Analysis," *Psychoanalytic Review* 33 (1946): 399-415 (qtd. In Holland, 270), in which it is argued that "Caliban shows the bestiality Prospero has repressed, and Prospero does not like him because he will not be repressed; that is, unlike Ariel and Miranda, he will not submit to Prospero's demands for gratitude."

20. See footnote 1.

21. See also Barker and Hulme, footnote 1.

22. Aristotle, *Politics*, trans. Carnes Lord (Chicago: University of Chicago Press, 1989).

23. See Brown, 62-63, for a discussion of the power of the colonizer over the sexuality of a subject people.

24. An instance if language used to enslave or subject is not new in Shakespeare; a striking example is Richard III's wooing of the widow Anne. See chapter 3, part 2, "Thy Self is Self-Misus'd."

25. *William Shakespeare*, 94-95.

26. *Shakespeare's Living Art*, 287, 298.

27. Paul Cantor, "Prospero's Republic: The Politics of Shakespeare's *The Tempest*," in *Shakespeare as a Political Thinker*, eds. John Alvis and Thomas G. West (Durham: Carolina Academic Press, 1981), 244.

28. Lionel Trilling, *Sincerity and Authenticity* (Cambridge: Harvard University Press, 1972), 42, n.1.

29. Michel de Montaigne, *The Essays of Michael Lord of Montaigne*, trans. John Florio, 3 vols. (New York: E. P. Dutton, 1928), 1:215-229). "It is a nation, would I answer *Plato*, that hath no kinde of traffike, no knowledge of Letters, no intelligence of numbers, no name of magistrate, nor of politike superioritie; no use of service, of riches or of povertie, no contracts, no successions, no partitions, no occupation but idle; no respect of kindred, but common, no apparell but naturall, no manuring of lands, no use of wine, corne, or mettle. The very words that import lying falsehood, treason, dissimulations, covetousnes, envie, detraction, and pardon, were never heard of amongst them" (220).

30. Harry Epstein, "The Divine Comedy of *The Tempest*," *Shakespeare Studies 8*: 294, 1972.

31. Gonzalo could serve as Shakespeare's dramatic envisioning of Montaigne. Aside from the fact that Gonzalo's speech is taken directly from the *Essays*, his manner of expressing truths is, like the skeptic's, digressive and indirect.

32. Stephen Orgel, ed., *Jonson: The Complete Masques* (New Haven: Yale University Press, 1969), 2.

33. Such a materialist understanding of knowledge is clearly observed by Plutarch in his "Life of Alexander." Alexander, finding that his tutor Aristotle had published some of his teachings, admonished him: "Thou hast not done well to put forth the Acroamatical Sciences. For wherein shall we excel other, if those things which thou hast secretly taught us be made common to all? I give thee to understand, that I had rather excel others in excellency of knowledge than in greatness of power," *Lives 5*: 260-261. This is the opposite view from that of knower as possessor attributed to Socrates by Xenophon, see footnote 13.

34. There is an echo here of Faustus's desperate vow, "I'll burn my books," *Dr. Faustus*, V.iii.200, in Marlowe.

35. For a statement of this see Emile Montegut, as cited in *The New Variorum Edition of Shakespeare: The Tempest*, ed. Horace Howard Furness (Philadelphia: J. B. Lippincott & Co., 1920), 359-60).

36. Aristotle, *Metaphysics*, trans. Hippocrates G. Apostle (Bloomington: Indiana University Press, 1975), 982b12-21. Seth Benardete provides a commentary in "On Wisdom and Philosophy: The First Two Chapters of Aristotle's *Metaphysics A*," *Review of Metaphysics 32*, no. 2 (December 1978). "Wonder is a certain kind of conscious neediness (*aporia*); it thus looks like the neediness which the productive arts satisfy; but unlike that neediness it is wholly selfless and thus looks like the natural desire to know. . . . The wonderful is that which shows the hiddenness of the unhidden" (213-214). This "hiddenness of the unhidden" is well expressed when Miranda exclaims "O brave new world" on discovering those who betrayed her father (V.i.183).

37.   By charmes I make the calme Seas rough, and make y rough Seas plaine
     And cover all the Skie with cloudes, and chase them thence again.
     By charmes I rayse and lay the windes, and burst the vipers jaw,
     And from the bowels of the Earth both stones and trees doe drawe.

Whole woods and Forestes I remove: I make the Mountaines shake,
And even the Earth it selfe to grone and fearfully to quek.
I call up dead men from their graves: and thee O lightsome Moone
I darken oft, though beaten brasse abate thy perile soone
Our sorcerie dimmes the Morning faire, and darkes y Sun at Noone.

Ovid, *The Metamorphoses*, trans. Arthur Golding, gen. Ed. J. I. M. Cohen (Carbondale, IL: Southern Illinois University Press, 1961), 142.

38. See this Shakespearean characterization of time in the Sonnets, discussed in chapter 4.

39. Milton, "Prolusion VII: 'Learning Makes Men Happier Than Does Ignorance,'" in *Complete Poems and Major Prose*, ed. Merritt Y. Hughes (Indianapolis: The Bobbs-Merrill company, 1978), 625. It also comments on the philosopher-king who rules Plato's *Republic*, to whom Prospero has been compared (see Cantor in Alvis).

40. Robert Egan, "This Rough Magic: Perspectives of Art and Morality in *The Tempest*," *Shakespeare Quarterly* 23 23 (1972): 175, 177. See also George Wilson Knight's *The Imperial Theme*.

41. Stephen Orgel, "Prospero's Wife," *Representing the English Renaissance*, ed. Stephen Greenblatt (Berkeley: University of California Press, 1988), 255.

42. J. M. Gregson, *Public and Private Man in Shakespeare* (Totowa, NJ: Barnes & Noble, 1983), 249.

43. French, 322-323, 341.

44. Jean-Paul Teytaud, "Catharsis Comique et Reconaissance Dramatique Dans *La Tempête*," *Etudes Anglais*, (Avril-Juin 1968) 21.2: 119.

45. William Shakespeare, *Comedies, Histories and Tragedies*. A facsimile edition, ed. Helge Kokeritz (New Haven: Yale University Press, 1954), A3.

Chapter 6

Conclusion: Time's Tyranny

The combination of Prospero's detachment and his performed moral indignation diminishes the resistant voice of Caliban who alone insists that Prospero is a tyrant. To understand how *The Tempest* expands Shakespeare's exploration of tyranny it is necessary then to see clearly the relation between Prospero and Caliban. Is it that Caliban cannot see the goodness of Prospero's project and how he may benefit from it? Or is it that Caliban recognizes the importance of self-rule? Prospero's "project" entirely ignores what Caliban wants, which is to people his island and to choose his master and his gods. Prospero wishes to provide himself peace for contemplation and to secure Miranda's future. Originally Caliban was treated equally, and shared his knowledge of the island, but, for his attempted rape of Miranda, Prospero enslaved him.

Is tyranny inevitable when there is no good held in common? Prospero might have allowed Caliban his freedom, but he would remain a danger, as his conspiracy (when he is forgotten by Prospero) proves. When, as in this case, there is no common good, it seems it becomes impossible to distinguish between a good ruler and a tyrant.

How does Shakespeare then distinguish tyranny at all? Prospero's actual crimes are far from those of Macbeth, Richard, or Leontes, but what makes him superior to them, aside from an intuitive response to his Art as some form of white magic? No matter how many needs or desires are satisfied under a tyrant, servitude diminishes the individual and denies the fulfillment of human potential. Caliban and Stephano both celebrate their temporary enfranchisement: "Freedom, high-day! high-day freedom!" (II.ii.186) "Thought is free (III.ii.121). The importance of ruling oneself, being one's own person, is connected to the problem of the tempest-tossed ship presented in the first scene; shouldn't those who know how to rule, rule (the Boatswain)? This returns to the question posed between Malcolm and Macduff: Does legitimacy matter? If we are to believe the Boatswain, only those who know how to exercise power may legitimately claim to rule: "king" is just a name. An awareness of the strength of Caliban's desire to be free (even if this freedom is only the freedom to choose a new master), shows the dangers of the forceful repression of such desire.

Prospero's Art provides a partial solution because his poetry allows him to persuade others to do what he wishes rather than forcing them to it. The tempest and anti-masque elicit from Alonso "heart-sorrow" and repentance, the arranged meeting of Ferdinand and Miranda engenders romantic love (made surer by Prospero's apparent opposition), and the masque keeps the lovers at a game of chess. This poetic form of persuasion is indirect rule because it induces others to choose freely what Prospero wants them to choose. But even this form of indirect rule does not make Caliban obedient.

The idea that those who know how to rule deserve to rule is expressed at several points in *The Tempest*. This view provides the basis for Macbeth's and Richard's claims to their thrones and Leontes's claim to know and judge Hermione's guilt. Such a view obviates the need for any formal legitimacy; Macbeth should rule Scotland because he is its most competent defender, and Richard should rule England because he knows how to preserve the state.[1] The accident of birth, which placed them at several removes from the thrones of Scotland and England, should be ignored in favor of their superior competence. Nonetheless, a lack of formal legitimacy undermines the grounds on which they claim obedience and subjection. Macbeth simply and foolishly ignores such legitimation (depending on the Witches), but Richard goes so far as to slander his mother to give his claim to the throne greater substance. Leontes publicly defies the supreme religious authority in Sicilia. Caliban's complaint against Prospero, that he is a usurper, explains why conventional legitimacy matters, since he embodies the strong impulse towards self-rule and belief that such self-rule is possible. The common desire to be free is importantly satisfied by the legitimation of power. "Legitimation" comes from a prior implicit or explicit agreement.

In *Macbeth*, Duncan was in the process of such legitimation by establishing a hereditary monarchy in place of an elective one. Shakespeare selects this delicate point in Scottish history to show the stark conflict of claims to rule based on genuine merit and those based on an artificially created standard. Macbeth's utter disregard of the trappings of authority (heightened in the play by his consorting with the Witches) loses him the support of the Scots nobility and even his loyal soldiers. Macbeth's martial superiority is more than matched by Malcolm's attention to the development of a hereditary monarchy in Scotland. Malcolm learns in England the importance of investing a monarchy with divine sanctions (the curing of the King's Evil) in order to solve the Macbeth problem. The first presentation of Macbeth is as a greatly honored hero, deserving of high office; his genuine merit explains his devastation at obtaining only "mouth-honor."

Richard III is far more self-conscious and attentive to the trappings of legitimacy, with greater success: his army does not desert him, though he is betrayed by some of the nobility. Richard is more politically astute than Macbeth and grasps immediately the importance of divine sanction as well as hereditary legitimacy to assuring the throne. He stages his acceptance of the crown to give the appearance of religious sanction and slanders his parents to strengthen his own hereditary claim. Richard ought to be a highly successful tyrant since he has mastered Machiavelli and knows how to rule by appearing weak, but his performance falters. Unlike Macbeth, Richard does not believe himself superior to others; in fact he believes himself physically inferior. His advantage is that he thinks more clearly about politics: but this knowledge is available to everyone who does not suffer from "confusion of the brain." Richard's performance falters because he finds that the foundation of his desire for absolute power is the desire for revenge on nature rather than an indifference to it. According to Shakespeare's criticism of Machiavelli, this is the common delusion of his pupils: that they believe they may conquer nature by regarding it indifferently and yet their desire to conquer it attaches them to it. Shakespeare exposes this fundamental political problem in Machiavelli's political science. The danger is that Machiavelli opens his political science to everyone (both to princes in *The Prince* and to those who would be princes in *The Discourses*), even those with vengeful natures such as Richard. Shakespeare, unlike many modern interpreters of Machiavelli, appears to have taken him very seriously as a teacher of evil, and as an opponent.

Macbeth and Richard both aspire to be founders without concern for progeny because founders have the greatest honors. This leads to their most atrocious crimes: the murder of Macduff's wife and children and the murder of the Princes in the Tower. Each has deep insights in moments of passion, but these fade against the horizons of their ambitions.[2]

Macbeth's fate describes an easily visible path to tyranny, that of the public-spirited lover of honor, someone who would not be expected to harm the state. The authoritative man, authoritative because unbeatable on the field of battle and so the necessary prop of any regime, must often be subordinate to men whom he considers his inferiors—inferior in the virtues of a man: courage, strength, and the ability to withstand pain and to deliberate under the press of extreme danger. Macbeth is the problem Duncan overlooks in founding his hereditary monarchy. Malcolm, with the help of England and the example of his father's mistakes, succeeds in ruling his Macbeth, Macduff.

Macbeth and Richard acknowledge themselves as tyrants. Macbeth in doing so falls into despair, but Richard is coolly appreciative of his lust for power while remaining indifferent to his moral position. Richard makes crime look comic. He loses his composure only once, when he begins to recognize that his carefully worked out ideology of nature may have entrapped him, but the mask is quickly reassumed.

In *The Winter's Tale*, Leontes, King of Sicilia, does not view himself as a tyrant at all. As he says, were he a tyrant he would have all opponents killed. But one need not be openly bloody to be termed a tyrant in Shakespeare. Leontes is faced with the same problem facing Duncan, Macbeth and Malcolm: How does one lend greater than human authority to the will of the monarch? How can monarchic decrees be given more than arbitrary force? As Malcolm learns from King Edward in England, religious authority lends great power to the throne by inspiring awe. Leontes requires this authority to support his punishment of what he believes to be an erotic crime. But he sends to the Oracle, not for verification of his own opinion, but in order to lessen the upheaval his punishment of Hermione would cause, and to dispel the notion that he is a tyrant. This casual regard for the religious sanction causes him publicly to reject the gods when they contradict his interpretation of events. This act confirms him as a tyrant.

There are circumstances (such as those of Macbeth and Richard) when the one who knows best how to rule for the common good undermines it. If we are to judge by competence, Prospero deserves to rule (given how many of his "subjects" he is able to benefit) even more than Macbeth or Richard, but he is still an illegitimate ruler of the island. Prospero differs from the other three tyrants in that he manages to step on others without undermining himself. He is the most successful of these four Shakespearean tyrants. Why?

Prospero's Art acknowledges the recalcitrance to reason in human nature; his wisdom allows him to see that Caliban cannot always be kept subordinate. *The Tempest* explores the relation between the art of rule and of language. Prospero has the power to convince by his Art, but Caliban's cursing represents the limits of this power. He cannot always allow Caliban to choose freely since he will choose with no regard for the wills or desires of others (his attempted rape of Miranda). Like Sebastian and Antonio, he must be constrained, which involves the exercise of apparently tyrannical power. But Prospero, more than the three other tyrants, is carefully attentive to appearances; with all but the conspirators, he encourages an obedience resulting from the educative process of his Art. In the end he acknowledges the limits of his power in acknowledging "this thing of darkness," Caliban, and asks forgiveness for the necessity of his "rough magic."

As Richard III shows Shakespeare's rejection of Machiavelli, Prospero offers his modification of Aristotle's strict definition of tyranny as any rule that is not exclusively in the common interest.[3] For Aristotle the tyrant can be someone concerned with his own good only when it coincides exactly with the common good. Machiavelli's king is a political scientist who is by necessity a tyrant, though the word becomes emptied of meaning in his thought. Aristotle's king is a political philosopher who rules and in ruling sacrifices his own interest to the common interest. For Shakespeare, tyranny appears as a real and unavoidable political phenomenon, but one which may be transformed by conscious concealment of its unjust foundations.

Macbeth and Leontes share the desire to be loved or honored by others regardless of the worth of their opinions (like Caliban, who initially cares less about the fineness of a master than that he be able to choose one freely). There is a discrepancy between the tyrant's view of his abilities and what he deserves and the views of those around him (Calibans' attempt on Miranda). Each of the four tyrants in these plays believes himself superior to those around him, and believes that those around him see less clearly than he does. Macbeth believes himself deserving of the highest honors in Scotland, because he is most courageous in battle. Richard does not believe himself a superior man (he admits that Edward VI was a finer man than he), but he does believe himself more relentless and possessed of greater political insight. Leontes presumes himself morally superior to others and to the gods, gifted with divine intuitions about hidden motives and actions. Prospero claims superiority on the basis of the power of his "Art." The scope and persistence of Macbeth's, Richard's, and Leontes's claims to rule by merit are like Caliban's tyrannicidal plot. They are different versions of the "Caliban" problem. They recognize the fact that in order to completely control one's own life and gratify strong passions for honor, revenge, and love, one must control other's lives and bring them into the service of the satisfaction of their desires. In general it appears from these plays that the tyrant, unlike other desiring beings, finds no way to limit what he wants. He uses up those on whom he depends. Believing in his own achieved self-sufficiency, he does not recognize his dependence on others at all.

This "Caliban" problem stresses the importance of reticence about the injustices a ruler commits, just as Prospero neglects to mention Caliban at the end of the play. If perfect achievement of the common good is not possible, if a "thing of darkness" always exists, political injustice will persist. But it is when such injustice is publicly vaunted that it is most degrading (Macbeth's consulting the Witches, Richard's conversation with Queen Elizabeth, and Leontes's defiance of the Oracle). An alternative to the harsh rule of Caliban's slavery is Prospero's soft mind-control. Those on whom he practices it are prompted to reflect on themselves, and what they truly desire. It is opposed to the modern alternative of intellectual terror suggested by Orwell's *1984*: according to Big Brother, terror makes you see what you ought to desire. Prospero is, to this extent, Shakespeare's gesture towards the modern ideological tyranny that reforms from inside. But Prospero's mind-control induces rather than compels when it can: his Art, as in the initial tragedy performed for Miranda, is designed to charm and educate those responsive to it.

The tyrant's actions reflect a refusal to accept mortality, a desire to preserve the moment of absolute power. One aspect of this is the recurrent lack of concern for children that is connected in the plays with the wish for immortality. These tyrants, attentive to securing absolute political power, peculiarly avoid the question of how they will found a line: a question connected with acknowledgment of their own mortality. Macbeth destroys Banquo's and Macduff's line but does not consider his own childlessness. Richard, constantly rethinking the politics of his marital status, never seems to consider what will happen to the throne beyond his lifetime. Leontes's actions willfully destroy his children and the assured succession in Sicilia emphasized in the first scene of the play. Prospero, however, says he acts only on Miranda's behalf and vows reflectively on his return to Naples that "every third thought" will be his grave.

Shakespeare sees tyranny as the greatest political danger, most common, and as at the heart of human unhappiness. The exaggerated proportions of the tyrant—the large injustice of his desires and means of satisfying them—magnify this problem. To the tyrant the universe seems cold, and keen awareness of this indifference intensifies his impetus to situate himself firmly in the world, which requires satisfaction of expansive desires for love and honor. Why not choose tyranny? What is the basis for a rejection of tyranny? The simple answer is that it is a tragic way of life as Macbeth, Richard, and, in part, Leontes show. Lydgate's *Fall of Princes* and *The Mirror for Magistrates* modeled after it, both emphasize this tragic aspect showing the certain humiliation of tyrants in order to discourage the ambitious from attempting to oppress others. But their caricatures of tyrants, like Auden's cryptic portrait of the evil tyrant who murders children in his displeasure, place tyranny at a distance from the spectrum of human experience.

Shakespeare's tyrants are not freaks of art. He achieves a poise between showing the ugliness and horror of tyranny (in Macbeth's murders of the Macduff children and Richard's murder of the Princes, Leontes's command to burn and then expose his daughter), and making the phenomenon of tyranny comprehensible. We are allowed to see why Macbeth would believe he ought to rule Scotland, why Richard would want to test his mind against fortune and nature to rule England, why Leontes would aspire to a perfect moral purity, and why Prospero would try to suppress Caliban. A poet can achieve this poise in dramas of tyranny between repelling and puzzling an audience, so that the audience is neither completely horrified by tyranny nor analytically distanced from it. This poise is kept by showing how tyrannical desires are not aberrant but common. Shakespeare's insistence on the variety and levels of tyranny forces to our attention the fact that nearly all human beings are, in some important way, tyrannical. Why is there this private, unhappy attraction to absolute power? Tyrannical passions emerge from the discrepancy between one's estimation of one's talents and the estimation of others, which provides the basis for a fierce seeking of power as a good, however imperfectly perceived.

The tyrannical impulse, common to all, is fully realized by few, according to Shakespeare. Most have greater affinities with the petty tyrants of the comedies. A select number are capable of tyranny on the grand scale of Shakespeare's tyrants, which requires great passion, something only poorly characterized by the word "ambition." The final paradigm for tyranny in Shakespeare is Time, to which even Prospero's Art is subject. He cannot choose when his "project" begins or ends: Fortune affords him an opportunity and he has four hours in which to realize his intentions. Shakespeare records his own tyrant in the Sonnets urging, as always, defiance along with understanding:

> But wherefore do not you a mightier way
> Make war upon this bloody tyrant Time?
> (16.1-2)

Notes

1. His brother, Edward, inclines towards a soft piety, like that which Shakespeare critically dramatizes in the *Henry VI* plays. The meekness of his post-marital years is like Duncan's effeminacy in *Macbeth*.

2. Shakespeare's lengthiest treatment of the problem of the legitimation of a usurper is, of course, in the Henriad. Henry V asserts the success of such a project when he proclaims, "We are no tyrant, but a Christian king" (I.ii.241). That it is Henry V not Henry VI who is able to say this suggests that Shakespeare regarded such a successful conversion as very difficult during the reign of the usurper himself.

3. Rousseau comments on the strict classical view of tyranny in Book 3, chapter 10, "On the Abuse of Government and Its Tendency to Degenerate" in *The Social Contract*: "It is true that Aristotle, *Nicomachean Ethics* Book VII, chapter x, distinguishes between tyrant and king by the fact that the former governs for his own utility and the latter solely for the utility of his subjects. But besides the fact that generally all the Greek authors used the term tyrant in another sense as is best seen in Xenophon's *Hiero*, it would follow from Aristotle's distinction that since the beginning of the world, not a single king would as yet have existed," ed. Roger D. Masters, trans. Judith R. Masters (New York, St. Martin's Press, 1978), 98.

Bibliography

Primary Sources

Shakespeare, William. *Macbeth*. The Arden Shakespeare. Ed. Kenneth Muir. London: Methuen, 1962.

———. *Macbeth*. A New Variorum Edition. Ed. Horace Howard Furness. Philadelphia: J. B. Lippincott Co., n.d.

———. *Richard III*. The Arden Shakespeare. Ed. Antony Hammond. London: Methuen, 1981.

———. *Richard III*. A New Variorum Edition. Ed. Horace Howard Furness. Philadelphia: J. B. Lippincott Co., n.d.

———. *The Tempest*. The Arden Shakespeare. Ed. Frank Kermode. London: Methuen, 1954.

———. *The Tempest*. A New Variorum Edition. Vol. 4. Ed. Horace Howard Furness. Philadelphia: J. B. Lippincott Co., 1895.

———. *The Winter's Tale*. The Arden Shakespeare. Ed. J. H. P. Pafford. London: Methuen, 1954.

———. *The Winter's Tale*. A New Variorum Edition. Philadelphia: J. B. Lippincott Co., 1898.

Secondary Sources

Adelman, Janet. "'Born of Woman': Fantasies of Maternal Power in *Macbeth*." *Cannibals, Witches, and Divorce: Estranging the Renaissance*. Ed. Marjorie Garber. Baltimore: The Johns Hopkins University Press, 1987.

Alvis, John, and Thomas G. West. *Shakespeare As Political Thinker*. Durham, NC: Carolina Academic Press, 1981.

Anderson, Perry. *Lineages of the Absolutist State*. London: NLB, 1974.

Aquinas, St. Thomas. *Introduction to St. Thomas Aquinas*. Ed. Anton C. Pegis. New York: The Modern Library, 1948.

———. *The Political Ideas of St. Thomas Aquinas: Representative Selections*. Ed. Dino Bigongiari. New York: Hafner Publishing Co., 1953.

Arendt, Hannah. *Totalitarianism*. Part 3 of *The Origins of Totalitarianism*. New York: Harcourt Brace Jovanovich, 1968.

Aristotle. *Metaphysics*. Trans. Hippocrates G. Apostle. Bloomington, IN: Indiana University Press, 1975.

———. *Nicomachean Ethics*. Trans. Hippocrates G. Apostle. Grinnell, IA: The Peripatetic Press, 1984.

———. "Poetics." *Aristotle*. Loeb Classical Library. 23 vols. Vol. 23. Trans. Hamilton Fyfe. Cambridge: Harvard University Press, 1973.

———. *Politics*. Trans. Carnes Lord. Chicago: University of Chicago Press, 1984.

Armstrong, William A. "The Elizabethan Concept of the Tyrant." *Review of English Studies* 22.87 (1946): 161-181.

———. "The Influence of Seneca and Machiavelli on the Elizabethan Tyrant." *Review of English Studies* 24.93 (1948): 19-35.

Auden, W. H. *The Dyer's Hand*. New York: Vintage Books, 1968.

———. *Selected Poetry of W. H. Auden*. 2nd ed. New York: Vintage Books, 1970.

Augustine. *City of God*. Ed. David Knowles. New York: Penguin Books, 1977.

Bacon, Francis. *Essays*. World Classics Library. London: Oxford University Press, 1975.

Barber, Benjamin, and Michael J. Gargas McGrath, eds. *The Artist and Political Vision*. New Brunswick: Transaction Books, 1982.

Barber, C. L. *Shakespeare's Festive Comedy*. Princeton: Princeton University Press, 1959.

———. "Thou That Beget'st Him That Did Thee Beget." *Shakespeare Survey* 22 (1969): 59-67.

Barroll, J. Leeds. *Artificial Persons: The Formation of Character in the Tragedies of Shakespeare*. Columbia, SC: University of South Carolina Press, 1974.

Belsey, Catherine. *The Subject of Tragedy: Identity and Difference in Renaissance Drama*. New York: Methuen, 1985.

Benardete, José. "Macbeth's Last Words." *Interpretation 1* (summer 1970): 61-83.

Benardete, Seth. "On Wisdom and Philosophy: The First Two Chapters of Aristotle's *Metaphysics A*." *Review of Metaphysics* 32.2 (1978): 205-215.

Biggins, Dennis. "Sexuality, Witchcraft, and Violence in *Macbeth*." *Shakespeare Studies 8* (1975): 255-277.

Bloom, Allan, with Harry V. Jaffa. *Shakespeare's Politics*. Chicago: University of Chicago Press, 1964.

Bradbrook, Muriel C. *The Growth and Structure of Elizabethan Comedy*. London: Chatto and Windus, 1955.

Bradley, A. C. *Shakespearean Tragedy*. London: Macmillan, 1957.

Buchanan, George. *The Powers of the Crown in Scotland [De Jure Regni Apud Scotos]*. Trans. Charles Flinn Arrowood. Austin: University of Texas Press, 1949.

Bullinger, Henrie. *The Tragedies of Tyrantes Exercised upon the Church of God, from the birth of Christ unto this present yeere, 1572*. Containing the causes of them, and the just vengeance of God upon the authours. Also some notable convertes and exhortations to pacience. Written by Henrie Bullinger and now Englished. London: William How, for Abraham Weale, dwelling in Paules Churchyard at the sign of the Lamb, 1575.

Bullough, Geoffrey. *The Major Tragedies: Hamlet, Othello, King Lear, Macbeth*. Vol. 7 of *Narrative and Dramatic Sources of Shakespeare*. 8 vols. New York: Columbia University Press, 1973.

Calderwood, James L., and Harold E. Toliver. *Essays in Shakespearean Criticism*. Englewood Cliffs, NJ: Prentice-Hall, 1970.

Calvino, Italo. *Italian Folktales*. Trans. George Martin. New York: Pantheon Books, 1980.

——. *Six Memos for the Next Millenium*. Cambridge: Harvard University Press, 1988.

——. *The Uses of Literature*. Trans. Patrick Creagh. New York: Harcourt Brace Jovanovich, 1986.

Campbell, Lily B., ed. *The Mirror for Magistrates*. Cambridge: Cambridge University Press, 1938.

——. *Shakespeare's Histories: Mirrors of Elizabethan Policy*. San Marino, CA: Henry E. Huntington Library, 1947.

Carlisle, Carol. "The Macbeths and the Actors." *Renaissance Papers 1958, 1959, 1960*. Durham: The Southeastern Renaissance Conference, 1961.

Castiglione, Baldesar. *The Book of the Courtier*. Trans. George Bull. New York: Penguin Books, 1986.

Cavell, Stanley. *Disowning Knowledge in Six Plays of Shakespeare*. Cambridge: Cambridge University Press, 1984.

Chabod, Federico. *Machiavelli and the Renaissance*. Trans. David Moore. New York: Harper and Row, 1958.

Chandler, Raymond. *Farewell, My Lovely*. Middlesex, England: Penguin, 1986.

Charleton, H. B. *Shakespearean Comedy*. New York: The Macmillan Company, 1938.

——. "Shakespeare's Politics and Politicians." The English Association Pamphlet No. 72. April 1929. Oxford: Oxford University Press.

Chepiga, Michael J. *Politics and the Uses of Language in Shakespeare's English History Plays*. Ann Arbor: UMI, 1976. #76-10, 158.

Churchill, George B. *Richard III up to Shakespeare*. Berlin: Mayer and Muler, 1900.

Cibber, Colley. *Richard III. a Tragedy*. Volume 2 of *Dramatic Works of Colley Cibber*. New York: AMS Press, 1966.

Clark, Arthur Melville. *Murder Under Trust or The Topical Macbeth and Other Jacobean Matters*. Edinburgh: Scottish Academic Press, 1981.

Coghill, Nevill. "The Basis of Shakespearean Comedy: A Study of Medieval Affinities." *Essays and Studies*. Vol. 3. London: Wyman and Sons, Ltd., 1950.

Coleridge, Samuel Taylor. *Coleridge's Complete Poetical Works*. Vol. 2. Ed. Hartley Coleridge. Oxford: The Clarendon Press, 1912.

——. *Lectures on Shakespeare*. Ed. T. Ashe. London: George Bell and Sons, 1900.

Colie, Rosalie. *The Resources of Kind: Genre-Theory in the Renaissance*. Ed. Barbara K. Lewalski. Berkeley: University of California Press, 1973.

Danby, John F. *Shakespeare's Doctrine of Nature: A Study of King Lear*. London: Faber and Faber, 1949.

Dean, John. *Restless Wanderers: Shakespeare and the Pattern of Romance*. Salzburg: Institute für Anglistik und Americanistik, University of Salzburg, 1979.

De Quincey, Thomas. "On the Knocking at the Gate in *Macbeth*." *The Norton Anthology of English Literature*. 5th ed. Vol. 2. New York: W. W. Morton, 1986.

Dollimore, Jonathan. *Radical Tragedy*. Chicago: University of Chicago Press, 1984.

Dollimore, Jonathan, and Alan Sinfield. *Political Shakespeare: New Essays in Cultural Materialism*. Ithaca: Cornell University Press, 1985.

Drakakis, John, ed. *Alternative Shakespeares*. New York: Methuen, 1985.

Eagleton, Terry. *Criticism and Ideology*. London: NLB, 1975.

——. *Shakespeare and Society*. New York: Schocken Books, 1967.

——. *William Shakespeare*. New York: Basil Blackwell, 1986.

Egan, Robert. "This Rough Magic: Perspectives of Art and Morality in *The Tempest*." *Shakespeare Quarterly* 23 (1972): 171-182.

Elyot, Sir Thomas. *The Book Named the Governor 1531*. A Scolar Press Facsimile. Ed. R. C. Alston. Menston, England: Scolar Press Limited, 1970.

Empson, William. *Essays on Shakespeare*. Cambridge: Cambridge University Press, 1986.

Epstein, Harry. "The Divine Comedy of *The Tempest*." *Shakespeare Studies* 8: 279-296, 1972.

Faber, M. D. *The Design Within: Psychoanalytic Approaches to Shakespeare*. New York: Science House, 1970.

Faggi, Vico. "Comé Macbeth è re Nicolo." *Il Ponte* 37.2 (1981): 221-224.

Ferguson, Margaret W., Maureen Quilligan, and Nancy Vickers, eds. *Rewriting the Renaissance: The Discourses of Sexual Difference in Early Modern Europe*. Chicago: The University of Chicago Press, 1986.

Figgis, John Neville. *The Divine Right of Kings*. Cambridge: Cambridge University Press, 1922.

French, Marilyn. *Shakespeare's Division of Experience*. New York: Summit Books, 1981.

Frey, David L. *The First Tetralogy: Shakespeare's Scrutiny of the Tudor Myth*. Paris: Mouton, 1976.

Frye, Northrop. *A Natural Perspective: The Development of Shakespearean Comedy and Romance*. New York: Columbia University Press, 1965.

Frye, Roland Mushat. *Shakespeare and Christian Doctrine*. Princeton: Princeton University Press, 1963.

Garber, Marjorie. *Dream in Shakespeare: From Metaphor to Metamorphosis*. New Haven: Yale University Press, 1974.

———. *Shakespeare's Ghostwriters: Literature as Uncanny Causality*. New York: Methuen, 1987.

Gasquet, Emile. *Le Courant Machiavelien dans la Pensée et la Littérature Anglaise du XVIe Siècle*. Paris: Didier, 1974.

Gentillet, Innocent. *Discours Contre Machiavelli*. Eds. A. D'Andrea and P. D. Stewart. Firenze: Casalini Libri, 1974.

Gervinus, Georg Gottfried. *Shakespeare Commentaries*. Trans. F. E. Bunnett. 5th ed. New York: Charles Scribner's Sons, 1892.

Goldberg, Jonathan. *James I and the Politics of Literature*. Baltimore: The Johns Hopkins University Press, 1983.

Greenblatt, Stephen. "Genre: The Forms of Power and the Power of Forms in the Renaissance." 15.1-2 (spring and summer 1982).

———. *Renaissance Self-Fashioning*. Chicago: The University of Chicago Press, 1980.

———. ed. *Representing the English Renaissance*. Berkeley: University of California Press, 1988.

———. *Shakespearean Negotiations*. Berkeley: University of California Press, 1988.

Gregson, J. M. *Public and Private Man in Shakespeare*. Totowa, NJ: Barnes and Noble Books, 1983.

Hall, Edward. *Chronicle*. London: Printed for J. Johnson et al., 1809.

Heilman, Robert B., ed. *Shakespeare: The Tragedies*. Englewood Cliffs, NJ: Prentice-Hall, 1984.

Henke, James T. *The Ego-King: An Archetype Approach to Elizabethan Political Thought and Shakespeare's Henry VI Plays*. No. 74. Salzburg: Institut für Anglische Sprache Und Literatur, 1977.

Hill, Geoffrey. "'The True Conduct of Human Judgment' Some Observations on *Cymbeline*." In *The Lords of Limit*. London: Andre Deutsch, 1984.

Hobbes, Thomas. *Leviathan*. Ed. Bernard Crick. New York: Penguin, 1983.

Holland, Norman N. *Psychoanalysis and Shakespeare*. New York: Farrar Straus and Giroux, 1979.

Hooker, Richard. *Of the Laws of Ecclesiastical Polity*. Book 1. Ed. R. W. Church. Oxford: The Clarendon Press, 1888.

Hoy, Cyrus. *The Hyacinth Room: An Investigation into the Nature of Comedy, Tragedy, and Tragicomedy*. New York: Knopf, 1964.

James I, King of England. "King James's Opinion of a King, of a Tyrant, and of the English Lawe, Rights, and Privileges In Two Speeches." The first to the Parliament, 1603, the second, 1609. London: Printed for R. Baldwin near the Black-Bull in the Old-Baily, 1689.

––––––. *The Political Works of James I*. Ed. Charles H. McIlwain. Cambridge: Harvard University Press, 1918.

John of Salisbury. *Policratus: The Statesmans Book*. Ed. Murray F. Markland. New York: Frederick Ungar Publishing Co., 1979.

Jorgens, Jack J. *Shakespeare on Film*. Bloomington: Indiana University Press, 1977.

Kahn, Coppelia. *Man's Estate: Masculine Identity in Shakespeare*. Berkeley: University of California Press, 1981.

Kantorowicz, Ernst H. *The King's Two Bodies*. Princeton: Princeton University Press, 1957.

Kemble, John Philip. *Macbeth and King Richard the Third: An Essay*. London: John Murray, Albemarle Street, 1817.

Kermode, J. Frank, ed. *Four Centuries of Shakespearean Criticism*. New York: Avon Books, 1965.

Kernan, Alvin B., ed. *Modern Shakespearean Criticism: Essays on Style, Dramaturgy, and the Major Plays*. New York: Harcourt Brace Jovanovich, 1970.

Knight, George Wilson. *The Crown of Life*. London: Methuen, 1952.

––––––. *The Imperial Throne*. London: Methuen, 1951.

––––––. *The Shakespearean Tempest*. London, Methuen, 1953.

Knights, L. C. *Further Explorations*. Stanford: Stanford University Press, 1965.

––––––. *Shakespeare: The Histories*. 1962. Longman House, Essex: Longman Group Ltd., 1971.

Kott, Jan. *Shakespeare Our Contemporary*. Trans. Boleslaw Taborski. London: Methuen and Co., Ltd., 1964.

Krieger, Murray. "The Dark Generations of Richard III." *Criticism 1* (1959): 32-48.

La Boétie, Étienne de. *Ouvres Politiques*. Les Classiques du Peuple. Paris: Éditions Sociales, 1963.

Landauer, Gustav. *Shakespeare*. Hamburg: Rutter and Loenig Verlag, 1962.

La Perrière, Guillaume de. *The Mirrour of Policie: A Worke nolesse profitable than necessarie, for all Magistrates, and Governours of Estates and Commonweales*. London: Printed by Adam Islip, 1598.

Lenz, Carolyn R. S., Gayle Greene, and Carol T. Neely, eds. *The Woman's Part: Feminist Criticism of Shakespeare*. Chicago: University of Illinois Press, 1983.

Lerner, Ralph, and Muhsin Mahdi, eds. *Mediaeval Political Philosophy*. Ithaca: Cornell University Press, 1972.

Levin, Harry. *Shakespeare and the Revolution of the Times: Perspectives and Commentaries*. Oxford: Oxford University Press, 1976.

Levin, Richard. "Feminist Thematics and Shakespearean Tragedy." *PMLA* 103.2 (March 1988).

Lewis, Wyndham. *The Lion and the Fox: The Role of Hero in the Plays of Shakespeare*. New York: Harper & Brothers Publishers, n.d.

A Lexicon Abridged from Liddell and Scott's Greek-English Lexicon. Oxford: Clarendon Press, 1974.

Lydgate. *Fall of Princes*. Ed. Henry Bergen. Washington: The Carnegie Institution of Washington, 1923.

Lyons, Bridget Gellert. "'Kings Games': Stage Imagery and Political Symbolism in *Richard III*." *Criticism: A Quarterly for Literature and the Arts* 20.1 (1978): 17-30.

Machiavelli, Niccolo. *The Comedies of Machiavelli*. Ed. and trans. By David Sices and James B. Atkinson. Hanover: University Press of New England, 1985.

———. *The Discourses*. Ed. Bernard Crick. Trans. Leslie J. Walker, S. J. Middlesex, England: Penguin Books, 1976.

———. *Machiavelli's The Prince: An Elizabethan Translation*. Ed. Hardin Craig. Chapel Hill: The University of North Carolina Press, 1944.

———. *The Prince*. Trans. Harvey C. Mansfield. Chicago: University of Chicago Press, 1985.

Mack, Maynard. *Killing the King*. New Haven, CT: Yale University Press, 1973.

Mannoni, Dominique O. *Prospero and Caliban: The Psychology of Colonization*. Trans. Pamela Powesland. New York: Frederick A. Praeger, 1956.

Mansfield, Harvey C., Jr. *New Modes and Orders*. Ithaca: Cornell University Press, 1980.

Marlowe, Christopher. *The Complete Plays*. Ed. J. B. Steane. New York: Penguin Books, 1978.

Marsilius of Padua. *Defensor Pacis*. Mediaeval Academy Reprints for Teaching. Trans. Alan Gewirth. Toronto: University of Toronto Press, 1980.

Marvell, Andrew. *The Poems of Andrew Marvell*. Ed. Hugh Macdonald. Cambridge: Harvard University Press, 1973.

Merchant, W. Moelwyn. "His Fiend-Like Queen." *Shakespeare Survey 19* (1966): 75-81.

Meyer, Edward. *Machiavelli and the Elizabethan Drama*. New York: Burt Franklin, rpt. Of Weimar Literarhistorische Forschungren, 1897.

Milton, John. *Complete Poems and Major Prose*. Ed. Merritt Y. Hughes. Indianapolis: The Bobbs-Merrill Company, 1978.

Montaigne, Michel de. *The Essays of Michael Lord of Montaigne*. 3 vols. Trans. John Florio. New York: E. P. Dutton, 1928.

More, St. Thomas. *The History of King Richard III*. Ed. Richard S. Sylvester. New Haven: Yale University Press, 1976.

———. *Utopia*. Ed. Edward Surtz, S. J. Trans. G. C. Richards. New Haven: Yale University Press, 1964.

Muir, Kenneth, and P. Edwards, eds. *Aspects of Macbeth*. Cambridge: Cambridge University Press, 1977.

Neill, Michael. "Shakespeare's Halle of Mirrors: Play Politics, and Psychology in *Richard III*." In *Shakespeare Studies 8*. (1975): 99-129.

Nelson, Thomas Allen. *Shakespeare's Comic Theory*. The Hague: Mouton, 1972.

Newell, W. R. "Tyranny and the Science of Ruling in Xenophon's *Education of Cyrus*." *The Journal of Politics* 45 (1983): 889-906.

Nichols, Mary Pollingue. "*The Winter's Tale*: The Triumph of Comedy Over Tragedy." *Interpretation* 9.2-3 (1981): 169-190.

Oliensis, Jane Rebecca. "*The Winter's Tale* and *Alcestis*." Harvard University. Thesis, 1979.

Olson, Paul A., gen. ed. *Ben Jonson's Literary Criticism*. Ed. James R. Redwine, Jr. Lincoln, NE: Nebraska University Press, 1970.

Orgel, Stephen, ed. *Jonson: The Complete Masques*. New Haven: Yale University Press, 1969.

Orwell, George. *1984*. New York: Harcourt Brace Jovanovich, 1983.

Ovid. *The Metamorphoses*. Trans. Arthur Golding. Gen. ed. J. I. M. Cohen. Carbondale, IL: Southern Illinois University Press, 1970.

Parker, Patricia, and Geoffrey Hartman, eds. *Shakespeare and the Question of Theory*. New York: Methuen, 1985.

Pettet, E. C. *Shakespeare and the Romance Tradition*. Brooklyn: Haskell House Publishers, 1976.

Plato. *Gorgias*. Trans. Terence Irwin. Oxford: Clarendon Press, 1979.

———. *The Republic*. Trans. Allan Bloom. New York: Basic Books, 1968.

Plutarch. *The Lives of the Noble Grecians and Romans*. Trans. By John Dryden. New York: The Modern Library, n.d.

———. *The Lives of the Noble Grecians and Romans*. Trans. Thomas North. Vol. 5-7. New York: The Limited Editions Club, 1941.

Pocock, J. G. A. *The Machiavellian Moment: Florentine Political Thought and the Atlantic Republic Tradition*. Princeton: Princeton University Press, 1975.

Ponet, John. *A Short Treatise of Politics Power*. Yorkshire England: The Scolar Press, Ltd., 1970.

Praz, Mario. "Machiavelli and the Elizabethans." *Proceedings of the British Academy*. Vol. 13. London: Humphrey Milford Amen House, 1928.

Raab, Felix. *The English Face of Machiavelli: A Changing Interpretation*. London: Routledge and Kegan Paul, 1964.

Rabkin, Norman. *Shakespeare and the Common Understanding*. Chicago: University of Chicago Press, 1967.

Raleigh, Walter, ed. *Johnson on Shakespeare*. London: Oxford university Press, 1925.

Richmond, H. M. *Shakespeare's Political Plays*. Studies in Language and Literature. New York: Random House, 1967.

Rousseau, Jean-Jacques. *Émile or On Education*. Trans. Allan Bloom. New York: Basic Books, 1979.

————. *The First and Second Discourses*. Trans. Robert and Judith P. Masters. New York: St. Martin's Press, 1978.

————. *The Social Contract*. Ed. Roger R. Masters. Trans. Judith P. Masters. New York: St. Martin's Press, 1978.

Sahel, Pierre. "Machiavelisme vulgaire et machiavelisme authentique dans *Macbeth*." *Cahiers Élisabéthains 14* (1978): 9-22.

Salgado, Gamini. *Eyewitnesses of Shakespeare*. London: Sussex University Press, 1975.

Salingar, Leo. *Shakespeare and the Traditions of Comedy*. Cambridge: Cambridge University Press, 1974.

Santayana, George. "The Absence of Religion in Shakespeare." In *Essays in Literary Criticism*. Ed. Irving Singer. New York: Charles Scribner's Sons, 1956.

Schwartz, Murray, and Coppelia Kahn. *Representing Shakespeare: New Psychoanalytic Essays*. Baltimore: The Johns Hopkins University Press, 1980.

"Scotland." *Encyclopedia Britannica*. 11th ed. 1911.

Shakespeare, William. *Comedies, Histories, and Tragedies*. A facsimile edition. Ed. Helge Kokeritz. New Haven: Yale University Press, 1954.

————. *Cymbeline*. The Arden Shakespeare. Ed. J. M. Nosworthy. New York: Methuen, 1969.

————. *Hamlet*. The Arden Shakespeare. Ed. Harold Jenkins. New York: Methuen, 1982.

————. *The Second Part of King Henry IV*. The Arden Shakespeare. Ed. A. R. Humphreys. New York: Methuen, 1966.

————. *The First Part of King Henry VI*. The Arden Shakespeare. Ed. Andrew S. Cairncross. London: Methuen, 1962.

————. *The Second Part of King Henry VI*. The Arden Shakespeare. Ed. Andrew S. Cairncross. London: Methuen, 1962.

————. *The Third Part of King Henry VI*. The Arden Shakespeare. Ed. Andrew S. Cairncross. London: Methuen, 1964.

————. *King Lear*. The Arden Shakespeare. Ed. Kenneth Muir. London: Methuen, 1975.

————. *Measure for Measure*. The Arden Shakespeare. Ed. J. W. Lever. London: Methuen, 1967.

——. *A Midsummer Night's Dream*. The Arden Shakespeare. Ed. Harold F. Brooks. London: Methuen, 1979.

——. *The Riverside Shakespeare*. Ed. G. Blakemore Evans et al. Boston: Houghton Mifflin Company, 1974.

Sharpe, Kevin, and Steven N. Zwicker, eds. *Politics of Discourse: The Literature and History of Seventeenth-Century England*. Berkeley: University of California Press, 1987.

Sher, Antony. *Year of the King*. London: Chatto and Windus, 1985.

Smith, D. Nichol, ed. *Shakespeare Criticism: 1623-1840*. London: Oxford University Press, 1961.

Smith, Hallett. *Shakespeare's Romances*. San Marino, CA: The Huntington Library, 1972.

Smith, William, ed. *A Dictionary of Greek and Roman Biography and Mythology by Various Writers*. 3 vols. New York: AMS Press, 1967.

Spencer, Theodore. *Shakespeare and the Nature of Man*. New York: The Macmillan Company, 1942.

Spenser, Edmund. *Complete Poetical Works*. The Cambridge Edition of the Poets. Ed. R. E. Neil Dodge. New York: Houghton Mifflin, 1908.

Spevak, Martin, ed. *The Harvard Concordance to Shakespeare*. Cambridge: Harvard University Press, 1969.

Steele, Robert, ed. *Three Prose Versions of the Secreta Secretorum*. Early English Text Society Extra Series 74. London: Kegan Paul, 1898.

Strachey, Lytton. *The Shorter Strachey*. Eds. Michael Holroyd and Paul Levy. Oxford: Oxford University Press, 1980.

Strauss, Leo. *Natural Right and History*. Chicago: The University of Chicago Press, 1971.

——. *On Tyranny*. Ithaca: Cornell University Press, 1968.

Taylor, Michael. "Ideals of Manhood in *Macbeth*." Études Anglaises 21 (1968): 338-48.

Tennenhouse, Leonard. *Power on Display*. New York: Methuen, 1986.

Teyaud, Jean-Paul. "Catharsis Comique et Reconnaissance Dramatique Dans *La Tempête*." Études Anglaise 21.2 (April-June 1968): 113-124.

Tillyard, E. M. W. *Shakespeare's History Plays*. New York: Collier Books, 1944.

——. *Shakespeare's Last Plays*. London: Chatto and Windus, 1954.

Todorov, Tsvetan. *The Fantastic: A Structural Approach to a Literary Genre*. Trans. Richard Howard. Cleveland: The Press of Case Western Reserve University, 1973.

Tolstoy, Leo. *Recollections and Essays*. Trans. Aylmer Maude. London: Oxford University Press, 1961.

Ure, Peter. *Elizabethan and Jacobean Drama*. Liverpool: Liverpool University Press, 1974.

Watson, Robert N. *Shakespeare and the Hazards of Ambition*. Cambridge: Harvard University Press, 1984.

Wilson, E. C. *Shakespeare, Santayana, and the Comic*. University, AL: University of Alabama Press, 1973.

Winstanley, Lilian. *Macbeth, King Lear, and Contemporary History*. New York: Octagon Books, 1970.

Xenophon. *Cyropaedia*. Loeb Classical Library. 7 vols. Vols. 5-6. Trans. Walter Miller. Cambridge: Harvard University Press, 1968.

———. *Memorabilia, Oeconomicus, Apology, Symposium*. Loeb Classical Library. 7 vols. Vol. 4. Trans. E. C. Marchant. Cambridge: Harvard University Press, 1979.

———. *Scripta Minora*. Loeb Classical Library. 7 vols. Vol. 7. Trans. E. C. Marchant. Cambridge: Harvard University Press, 1984.

Index

About the Author

Mary Ann McGrail holds a doctorate in Renaissance literature from Harvard University and has taught at Kenyon College, Catholic University, and Boston University. She is the editor of *Shakespeare's Plutarch*. She also holds a J.D. from the University of Virginia and is currently a law clerk for the Honorable Richard S. Arnold of the Eighth Circuit Court of Appeals.

CPSIA information can be obtained at www.ICGtesting.com
Printed in the USA
BVOW080101030113

309659BV00010B/286/P